Scarecrow Studies in Young Adult Literature
Series Editor: Patty Campbell

Scarecrow Studies in Young Adult Literature is intended to continue the body of critical writing established in Twayne's Young Adult Authors Series and to expand it beyond single-author studies to explorations of genres, multicultural writing, and controversial issues in young adult (YA) reading. Many of the contributing authors of the series are among the leading scholars and critics of adolescent literature, and some are YA novelists themselves.

The series is shaped by its editor, Patty Campbell, who is a renowned authority in the field, with a thirty-year background as critic, lecturer, librarian, and teacher of YA literature. Patty Campbell was the 2001 winner of the ALAN Award, given by the Assembly on Adolescent Literature of the National Council of Teachers of English for distinguished contribution to YA literature. In 1989 she was the winner of the American Library Association's Grolier Award for distinguished service to young adults and reading.

1. *What's So Scary about R. L. Stine?* by Patrick Jones, 1998.
2. *Ann Rinaldi: Historian and Storyteller*, by Jeanne M. McGlinn, 2000.
3. *Norma Fox Mazer: A Writer's World*, by Arthea J. S. Reed, 2000.
4. *Exploding the Myths: The Truth about Teens and Reading*, by Marc Aronson, 2001.
5. *The Agony and the Eggplant: Daniel Pinkwater's Heroic Struggles in the Name of YA Literature*, by Walter Hogan, 2001.
6. *Caroline Cooney: Faith and Fiction*, by Pamela Sissi Carroll, 2001.
7. *Declarations of Independence: Empowered Girls in Young Adult Literature, 1990–2001*, by Joanne Brown and Nancy St. Clair, 2002.
8. *Lost Masterworks of Young Adult Literature*, by Connie S. Zitlow, 2002.
9. *Beyond the Pale: New Essays for a New Era*, by Marc Aronson, 2003.
10. *Orson Scott Card: Writer of the Terrible Choice*, by Edith S. Tyson, 2003.
11. *Jacqueline Woodson: "The Real Thing,"* by Lois Thomas Stover, 2003.
12. *Virginia Euwer Wolff: Capturing the Music of Young Voices*, by Suzanne Elizabeth Reid, 2003.
13. *More Than a Game: Sports Literature for Young Adults*, Chris Crowe, 2004.
14. *Humor in Young Adult Literature: A Time to Laugh*, by Walter Hogan, 2005.
15. *Life Is Tough: Guys, Growing Up, and Young Adult Literature*, by Rachelle Lasky Bilz, 2004.
16. *Sarah Dessen: From Burritos to Box Office*, by Wendy J. Glenn, 2005.
17. *American Indian Themes in Young Adult Literature*, by Paulette F. Molin, 2005.
18. *Gay and Lesbian Literature for Young Adults*, by Michael Cart, 2005.

American Indian Themes in Young Adult Literature

Paulette F. Molin

Scarecrow Studies in
Young Adult Literature, No. 17

THE SCARECROW PRESS, INC.
Lanham, Maryland • Toronto • Oxford
2005

SCARECROW PRESS, INC.

Published in the United States of America
by Scarecrow Press, Inc.
A wholly owned subsidiary of
The Rowman & Littlefield Publishing Group, Inc.
4501 Forbes Boulevard, Suite 200, Lanham, Maryland 20706
www.scarecrowpress.com

PO Box 317
Oxford
OX2 9RU, UK

British Library Cataloguing in Publication Information Available

Library of Congress Cataloging-in-Publication Data

Molin, Paulette Fairbanks.
    American Indian themes in young adult literature / Paulette F. Molin.
        p. cm. — (Scarecrow studies in young adult literature, ; no. 17)
    Includes bibliographical references and index.
    ISBN 0-8108-5081-8 (hardcover : alk. paper)
    1. Young adult literature, American—History and criticism. 2. Indians in litera-
ture. 3. American literature—Indian authors—History and criticism. 4. Indians of
North America—Biography—History and criticism. 5. Young adults—Books and
reading—United States. 6. Indians of North America—Intellectual life. 7. Indians
of North America—Historiography. I. Title. II. Series.
    PS173.I6M65 2005
    810.9'352997—dc22

                                                              2004026420

⊗™ The paper used in this publication meets the minimum requirements of
American National Standard for Information Sciences—Permanence of
Paper for Printed Library Materials, ANSI/NISO Z39.48-1992.
Manufactured in the United States of America.

This book is dedicated to the memory of Lee Francis, the founding director of Wordcraft Circle of Native Writers & Storytellers, who worked tirelessly seeking to ensure that Native voices—past, present, and future—are heard throughout the world.

It is also dedicated to my nieces and nephews and young adults everywhere.

The Indians survived our open intention of wiping them out, and since the tide turned they have even weathered our good intentions toward them, which can be much more deadly.

—John Steinbeck

For most people, serious learning about Native American culture and history is different from acquiring knowledge in other fields, for it requires on initial, abrupt, and wrenching demythologizing. One does not start from point zero, but from minus ten, and is often required to abandon cherished childhood fantasies of super-heroes and larger-than-life villains.

—Michael Dorris

Contents

PART 3 NONFICTION

Acknowledgments

I first began formally evaluating materials written about Native peoples while directing an American Indian culturally based curriculum project in Minneapolis during the 1970s. This Indian-initiated project developed out of alarm over the high dropout rates of Indian students, the absence of Indian teachers in classrooms, and the use of instructional materials that regularly erased or disparaged Native peoples. Our project sought to address these issues through a variety of means, including efforts to increase the number of Native teachers in classrooms and the development and implementation of culturally based instruction, including courses in tribal languages. Part of the work centered on evaluating books about Indians for possible use in classrooms. Critical to these efforts were groundbreaking publications such as *Textbooks and the American Indian* by Rupert Costo and Jeannette Henry, *Unlearning "Indian" Stereotypes* by the Council on Interracial Books for Children, and *American Indian Authors for Young Readers* by Mary Gloyne Byler. I especially appreciate the teachers, parents, students, artists, consultants, and interns with whom I was privileged to work, among them Nancy Merrill, who helped write the proposal for the project; Kay Gamble, who taught students and developed curriculum; Nancy Hands Kraus, who helped extend the work to another setting; Diana Beaver, Nina Ross, and Kathleen Westcott, who were among the interns preparing to become classroom teachers; Susan Gurnoe Weinlick, who typed endless curriculum drafts; and the late Susan Weyaus, one of our Native language teachers. I deeply appreciate all of them, including those who have provided ongoing friendship since that period.

Arlene Hirschfelder has also served an important role in this work. I first became acquainted with Arlene through her writing in *Unlearning "Indian" Stereotypes*, but was later privileged to meet her in person in New York City. Since our initial meeting, we have embarked on a number of writing projects together. I greatly value her friendship and support, including her vital role with this book. Besides meeting Arlene while living in New York, I regularly found my way to the former Title IV, or Indian education program, tucked away in a public school in upper Manhattan. That program, sharing similarities with others across the country, fought an uphill battle to counteract the school treatment of American Indians as peripheral to the regular instructional program. Yvonne (Beamer) Dennis, Stephanie Betancourt, Wanda Hunter, and Annie Teamer were among the program's staff members.

After moving to Virginia, I had the opportunity to meet Mary Gloyne Byler, one of the authors our Minnesota project staff had regularly recommended to teachers. I appreciate her contributions to my work, including that at Hampton. This is also to thank K. Tsianina Lomawaima for sharing her discerning letter about *My Heart Is on the Ground* to Scholastic with me, for commenting on my writing, and for her involvement and support during earlier work together on boarding school research. Her example is always exemplary. Oyate, the Berkeley-based organization that works to see that Native lives and histories are accurately portrayed, provides essential educational services. Besides evaluating books, Oyate's work includes publishing a catalog and maintaining a resource-rich website. Wordcraft Circle of Native Writers & Storytellers, another organization that fosters Native work and Native voices, keeps the circle growing. I appreciate Debbie Reese's insights and work and Barbara Landis at Carlisle. Thank you to Carole and O. L. Durham for their friendship but also for keeping Kathy Kerner's book, *They Taught You Wrong*, in print and circulating. This is also to thank Patty Campbell for her patience and support as I worked on this book. I appreciate the assistance of the staff members of the Hampton Public Library, especially in response to my steady stream of interlibrary loan requests.

As always, my family is first in my heart. Larry is the best—always a supportive presence in my life. My mother, who attended the Pipestone boarding school, personifies that legacy, but much more. My great-niece Shannon was in my care when I began research for this book. This work is for her, Britney, Amber, Paulette, Lindsey, Mikey, Tom, Tim, Sean, and all the rest of our relatives. May they always find teachers, books, and stories devoted to tribal lives and communities that help pave the way to healthy futures.

Foreword

Arlene Hirschfelder

For several days, I pondered ways to begin the foreword to Paulette Molin's book. When I finally sat down at the computer to begin writing, I heard my Westy barking at the front door. The letter carrier had just delivered the mail. Among the letters and catalogues, I spotted the latest issue of *National Geographic* (September 2004). A quick scan of articles listed on the cover revealed one entitled "The New Face of the American Indian" that leads to an article by Joseph Bruchac, an author of Abenaki descent. A quick look-see of "Indian Country," the large supplemental map tucked inside the magazine, showed a wealth of historical and current socioeconomic information. One side of the map includes "Portraits of Pride," a border of sixteen images of Native people from 1790s to the current time. Four writers are pictured: Sherman Alexie, Spokane/Coeur D'Alene; Vine Deloria, Dakota; Winona LaDuke, Anishinaabe; and N. Scott Momaday, Kiowa. No question I needed to read Bruchac's piece before returning to the keyboard. Good thing I did.

What, you ask, does Joseph Bruchac's article and accompanying map have to do with Paulette Molin's study of American Indian themes in young adult literature? Plenty! Molin analyzes American Indian characters and themes in young adult literature, both fiction and nonfiction authored by Indians and non-Indians. She discusses several of Bruchac's young adult novels as well as his nonfiction treatments of important events in Native history. Her analysis shows that Bruchac does his homework *before* he sets words to page so he can be "absolutely true" to the story and its sources. Before writing *The Journal of Jesse Smoke, a Cherokee Boy, Trail of Tears, 1838*, Bruchac spent years studying source material as well as consulting with contemporary Cherokee writers, artists, and storytellers. The same prodigious effort went into another Bruchac young adult novel, *Sacajawea: The Story of Bird Woman and the Lewis and Clark Expedition*. He researched explorers' journals and consulted with the tribal historian of the Wind River Shoshones. A contemporary descendant of Sacajawea read and commented on his manuscript. For *The Winter People*, an historical novel that deals with the decimation of the Abenaki village of St. Francis in 1759, Bruchac incorporated "tribal sources to present a pivotal event from untold perspectives."

Reading Paulette Molin's descriptions of Joseph Bruchac's research methods resonated with me. Like him, I did homework *before* writing *Photo Odyssey: Solomon Carvalho's Remarkable Western Adventure 1853–54* (included in one of Molin's nonfiction chapters). My research took me to archives in Berkeley, California and Baltimore, Maryland where I poured over primary source materials. It required consultations with experts in Lenape history, Jewish history, daguerreotype photography, and the botany of grasslands in central North America. Lengthy phone calls with Carvalho's great-great-granddaughter were invaluable.

Bruchac and a number of other authors identified by Molin (especially in her chapter "Nonfiction: American Indian Life Stories") have also written novels, nonfiction books, and autobiographies dealing with contemporary realities of American Indian people. Since one can easily make a case that Native people are perhaps one of the least understood of all those who make up the tapestry of American life, owing in part to the paucity of literature about their lives today, Molin's commentary makes it clear that authors should and could do homework and write about contemporary times. This focus is undeniably important. Since so many Americans (teens included) believe Native people lived and died in the past, it's significant that writers like Cynthia Leitich Smith and Virginia Driving Hawk Sneve, among others, have chosen to set their works in the here and now. As renowned scholar Ella Deloria (Dakota) put it so well in *Speaking of Indians* (1944): "All that which lies hidden in the remote past is interesting . . . but not so important as the present and the future."

Molin's study identifies authors who fail to do the appropriate home-work when they set out to write either an historical or contemporary novel or a nonfiction work. Some fail to question whether their sources are reputable. Some fail to question when the sources were written. Some fail to find qualified expert readers with extensive knowledge to critique their manuscripts *before* they are published. And some authors who do receive comments from experts choose not to incorporate rec-ommended changes. In one chapter, Molin deals exclusively with the controversy surrounding *My Heart Is on the Ground*, a fictionalized di-ary of "Nannie Little Rose, a Sioux Girl" written by Ann Rinaldi. The author chose not to follow up on the suggestions of Genevieve Bell, her fact checker (whom she thanked in her acknowledgments). After its publication, Rinaldi's fictionalized diary received a fair amount of crit-icism from Indian and non-Indian scholars with extensive knowledge of boarding schools and Lakota culture and history. Bell wrote:

I completely sympathize with the critical review of Rinaldi's work that has proliferated both on the Internet and off it. There is much in the book that is offensive, and I did say so to Scholastic. Indeed, there is much more in this book that is offensive that I missed, which is why I urged Melissa Jenkins [of Scholastic] to get a Lakota person to read it. She knew that I was not Native American. However, I also contracted with Scholas-tic to fact-check the manuscript and thought it only appropriate that my name be attached to that act. Again, I can only reflect on the naiveté that made me think that my comments would be taken seriously enough to change the course of the publication. I am deeply sorry that they did not. And I apologize for the offense that I have given, however, inadvertently.[1]

In addition to analyzing works of authors who undertake (and don't undertake) extensive homework before attempting to write their books, Molin discusses reviewers of books with American Indian themes. She shows how too many reviewers reinforce, and even honor, stereotypical works, perpetuating notions of white dominance and superiority. For those teachers, librarians, parents, and others concerned with factual and cultural accuracy and who depend on reviews to suggest reliable works, it's frustrating to read book reviews that commend good writing and ignore bad scholarship. It's frustrating to read book reviews that celebrate artful writing and sidestep demeaning vocabulary, stereotyping in text and illustrations, and distorted Eurocentric history. It's frustrating to read book reviews that applaud literary quality and ignore the social context and impact of a book. Naomi Caldwell-Wood and Lisa A. Mitten addressed this point back in 1991:

> Over the years, the most frequently asked questions by librarians concerning books on Native Americans have centered around the ideas of "How can I personally tell good books on Indians from bad?" and "Where can I find reliable reviews?." Neither of these are as simplistic as they sound. Reviews abound in the usual sources for books dealing with Native peoples, but most are written from a literary angle, or from a children's/YA literature perspective.[2]

The same year Kathleen T. Horning and Ginny Moore Kruse of the Cooperative Children's Book Center, School of Education, University of Wisconsin at Madison noted that:

> most children's book editorial departments are composed of people whose backgrounds are Euroamerican, and most children's and young adult book review journals use reviewers whose understanding of races and cultures other than their own is shaped by the prevailing images and ideas in the dominant experience.[3]

The problem also rests in part with American education. In her November 1999 *School Library Journal* piece, educator Debbie Reese wrote:

> As a society we receive little formal education about Native Americans that provides us with sufficient knowledge to be able to notice errors [in books]. If finding reviewers with expertise is difficult, it may be necessary to note in the review that the reviewer has attended to literary elements but cannot comment with authority on a book's factual or cultural authenticity.[4]

A year later, in her study "Contesting Ideology in Children's Book Reviewing" (*Studies in American Indian Literature*, vol. 12, no.1, Spring 2000: pp. 37–55), Reese points out that librarians would like to see more "people of color" (and that of course includes Native Americans) involved in authoring, illustrating, publishing, and reviewing books with American Indian themes.

So what can book reviewers do when they don't have time to consult several reputable sources, can't track down facts about the cultures and histories of hundreds of Native nations in North America, and are bereft of expertise? And how do librarians and teachers find appropriate young adult nonfiction and novels with American Indian themes for their collections and classrooms? The answer for all: Do some homework. Read Paulette Molin's *American Indian Themes in Young Adult Literature*. Her analyses of plots, American Indian characters, themes, and settings in fiction and nonfiction written for young adults provide invaluable tools to help evaluate literature about American Indians.

NOTES

1. Genevieve Bell, "The Politics of Representation: A Response to the Publication of Ann Rinaldi's *My Heart Is on the Ground*," 1999. Available online at http://home.epix.net/~landis/review.html (accessed August 24, 2004).

2. Naomi Caldwell-Wood and Lisa A. Mitten, *"I" Is Not for Indian: The Portrayal of Native Americans in Books for Young People: Selective Bibliography and Guide*. Program of the ALA/OLOS Subcommittee for Library Services to American Indian People, American Indian Library Association, Atlanta, Georgia, June 29, 1991. Available online at www.nativeculture.com/lisamitten/ailabib.htm, 1 (Accessed August 24, 2004).

3. Kathleen T. Horning and Ginny Moore Kruse, "Looking into the Mirror: Considerations behind the Reflections," in *The Multicolored Mirror: Cultural Substance in Literature for Children and Young Adults*, ed. by M. V. Lundgren (Fort Atkinson, WI: Highsmith, 1991), 7.

4. Debbie Reese, "Authenticity and Sensitivity: Goals for Writing and Reviewing Books with Native American Themes," *School Library Journal* (November 1999), 36.

Part One

Contemporary Literature

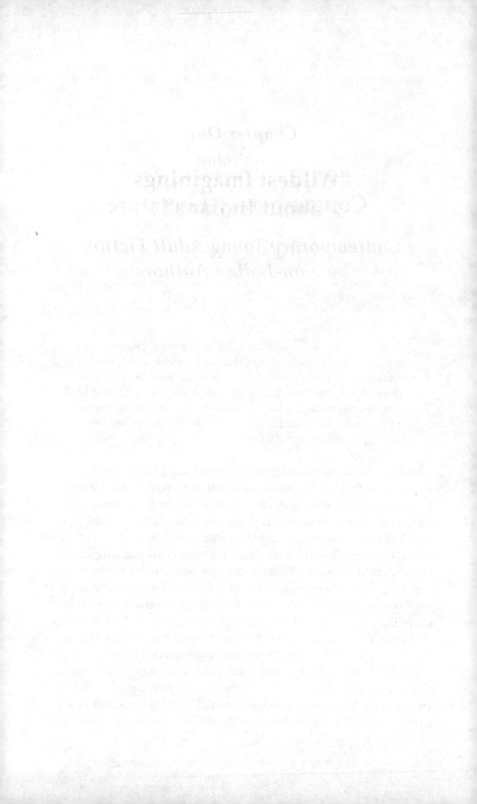

Chapter One

"Wildest Imaginings about Indians"

Contemporary Young Adult Fiction by Non-Indian Authors

> There are plenty of "good" books—i.e. well-written, exciting, from respected authors, much-loved by their readers, with well-developed characters—that are terrible when examined with the criteria of whether the Native American(s) depicted in them are accurately or even humanly portrayed. For the most part, this criticism is directed at fictional works, where the greatest stereotypes and wildest imaginings about Indians still hold sway.[1]

These statements by Naomi Caldwell-Wood and Lisa A. Mitten of the American Indian Library Association still apply to too many works of fiction depicting Native Americans. Such novels, including those written for young adults, often present Euro-American views cloaked in the words of imaginary Indians, introduce characters who assume expertise about Native life based on a few visits to a tribal community, incorporate out-of-context elements of tribal culture for questionable purposes, present portrayals and perspectives that ring false to Native Americans, and reinforce stereotypes. Furthermore, the plots they devise are for the benefit of Euro-American audiences, not tribal communities. Such books are disappointing, especially given the critical need for strong, accurate portrayals of contemporary Native peoples in young adult fiction.

Robert Lipsyte, highly respected columnist and award-winning sports reporter for the New York Times, is one such writer. A 2001 recipient of the Margaret A. Edwards Award, Lipsyte is the author of a series of novels with Native American themes, *The Brave*, *The Chief*, and

Warrior Angel.[2] These books center on boxing and incorporate some of the characters from Lipsyte's earlier novel, *The Contender*, "one of the very first realistic novels about contemporary teenagers and a book that has been required reading in many American schools for the past three decades."[3] Writing in *Warrior Angel*, Robert Lipsyte sums up the early life of his protagonist Sonny Bear, a young boxer from the fictional Moscandaga Reservation in New York:

> Moving from the Reservation near Sparta in Upstate New York to Boston to Minneapolis to Santa Fe to Santa Cruz, California, as a kid while his mother tried to sell the jewelry she designed and made. Always coming back broke to the Res and his great-uncle Jake's auto junkyard. Hiding in the backs of old wrecked cars, drawing pictures he tore up before anyone could see them. Helping Jake find parts in the old cars for his customers. Dropping out of Sparta High School after he was kicked off the football team. He had slugged a teammate, an elephant-assed tackle who had called him Tonto. Didn't like football anyway. Too many rules. A white man's game. (*Warrior Angel*, 61)

This novel picks up where the two earlier books, the stereotypically titled *The Brave* and *The Chief*, left off. Sonny Bear, the son of a Moscondaga mother and a white father killed in Vietnam, first appears in *The Brave*. Named George Harrison Bayer after his mother's favorite Beatle, Sonny comments in the text: "My dad's name was B-a-y-e-r, people pronounced it bear, so that's the way my mom started spelling it when we went to pow-wows" (*Brave*, 124). Leaving the reservation at the age of seventeen with the intention of lying about his age and enlisting in the Army, he heads for New York City. A short time later, he runs afoul of the law by carrying drugs for a Times Square dealer and runs into tough cop Alfred Brooks, the boxing protagonist of *The Contender*. Brooks sees Sonny as a potential contender, "A guy coming up, willing to bust his tail and take his lumps to find out just how far he can go" (*Brave*, 111). By the end of *The Brave*, Sonny Bear has triumphed in boxing, but like Olympian Jim Thorpe, he is stripped of his official title. Lipsyte, who has also written a biography about Thorpe for young readers, then has Sonny Bear or "the Tomahawk Kid" battle his way to a heavyweight championship in *The Chief*. By *Warrior Angel*, "the youngest heavyweight champion in history" has lost his spirit until a mentally disturbed teenager, Richard Starkey, helps rescue him.

The fictional Moscondaga reservation shares similarities, especially in name and location, with the Onondaga reservation near Syracuse, New York. However, Lipsyte writes that the setting is not Iroquois. He comments: "They called Sonny a young chief, which he certainly was not, of the Iroquois, to which the Moscondaga do not belong" (*Chief*, 218). Writing through an imaginary insider, Lipsyte reinforces numerous stereotypes. He uses the term "res" to refer to the reservation, a term used by many American Indians and often rendered "rez" in print. Writer Sherman Alexie comments on the pitfalls of outsiders using the term in a review of Ian Frazier's nonfiction book *On the Rez*: "A white man using the word 'rez' to describe the reservation is the equivalent of a white man using the word 'hood' to describe a black inner-city neighborhood. It implies a degree of cultural familiarity that is very rare."[4] Alexie points out that "Frazier's formal use of 'the rez' marks him as an outsider eager to portray himself as an insider, as a writer with a supposedly original story to tell and as a white man who is magically unlike all other white men in his relationship to American Indians" (Alexie, 3). Besides his stereotypical book titles and use of an insider term, Lipsyte works the clichéd torn-between-cultures theme with his protagonist Sonny Bear, who asserts: "Whose people? I'm an Indian up here, but when the chiefs sit in the Long House and tell their secrets, I'm just a mixed-blood white boy" (*Brave*, 10). "Shove that tired old Redskin crap," he later comments, "I'm not anything anymore. Not Indian, not white" (*Warrior Angel*, 1). Sonny Bear also complains: "Both sides treated me like a cracker until I was champ" (*Warrior Angel*, 105). Lipsyte frames and defines American Indian identity issues from an outsider's perspective, not in tribal terms of sovereignty, culture, enrollment, descent, and upbringing, which are far more complex.

While spouting negative stereotypes against American Indians as an imaginary insider, Sonny Bear wears markers that would announce, if not broadcast, his Moscondaga identity (black ponytail, "exquisite" Indian belt and beaded headband). His physical appearance suggests that he embraces his indigenous heritage, but his disparaging comments parallel those of racist outsiders: "This is just the kind of dumb Redskin lipflap you need to leave behind," "Later on the redskin crap," and "No Redskin crap" (*Brave*, 15; *Chief*, 5; *Warrior Angel*, 107). Sonny also proclaims: "I am Sonny Bear, a member of the Moscondaga Nation. This is how we wear our hair" (*Brave*, 64). Although mostly raised on the reservation by his great-uncle Jake, he has harsh words for this elderly relative, telling him at one point: "I'm sick of your dumb Indian talk" (*Brave*, 13). In another passage, he comments: "Won't miss anybody on this raggedy Reservation, especially a crazy old man waiting for the buffalo to come back" (*Brave*, 16). In the novels, Jake is the character who takes care of Sonny, providing a home and instruction in family history and tribal culture. One of his teachings concerns Moscondaga runners, stereotypically named the Running Brave Society in Lipsyte's fiction. Lipsyte portrays Sonny Bear as "the last one with the blood of the Running Braves," the vanishing, last-of-their-kind Indian theme of so much fiction. In reality, running societies have a long history in American Indian nations, a rich tradition documented in Peter Nabakov's nonfiction book, *Indian Running*.[5] Lipsyte correctly identifies some of the roles of such runners as "a courier, a diplomat, a warrior, a peace bringer, always on call to the Nation, always in training" (*Brave*, 67). Unfortunately, he undercuts any factual information by stereotyping and denigrating the society. At one point, for example, a character comments: "I decided that the Running Braves were just a redskin gang. Great-great-grandpa was probably a drunk run over by another drunk" (*Chief*, 48).

Lipsyte points out changing perceptions of American Indians through characters such as Martin Witherspoon, a black college student and would-be writer, who serves as one of Sonny Bear's sidekicks. Witherspoon's attitudes go from romantic to negative during the course of his exposure to the reservation and its people: "By the third and fourth trips, the stories got old and the Res looked like a raggedy slum of sagging cabins and rusted trailers. Jake's house was a shabby yellow box in a sea of rust and chrome. The Clan Mothers started to sound like nagging grandmas" (*Chief*, 48). Witherspoon, who assumes a cultural familiarity that rightfully belongs to the people of the reservation, manifests observations that are the flip side of the same coin. He makes jaded comments as a way of showing off the "expertise" he has acquired from visiting the Moscondaga Reservation. In other words, he believes himself so knowledgeable, and such an insider, he can disparage the people and the place. Actually, Witherspoon merely reveals himself as a too-typical outsider and bad guest, one who exploits and betrays his hosts. Lipsyte does refute some notions about Indians during the course of his books. When another character tries to romanticize Jake by saying,

"He's like a shaman," Sonny Bear responds: "He runs a junkyard on the Reservation" (*Brave*, 135). When a reporter asks Sonny his opinion of Indian rights, Alfred Brooks responds for him: "Ask him about Indian lefts. He's here to fight, not talk politics" (*Brave*, 154). In another passage, Lipsyte accurately observes: "The closer to the Res, thought Sonny, the more they hate Indians. For the first hour or so, he knew, no one would want to sit next to him" (*Brave*, 20).

"Sports-journalist Lipsyte writes authoritatively about the world of boxing," *Kirkus Reviews* noted of *The Chief*, "moving his story at a headlong pace with pulse-pounding action scenes and providing characters with cocky dialogue; by concluding moments before Sonny enters the ring, he forces readers to consider his larger themes."[6] While that assessment rings true, Lipsyte's authoritativeness does not extend to his protrayal of Native Americans.

Native American themes are also at the heart of numerous novels written by Will Hobbs, the popular, award-winning author of young adult fiction. *Bearstone*, for one, is the coming-of-age story of Cloyd Atcitty (yes, Cloyd, not Lloyd), a troubled Ute-Navajo fourteen-year-old who grew up with his grandmother and a sister in Utah and spent time in a Ute group home in Colorado.[7] Cloyd's Ute mother died "getting him born" and he had never known his Navajo father, but wondered about him his whole life. In the opening scene of the book, Cloyd runs away from a Ute group home and hitchhikes to Window Rock, Arizona, in search of his father, only to find him brain dead in a hospital. The teenager is placed on a large ranch owned by elderly widower Walter Landis, in southwestern Colorado, near an area "all wilderness for a hundred miles and more" (*Bearstone*, 6). The book details the ups and downs of the relationship between the Indian "bad kid" and the white man "who didn't act like other grown-ups" (*Bearstone*, 8). One of the strengths of the book is the setting, the ancestral homeland of Cloyd's Ute people, who "knew every stream, places so out of the way that white men still hadn't seen them" (*Bearstone*, 12). Another is the action/adventure theme, where Cloyd rides a horse, hikes, and explores the mountains that were home to Utes "until gold was discovered there and the white men wanted them out of the way" (*Bearstone*, 12).

The book's depiction of Utes includes generalizations such as "Walter knew the Utes weren't big talkers" and stereotypical descriptions of Cloyd—"I think he's at least half-wild"—and his grandmother—"A Ute woman in the old style, she was dark, earthy, and large, the mainstay of her diet being frybread" (*Bearstone*, 39, 8, 64). In addition, Cloyd's female relatives—grandmother, mother, and sister—are nameless and mostly voiceless in the text. Although Cloyd's sister writes to him, little information is provided about her, only that she is a boarding school student. A section of the book that is especially problematic is Cloyd's handling of an ancient burial bundle. Although he remembers his grandmother's admonition to treat such areas with respect, Cloyd "probed with his fingers. Turkey feathers and fur, probably rabbit: hundreds of tiny bits of feather and fur wrapped around cords of yucca fiber. A blanket, a whole blanket in the style of the Ancient Ones" (*Bearstone*, 14). Folding the blanket back, he uncovered the remains of an infant. In the same area, Cloyd also happened upon a piece of pottery, a jar, that he "brought into the open where he could see it" (*Bearstone*, 15). Inside the jar was a small, carved turquoise bear that Cloyd took out and kept, hence the bearstone of the novel's title. The problem with this depiction is that disturbing a burial site is desecration, including handling or removing any objects from it. The author justifies this by writing: "Cloyd turned the smooth blue stone in his hand. He felt he was meant to cross the cliff and find this stone. He had earned this bear-stone; his grandmother would understand. She was the only person he knew who remembered the old ways and believed in their power" (*Bearstone*, 16). Desecration of ancient sites, such as that depicted in the novel, is a very real problem. Having a character justify such an act, no matter how well intentioned, conveys a message of approval.

A sequel to this book is *Beardance* (the title taken from the Ute Bear Dance), in which Hobbs picks up the story where it ended in *Bearstone*.[8] In this continuation of the saga, Cloyd returns to the mountains with his elderly foster parent Walter. While the older man searches for a lost treasure of Spanish gold, Cloyd hopes to find surviving grizzly bears in the mountains. During the course of the story, they meet Ursa, a biologist from the Tlingit tribe in Alaska, who is also searching for grizzlies in the Colorado mountains. Hobbs, who depicts her as a trained professional who uses her training to help protect bears, nonetheless undercuts this positive portrayal by referring to her as "grizzly woman" throughout the text. Bear cubs, too, are nicknamed "Cocoa and Brownie," even though they are not pets, but animals living in their own habitat. In these novels, Ute ceremonial life is taken out of its tribal context and applied to the teenage "insider" protagonist, who uses it without the guiding wisdom and preparatory training of qualified practitioners. In his review of this book for *School Library Journal*, Todd Morning commented: "This novel works as an effective adventure story, an exploration of the Ute Indian culture, and a natural-history lesson rolled into one, all set in the rarefied atmosphere of the Continental Divide."[9] Used in conjunction with reliable information about Ute culture, it does.

The bear, ubiquitous in name or presence in American Indian-themed fiction for young adults, also figures in Ben Mikaelsen's *Touching Spirit Bear*.[10] This novel is loosely based on a well-publicized event described by author Wendy Leopold, who writes: "Images of Indians as 'exotics' were reinforced in 1994 with a spate of stories around the country about two Tlingit youth 'banished' to a remote Alaskan island for robbing and severely beating a Seattle area pizza delivery man. At a time when the U.S. government was debating removing the Tlingits from federal recognition, media stories ignored the [termination] threat" confronting the tribal nation.[11] Drawing from this incident and information about a pilot sentencing circle project in Minnesota, Mikaelsen centers his novel on a teenager named Cole Matthews, "an innocent-looking, baby-faced fifteen-year-old from Minneapolis who had been in trouble with the law half his life" (Mikaelsen, 5). After viciously attacking a class-mate to the point of permanent physical damage, Cole is placed in a de-tention center and faces a prison sentence. While detained, he comes in contact with Garvey, a Tlingit youth probation officer, who offers the al-ternative of a new trial program, Circle Justice, "a healing form of jus-tice practiced by native cultures for thousands of years" (Mikaelsen, 10). Feigning an attitude change, Cole applies to the Circle and the members banish him to a remote Alaskan island for a year. Shortly af-ter stepping on shore, he torches the shelter built for him by Edwin, a Tlingit elder, and tries to escape by swimming away from confinement. Cole ends up tangling with a great white Spirit Bear, but survives to tell the tale. Found injured and nearly starved by Garvey and Edwin, the teenager spends months recuperating before facing the justice system again. He then returns to the island, this time intent on changing his life.

As Joel Shoemaker writes in his review in *School Library Journal*, "Mikaelsen's portrayal of this angry, manipulative, damaged teen is dead on. Cole's gradual transformation into a human kind of being

happens in fits and starts. He realizes he must accept responsibility for
what he has done, but his pride, pain, and conditioning continue to in-
terfere."[12] He achieves his realization through a form of justice that involves victim offender, and other members of the community. "Circle
Justice tries to heal, not punish," as Garvey explained to Cole. "Your
lawyer might take you to a zoo to help you appreciate animals more.
The prosecutor might have you watch a veterinarian operate for a day
to realize the value of life. The judge might help you on the weekend to
make birdhouses as repayment to the animal kingdom for something
you destroyed. Even neighbors might help in some way" (Mikaelsen,
11). This story is at its best in portraying a disaffected youth and the
parents and system that fail him. Its weaknesses lie in the plausibility of
some of the scenarios, such as the likelihood of a non-Indian juvenile
offender in Minneapolis being transported and banished to an Alaskan
island under Tlingit jurisdiction, the chances of *anyone* winning a fight
with a powerful bear, and the odds of Cole's victim joining him on the
island. Unfortunately, there is little information about the Tlingit, past
or present. Garvey and Edwin appear as secondary characters in the
novel, serving as teachers and helpers to move Cole along his journey
to redemption. "Although the [actual] incident got attention nationwide," Leopold writes, "almost no stories about it provided a cultural
context for the banishment. Instead of focusing on Tlingit judicial tradition, the Tlingits' battle for federal recognition or even the fate of the
two youth, the stories focused on the authenticity of the local judge who
said he was a Tlingit tribal judge" (Leopold, 3). Similarly, *Touching
Spirit Bear* does not address most of these issues, but can stimulate a
discussion of them. With Tlingit help, the novel's protagonist ultimately
fulfills the Japanese proverb in the novel's frontispiece, "Fall seven
times, stand up eight."

A. E. Cannon's novel *The Shadow Brothers*, also set in Utah, is the
story of Marcus Jenkins and his foster brother Henry Yazzie.[13] The
coming-of-age story, an American Library Association Best Book for
Young Adults, focuses primarily on the lives of the sixteen-year-old
brothers during their junior year in high school. *School Library Journal*
notes, "Cannon has written a read-it-again story on a not-everyday
topic."[14] The "not-everyday topic" is better known to Native Americans
who participated in the Indian Student Placement Services program of the
Church of Jesus Christ of Latter-Day Saints. This program, which began

in 1947 and focused primarily on Navajo children, placed tribal youth in Mormon homes during the school year. By the time it began phasing out in the 1970s, thousands of Native young people had participated. The program became controversial, in part because of the removal of children from their own families and cultures to assimilate them into mainstream culture, but also because it served as a means to proselytize. In contrast, proponents of the foster arrangements contended that they provided impoverished Indian students with educational opportunities they otherwise lacked. *Silent Courage, An Indian Story: The Autobiography of George P. Lee, A Navajo* offers a firsthand perspective of this program.[15] Lee, one of the program's first recruits, includes information about the family and societal circumstances that propelled him into foster care. The Indian Student Placement Services program ended, in part, because of increased educational opportunities on the Navajo Reservation. In addition, Congress passed the Indian Child Welfare Act in 1978, which established standards for the placement of Indian children in foster or adoptive homes, affirming tribal jurisdiction.

Cannon sets her fiction in Lake View, Utah, where Marcus, the narrator of the novel, lives with his Mormon mother, a psychiatrist father originally from Boston, and his young sister Julia. Henry entered the Jenkins home at the age of seven, shortly after the death of his mother. His father Lennie, a tribal policeman on the Navajo Reservation, was an old friend of Marcus's dad. "Lennie Yazzie called my parents the summer before my second-grade year to ask if Henry could live with us and go to school with me," Marcus explains. "Lake View is a small but fairly affluent community between Salt Lake City and Provo. The schools have a good reputation, and Lennie said that's what Henry needed, since he was practically a genius" (Cannon, 21). Henry's perspectives are directly revealed on occasion, primarily when Marcus finds and reads one of his student essays. Entitled "The Me Nobody Knows," Henry wrote, "Wakara High School, where the students are white and occasionally Hispanic—except for me. I am Native American and sometimes when I wake in the middle of the night, emerge from my cave of dreams, I think I am a symbol. I am a symbol of how complete the white man's victory was here" (Cannon, 8). Although Henry's firsthand viewpoints are rare, Cannon uses them as a tool to disparage another tribal group, within the same student essay: "The Utes used to roam this valley. Fierce, bold, clever—they made life miserable for the

Paiutes to the south, who grubbed their lives away in dirty hovels" (Cannon, 8). Hence, through this device, the Indian "insider," not Marcus, makes negative comments about other tribal peoples.

"Over the years," Cannon comments in *The Shadow Brothers*, "a number of Navahos have sent their kids to live with white families during the school year through the Mormon church's placement program" (Cannon, 21). In the novel, however, this program is not a factor. Besides characterizing the fictional placement as an arrangement between friends, Cannon incorporates other features that differ from the actual program. In contrast to the very real economic gaps of the program's participants and their hosts, the novel's two families represent comparable, though unequal, economic circumstances. Henry is also portrayed as an only child, a significant difference in family size from that reflected in the church program. While Cannon depicts the biological and foster fathers as longtime friends, participating children often met foster families for the first time through their placements. In the novel, Cannon makes only passing references to the Mormon faith, mainly in connection with Marcus's mother. With minimal coverage of the Mormon placement program and religion, the author avoids areas of potential controversy.

"Henry and me. Me and Henry." Marcus comments. "It's been that way forever. People even say our names together in the same way they say Tom-and-Jerry. It's always Marcus-and-Henry. Henry-and-Marcus" (Cannon, 15). Besides attending the same school, they share a room, buy a car (an old hearse) together, and compete against each other in academics and athletics. Cultural and racial differences, as well as Henry's homesickness, emerge from time to time in the narrative. At one point, Marcus gets a glimpse of what it means to be in the minority. On a trip to the Navajo Reservation, ogled by children in a trading post, he comments: "They kept staring at *me* like I was the strangest thing they'd ever seen. I looked around the store, and I realized that my dad and I were the only white people there, just like Henry had been the only brown person in our class the first day of school. Now I was the one from Mars" (Cannon, 30). Henry's adjustment is portrayed positively, with Marcus observing: "Henry doesn't go back to the reservation much now because he's too busy. . . . So Lennie comes up here a couple of times every year instead. I like Lennie. He's a very funny guy with a million great stories about being a reservation cop. . . . Still, they don't seem very much alike to me. You look at Lennie sitting there in his plaid cotton shirt with mother-of-pearl buttons, talking about rounding up sheep thieves, and you realize that he lives in a completely different world than Henry" (Cannon, 44). Marcus concludes that his foster brother is more Jenkins than Yazzie.

In the novel, though, Henry's Navajo background gradually comes to the forefront, with a pull from family. His aging grandfather, who had wanted Henry to stay at home, wishes to teach him tribal traditions before it is too late. The arrival of another Indian student at school also contributes to Henry's growing focus on identity issues. Asked to befriend Frank, a troubled transfer from another school, he is soon at odds with him. The two students not only represent different tribal groups, but opposite ways of adjusting to the white setting. The counselors at Frank's old school transferred him, figuring he and Henry would hit it off. "Don't you just love the irony of it, Marcus?" Henry asks. "An Indian is an Indian is an Indian" to the counselors. "There is no Navaho, no Hopi, no Ute, no Zuni, no Apache. Just brown skin. Just Indians" (Cannon, 62). Complicating their relationship, the two Indian teenagers are both portrayed as talented runners, who compete against each other in track. "We call boys like you apples." Frank erupts in one of their exchanges. "Red on the outside. White on the inside" (Cannon, 84). His anger is not surprising, given the circumstances young Native American students face in a school setting where they are vastly outnumbered. Caldwell-Wood and Mitten conclude of this book: "A well-done novel of a Navajo teen as told by his adoptive (non-Indian) brother. . . . Deals with issues many Indian kids face as novelties in their schools" (Caldwell-Wood and Mitten, 5). Nonetheless, it is best considered in the context of larger issues, such as foster care and cultural representation and continuity for American Indian communities.

James Bennett's *Dakota Dream*, another American Library Association Best Book for Young Adults, is the story of Floyd Rayfield, a white teenager who spent his life in foster homes and group homes, but believed his destiny was to become a Dakota Indian.[16] Hoping to someday have his name legally changed, Floyd sometimes signed his school assignments, "Charly Black Crow, AKA Floyd Rayfield." Besides adopting a new name, Floyd dyed his hair black "about once a month to get the red out" and had even tried to make his skin darker with tanning cream and walnut water (Bennett, 3). He also studied the Dakota culture and counted a ceremonial pipe and a pair of handmade moccasins among his most valued possessions. Floyd's penchant for using another name, wearing moccasins to school, advancing Dakota beliefs to a Baptist minister, writing unusual stories, and landing at the center of mishaps spell trouble for him with group home supervisors, school officials, and other authorities. Placed in a mental institution for observation and testing, Floyd runs away to the Pine Ridge Reservation in South Dakota.

The strength of Bennett's book is his sensitive depiction of a "hung-out kid," one shuffled from place to place and entangled in a web of bureaucratic institutions. "Since I'd never been to Joliet before, I didn't recognize any of the city landmarks," Floyd muses, "but Gates House looked familiar, anyway. It looked just like most of the dipshit places that are run by social services anywhere you go. It was a dull brick rectangle, with no porch and a few small windows. Not old, but real tacky. It looked like it didn't belong in the neighborhood. There was a parking lot in front, but no trees" (Bennett, 44). The supervisor of the house tells Floyd: "You may decorate your half of the room if you like with pictures or posters, but I don't allow any vulgar material. And you're not to make marks on the walls or deface them in any way" (Bennett, 45). Bennett skillfully captures the loneliness, coldness, and nuances of institutional life. In Floyd's observation, social workers came and went, leading him to conclude that the worst mistake a person could make in the system was to become attached to anyone.

Bennett's Native American themes, which are cliché ridden, are less compelling. While Floyd is depicted as a young man whose destiny it is to become a Dakota, this storyline has a familiar ring in tribal communities. Outsiders often seek to become Indian, flocking to Native communities in search of themselves or to find spiritual fulfillment. In an article entitled "The Tribe Called Wannabee: Playing Indian in America and Europe," scholar Rayna Green writes: "Almost from their very arrival in the Americas, Europeans found it useful, perhaps essential, to 'play Indian' in America."[17] This performance takes many forms, finding expression in literary texts, artifacts, enactments, and reenactments. "Some people," Green notes, "play Indian for a lifetime; others for brief, transient staged performances performed only in childhood or erratically and situationally over a lifetime" (Green, 118). Bennett's protagonist shares a number of these characteristics, from his dyed hair down to his moccasin-clad feet. "What it came down to was, I wanted to be an Indian," Floyd explains, "the way other kids want to grow up to be a policeman or a fire fighter, or whatever" (Bennett, 2). These aspirations are presented as parallel, a common mistake made by non-Indians, who often treat Indianness as a role or occupation instead of the human identity it is.

Illustrations for the cover of the book and a title page are stereotypical, featuring a typically generic Indian head. Names such as "Chief Bear-in-cave" and "a brave named Two-Claw" share the same characteristics. Bennett's depiction of Pine Ridge, actually home to the Oglala Lakota, is full of Euro-American perspectives. For instance, he has one character, Donny Thunderbird, voice the following "insider" comments: "A reservation is a place from the past. The Indian way of life is mostly history. . . . But Indians need help to live in the modern world" (Bennett, 13–14). Reservations were certainly established in the past, but they continue as present-day homelands. Furthermore, the Indian way of life is not "mostly history," but an ongoing contemporary reality. "One way that Indians need to become modern in is agriculture," Donny asserts, "and I've always been interested in crops and farming" (Bennett, 14). Actually, church missionaries and government agents promoted Euro-American farming on Indian reservations, in part, to change traditional land use patterns. This activity, advanced centuries ago in this country, disrupted tribal economies and was touted even when lands were demonstrably unsuited for agriculture.

Once Floyd reaches the Pine Ridge Reservation, thanks to a "borrowed" Kawasaki motorcycle and a ride part of the way, he quickly finds the spiritual experience he seeks. As scholar Vine Deloria writes: "A sizable number of people have come to American Indians, seeking to join tribal religious practices or take from the tribal traditions those things they find most attractive."[18] Assisted by the accommodating Chief Bear-in-cave, young Floyd embarks on a *hanblecheya*, or vision quest, commenting: "I was only twenty-four hours on the reservation, but it didn't get any more authentic than this" (Bennett, 42). The teenager completes a four-day vision quest during which he saw a complete tribal legend, quite a feat for anyone, much less an outsider on his very first visit to a Lakota reservation. The "chief" interpreted Floyd's Stone Boy vision with a flowery speech, commenting in part: "The grand thing about a destiny is that you learn it bit by bit, the way you learn a river. You love the Dakota and the values of the Dakota. You might say that's how the destiny begins. That's what puts you on the river, in your boat" (Bennett, 159). Floyd realizes his boat on the river of life means returning home to face the music, his vision quest reconciling him to his own community and world. His social worker, portrayed as a woman who went out on a limb for him, then arrives at Pine Ridge to escort him back.

Before Floyd leaves, Chief Bear-in-cave makes him an offer he cannot refuse. "Next summer, why not come here and work on the reservation? We have summer staff jobs for teenagers. . . . The work would be monotonous and the pay would be low. But you would spend the summer living and working among the Dakota. It might take you around another bend or two on the river, which might teach you more about your destiny" (Bennett, 176). Bennett thus interprets tribal life to serve the needs of an outsider. What about Lakota teenagers and their needs? As journalist Tim Giago points out, "The Oglala Lakota of the Pine Ridge Reservation and the Sicangu of the Rosebud Reservation have . . . unemployment as high as 60 percent and are within the boundaries of two of the poorest counties in America."[19] Furthermore, Bennett misrepresents and trivializes tribal citizenship, with Chief Bear-in-cave commenting: "If you pay your twenty-five dollars, and I write your name in the tribal enrollment book, who is to say that you are not Dakota?" (Bennett, 178). The tribal nation certainly could. It is possible to be adopted by an individual, but that person is not likely to be able to provide enrollment (that is, tribal citizenship). Tribal governments have jurisdiction in the matter of enrolling members of their respective nations, following established eligibility requirements as well as applicable rules and regulations. Outsiders, particularly in recognized tribes, cannot become tribal members by paying a fee and having their names recorded in a book. Nonetheless, Bennett concludes: "what a man is in his heart, that's what he truly is" (Bennett, 178). The idea that people can assume American Indian identity by what they hold in their hearts is self-serving, a convenient notion. It is not applicable to access to nationhood, tribal or otherwise. How does this work if the situation were reversed? Would Indians gain a new identity by holding it in their hearts? The reactions to that reversal can only be imagined. Bennett's protagonist, though, ends the novel with these words: "But mostly, I just thought about the one thing I was really sure of, and it gave me that peaceful, easy feeling: I was now an Indian" (Bennett, 182).

Colin Kersey also incorporates elements of fictional Native spirituality in his first novel, *Soul Catcher*, a combination horror and disaster narrative set in contemporary Seattle.[20] When an elderly shaman, Black Wolf, is brutally murdered by street toughs in that city, ancient forces of retribution hit the area in the form of deadly gale-force winds causing massive death and destruction. Kersey identifies this force as Williwaw ("an Eskimo spirit wind"), Taku (Inuit "legend of Taku"), or more generally, as a Native American spirit wind (Kersey, 200, 222). In the novel, it targets thirteen-year-old Evan Baker, "a boy with no ears," a deaf student with the power of second sight. Kersey's narrative is multiperspective, the story told by Evan and several other characters who fight against this lethal whirlwind, among them Evan's divorced mother Denise, a public relations representative; Billy Mossman, *Seattle Times* reporter-at-large; Paul Judge, an attorney from Montana's Crow Tribe; and Helen Anderson, a retired English teacher and survivor of one of Williwaw's strikes. "The story holds few surprises," *Publishers Weekly* notes, "and the explanation for why Evan has been singled out by Williwaw proves anticlimactic. Nevertheless, Kersey shows an aptitude for bringing characters to life, as well as for finding fresh possibilities in some of the genre's stalest ideas."[21]

The novel's stale ideas, unrelieved by fresh possibilities, extend to the Native American aspects of the book. The novel opens with a prologue centered on Black Wolf, a shaman, described by Kersey as "the last—the only one of his tribe who had not already died or surrendered to the white man's ways by moving to their cities" (Kersey, 4–5). This characterization of Native Americans is all too familiar, firmly rooted in vanishing Indian stereotypes. After the death of his wife, stereotypically dubbed Talks With Moon by the author, the shaman has no one to ease his loneliness or care for him. Although the couple had a daughter, Black Wolf disowned her after she moved away from home and married a white. "Once, many years before, she had come to visit him, bringing her half-breed children," Kersey writes, "but he had refused to see her. He stood inside the lodge door, listening to her sobbing entreaties with eyes pressed shut against the pain in his chest until, finally, she left" (Kersey, 5). Following the death of his wife, Black Wolf decides to journey to Seattle to find this daughter. Using money she had sent him over the years and he had refused to spend, Black Wolf leaves his ancestral home in Western Canada aiming to spend his remaining days of life with his urban family members.

Kersey's portrayal of Black Wolf is contradictory. Although he characterizes the shaman as refusing to have anything to do with his daughter, this rigid stance raises a number of questions. One is why Black Wolf would deny himself and his wife contact with their only child and their grandchildren. Another is why he would turn his back on descendants who could reverse his dying, last-of-his-kind status. This scenario is antithetical to Native love for children and family, strong tribal kinship ties, and a shaman's leadership role. Black Wolf's descendants could have carried the culture into the future, helping their family and community to grow and thrive. After years of alienation from his child, the shaman leaves home to search for her in the city. "The daughter of a Caribou shaman," in Black Wolf's estimation, "could not refuse him a warm fire and hot food to take the chill from his bones" (Kersey, 5). Kersey stereotypes the female role, expecting the daughter to treat her father better than he treated her, but also characterizing women as listening to men, bearing the young, dressing and cooking game, and dragging heavy carcasses and supplies on sledges. The shaman also speaks stereotypically, as in "You no sell heart" and "Black Wolf no sell necklace" (Kersey, 3). In Kersey's depiction, a drunken "outcast Indian" invites the shaman to share a bottle with these words, "Join powwow. We make big medicine" (Kersey, 6). Although Black Wolf's use of English is stereotypical at times, in other instances he speaks nearly as eloquently as Chief Seattle, who is quoted in the book and is an evident influence on the author. The shaman does not live to find his family in Seattle; instead, he is killed shortly after reaching the city. By the end of the book's prologue, Black Wolf had already summoned an avenging spirit wind to punish his murderers and to exact retribution for the desecration of the earth.

While most of the book's characters are non-Indians, another Native portrayal emerges in the person of Paul Judge, a thirty-five-year-old attorney from the Crow tribe in Montana. Kersey depicts Paul as an isolated and lonely man, who had lost his parents and grandmother from his life. Paul's father, in this portrayal, was a miner who "never came home until he was drunk" (Kersey, 142). The last time Paul saw his parents was when he was five or six years of age, following a fight in which his father hit his mother and "dragged her outside, screaming" (Kersey, 142). After Paul's grandmother arrived to rescue him in Butte, Montana, he lived with her at Lodge Grass on Montana's Crow Reservation. Paul, described as a Catholic who attended mission school, eventually won a scholarship to Gonzaga University. During his sophomore year in college, his grandmother died. After completing training in criminal law, Paul became a public defender in Seattle, handling mostly indigent cases. Besides being a loner, Paul is depicted as a single, available male with an attraction to the non-Indian Denise Baker and her son. He risks life and limb to help them survive the spirit wind, relying on his grandmother's teachings and spiritual assistance.

Ironically, given the other stereotypes in the book, Kersey portrays Paul as a man who is often the victim of racial slurs. In one encounter on a city street, a man comments of him, "It's Cochise," while another says, "How," raising a hand in salute (Kersey, 105). Kersey writes: "Paul ignored their drunken insults. Living in Seattle, you either got used to it or you moved on. The only Native Americans most people saw were the disenfranchised and downtrodden. The others, like himself, were too busy working, networking, and overcoming obstacles that most whites didn't have to think twice about. The end result was that people who wouldn't think about slurring a black, Latino, or Asian, slurred Indians without even realizing it" (Kersey, 106). In another incident, seeking help at a police substation, Paul is told by an officer, "I thought it was Indians who were supposed to be good at tracking," while another asks, "What's up, chief?" (Kersey, 162). Roberta Satiacum, a character who makes a brief appearance in the novel and is asked whether an Indian spirit is responsible for the mayhem, responds incredulously: "Are you kidding? If I said yes or even maybe, I'd be lucky to keep my job twenty-four hours. Make that twelve. My own children would disown me. Indians have taken a bad rap for too long as bloodthirsty savages without you quoting me saying something as stupid as that" (Kersey, 267–268).

Besides the mix of stereotypes, the novel is a mishmash of Northwest tribes, legendary beliefs, and supernatural forces. Paul ends up journeying to Makah tribal lands, in search of an ancient shaman living at "The Edge of the World." Kersey writes: ". . . the Edge people were a small tribe of perhaps a hundred Indians who claimed descendance from the distant Haida of the Queen Charlotte Islands in Canada" (Kersey, 212). There, Paul is attacked by twins, "two short, stocky men in their mid-twenties, dressed identically in buckskins and wearing mustaches—rare for Indians—and carved wooden helmets: one helmet was in the shape of an eagle, the other, displaying a longer beak, a raven" (Kersey, 226). Although this novel is set in contemporary times, these men brandish war clubs and try to kill Paul, another Indian, for going into their territory without an invitation. As Kersey writes, "Both men began circling him. The knife glinted in the moonlight. The other Indian gripped his war club" (Kersey, 227). The scene reinforces the idea that Indians, including contemporary people and their communities, are dangerous and violent. Even after announcing peaceful intentions, the Crow lawyer is attacked. "The one with the knife pressed it against his throat," Kersey writes. "Paul felt a trickle of warm blood roll down his neck. 'Now you die'" (Kersey, 227). Finally, he is taken to the chief, who explains the twins' behavior: "They believe there is still honor in fighting and bloodshed, as all Indians once did." (Kersey, 229). While generalizing to "all Indians," the author underscores the notion that Indian fighting was gratuitous, as well as ongoing, not for cause.

Following in the footsteps of authors such as Jean Craighead George, Will Hobbs, Scott O'Dell, and Gary Paulsen, MaryAnn Easley's *I Am the Ice Worm* is a survival story of the popular literary subgenre called the Robinsonade.[22] Named for Daniel Defoe's eighteenth century novel, *Robinson Crusoe*, contemporary Robinsonades are often set in the North American Arctic. "Its harsh weather, dangerous animals, and large, desolate, uninhabited areas," Jon C. Stott points out, "are ideally suited to the genre."[23] Easley's contribution to this subgenre centers on the experiences of protagonist Allison Atwood, a spoiled fourteen-year-old who travels from California to spend time with her mother in Alaska. Flying from Kotzebue in a single engine plane helmed by a bush pilot, the aircraft crashes after the wings ice up. Although the pilot dies, Allison survives to remain in the plane, which is intact enough to shelter her from the freezing cold, where it landed in a bluff of snow. Describing her situation, she comments: "At home, I'd know just what to do, but there were no emergency call boxes here I could walk to, no patrol cars cruising by, nothing but snow and ice. I listened, waiting to hear a search plane overhead. I listened, but no one came" (Easley, 22).

Eventually rescued, Allison comments: "When I opened my eyes, I saw something move outside the front window of the plane. It looked like a grizzly bear, big and furry. It was a man, dressed in fur from head to toe, and not like any I'd seen before. He was an Eskimo, but more primitive looking than the Eskimos I'd seen in Kotzebue" (Easley, 22).

Allison's rescuer is an Iñupiat trapper named Ikayauq, who conveniently happens upon the downed plane. Traveling by dogsled, he journeys with the teenager to his home village. Allison, who serves as a vehicle for Easley to write about the Iñupiat, expresses little or no gratitude to the people who help her survive her ordeal, instead demeaning their way of life. She describes the people as "primitive," their homes as "huts," and the food as "greasy" and "smelly." Although Allison shows some change and growth during the course of the novel, it is at the expense of the Iñupiat who take her into their homes and offer her hospitality. The scenario offered by Easley's novel is especially predictable to Native people, all too familiar with the exploitive attitudes and rude behaviors of outsider-tourists visiting their homes and communities. Negative images abound in Easley's descriptions of village life, including poverty and alcoholism, but she does little to address her own society's role in creating and per-petuating those conditions. A subplot involving Allison teaching sign language to Oolik, an outcast deaf villager, is self-serving. Although it is likely intended as a marker to show Allison's growth, it reinforces her at-titude of superiority in the novel. Allison and her mother have simply moved from shopping at malls to shopping for experiences in a culture different from their own. As reviewer Cyrisse Jaffee notes in her review of the book in *School Library Journal*, it is "a poorly executed story" with predictable events and superficial characters that are "sometimes stereotyped." Allison, in her view, "seems merely a device, never a fully realized and sympathetic character."[24]

In contrast to young adult novels with "the greatest stereotypes and wildest imaginings about Indians," *Bone Dance* by Canadian author Martha Brooks is a much better work of fiction.[25] Named an American Library Association Book of the Year, it also received the Ruth Schwartz Award (Young Adult), the Canadian Library Association Book of the Year Award for Young Adults, and was short-listed for the Mr. Christie's Book Award. "A writer known for complex, sensitive teen characters creates two more in this tale of lonely, grieving people finding what they need in each other," *Booklist* noted. "A lyrical, in-tensely felt romance."[26]

"Life is full of surprises, and sometimes the good ones and the bad ones get all bunched up together," seventeen-year-old protagonist Alexandra Marie Sinclair's Cree grandfather tells her in the novel (Brooks, 5). Set in Manitoba, the story focuses on Alexandra and another

central character, Lonny LaFreniere, a young man of the same age. Although living in different areas of Manitoba, the lives of these young
people eventually intersect. Alexandra and Lonny alternately tell the
story, using third person, past tense narration. Their lives unfold in the
novel's two divisions, "The Spirits" and "The Legacy." Alexandra's
life, centered in Winnipeg with her mother and Aunt Francine, is beset
with mourning. Besides the death of her beloved grandfather, she is
grappling with the void left by an absentee father, Earl McKay, a man
she knows primarily through the six letters he has sent her over the
years. When McKay dies and leaves her a cabin and land along Fatback
Lake in Manitoba's Lacs des Placottes Valley, Alexandra overcomes her
ambivalence to attend to her legacy. Lonny has powerful connections to
the same land, which was in his Métis stepfather's family for generations, and the source of guilt-ridden memories. He is haunted by the fact
that at age eleven he disturbed an Indian burial mound on the property,
believing his act of desecration caused his mother to die. Although
Lonny knows a weak heart ended her life, he blames himself for her
death and continues to avoid the area of land that his stepfather sold to
Earl McKay. It is not until Alexandra arrives that he is drawn back.

   In *Bone Dance*, dreams and waking visions permeate the narrative,
where they are treated as an everyday reality. Spirits alive in the land
and in the central characters, significant to the novel, are interwoven
with daily life. Brooks writes: "The ancestral LaFrenière log cabin,
once snug and sturdy, was as gray and sagging as an abandoned wasp's
nest. Behind that were the cut banks, the hills, and that particular one
with its Indian burial mound that everyone for miles around called Medicine Bluff. As always, the mound was rosy and beautiful in the fading
light of day. As always, [Lonny] could feel the presence of the furious
spirits rising around it" (Brooks, 7–8). His mother appeared to him
again and again, sometimes whispering, "Let the spirits dance. The land
will wake up and tell you things" (Brooks, 52). While Alexandra initially ignores the gift her father left her, her grandfather and Old Raven
Man appear to her in dreams. Encouraged and strengthened by their
help, she visits the property. Alexandra finds the cabin and land, but also
Lonny.

   Bone Dance's strongest Native character is Alexandra's Cree grandfather, a veteran of World War II, who had returned home from the con-
flict "disillusioned, fearful, and a little bit crazy" (Brooks, 28). His re-

sponse was to head far north and to lose himself running a trapline for nineteen years. He tells Alexandra: "That first winter I remember months and months of snow that cleaned out my spirit. I remember drinking tea made from boiled snow water. And smoking kinnikinnik with a man who told me to pay close attention to my dreams. They would tell me things, he said, that would be important to my life" (Brooks, 28). His dreams eventually took him to Alexandra's grandmother, a widow with two young daughters, and the couple married and remained together until her death. When she died, the loss profoundly affected him, leaving him fixated on her image and unable to eat or sleep. "I couldn't enjoy anything," he told Alexandra. "Not the blue sky. Or my garden. Or the birds singing. All I thought about . . . *continually*, was what I had lost." (Brooks, 42–43). It was not until later, and another dream, that he was able to begin to notice things again. He said: "I began to see your grandmother in your mother and in your aunt. Different little things they'd say and do reminded me of all the gifts of her life. And now I see her in the way you move your hands, little bug. And I feel grateful" (Brooks, 43). When Alexandra's "catastrophe" of a father disappeared, her grandfather helped the family out financially and was a strong presence in her life. "It was Grandpa who was there to help out," Alexandra remembers. "He bought their groceries and paid their rent. He'd shuffle through the door, practically every Saturday afternoon, grocery bags bouncing against his lame leg, and say, '. . . stop that studying for a while and take a rest. Let's make a little room on the table there. I noticed a special on oranges and chicken legs this week'" (Brooks, 37–38).

The Native ancestry of Alexandra and Lonny is primarily suggested in the text, implied rather than explained. Brooks provides hints in passages such as: "Alex's mom just stood, unanswering, perfectly composed, her Dene bones, her rich silken skin, her black hair pulled back with a four-directions beaded hair clip, her ears glinting with silver and turquoise earrings" (Brooks, 33). In Lonny's case, his friend Robert comments: "Wondered about that, with your Native ancestry and all. Been giving it some serious thought lately. Me and Charlene had a big long talk about your ancestry. And other stuff" (Brooks, 70). The fragmentary Native presence somehow parallels the family structures of the two main characters. "When he was small," Lonny comments, "before Pop, there had just been the two of them. Mom and him. Now there was just two again. Pop and him. Funny how life works out" (Brooks, 25). Although he is not Pop's biological son, Lonny has a strong family bond with him. Likewise, Alexandra's life shares similar features.

"A finely written, nimble book that implies that strangers can be bound," *Kirkus Reviews* notes, "sometimes, even before they meet."[27] Brooks herself has observed: "Each book I write takes form out of its own landscape and feel. I walk into those places in my mind, and wait for thunder to rumble, for lightening to flash, for any kind of sign that can help me pull a character, or two, or three or more, into my own spirit. Every journey I take with a book requires deep work, and therefore transforms me in some way."[28]

Most of the books considered here have the characteristics identified by Caldwell-Wood and Mitten earlier—"well-written, exciting, from respected authors, much-loved by their readers, with well-developed characters"—but are deficient when it comes to depicting Native Americans. The Native characters tend to be isolated from their own people, as in Lipsyte's caught-between-worlds Sonny Bear, Hobbs's foster child Cloyd Atcitty, Cannon's Henry Yazzie separated from the Navajo in a predominantly white community, and Kersey's last-of-his-kind Black Wolf and loner Paul Judge. When present at all, Native communities tend to be rendered stereotypically, as in Lipsyte's fictional Moscondaga Reservation ("this sad-sack reservation"), Bennett's Pine Ridge (not even a mention that it is the homeland of the Oglala Lakota), Kersey's Makah community ("You see before you a dying people"), and Easley's Alaska Native community ("a few huts clustered together"). In this fiction, non-Indian protagonists want something from these communities for themselves: Indian identity, spiritual enlightenment, help surviving, and "insider" experiences. A good number of these authors incorporate Euro-American perspectives using fictional Indian voices. These "insiders" then castigate other Indians (the Paiutes "who grubbed their lives away in dirty hovels") or solve Indian problems (a "warrior-diplomat" for the fictional Moscondaga Reservation, and farming at Pine Ridge). Indian social problems, but not Euro-American complicity in them, are ubiquitous in the majority of these novels, as in Lipsyte's characterization of Sonny Bear's mother, Kersey's depiction of Paul Judge's parents, and Bennett's description of Delbert in connection with Floyd's vision quest: "Besides being a little drunk, he was mostly interested in doing the chanting and burning the sage" (Bennett, 155). These novels, in the main, reflect static Euro-American perspectives.

NOTES

1. Naomi Caldwell-Wood and Lisa A. Mitten, comps., "Selective Bibliography and Guide for 'I' Is Not for Indian: The Portrayal of Native Americans in Books for Young People" (Program of the ALA/OLOS Subcommittee for Library Services to American Indian People. American Indian Library Association, 1991), 1. Available online at www.nativeculture.com/lisamitten/ailabib.htm (accessed August 7, 2004); hereafter referred to in text as Caldwell-Wood and Mitten.

2. Robert Lipsyte, *The Brave* (New York: Harper Trophy, 1991); *The Chief* (New York: Harper Trophy, 1993); *Warrior Angel* (New York: HarperCollins, 2003); hereafter referred to in text by their respective titles.

3. Robert Lipsyte, *The Contender* (New York: Harper Trophy, 1967). "Author Information." Available online at www.harpercollins.com/catalog/author_xml.asp?authorid=12397 (accessed August 9, 2004).

4. Sherman Alexie, "Some of My Best Friends," review of *On the Rez*, by Ian Frazier, *Los Angeles Times*, 23 January 2000, 1; hereafter referred to in text as Alexie.

5. Peter Nabokov, *Indian Running* (Santa Barbara, CA: Capra Press, 1981).

6. Review of *The Chief* by Robert Lipsyte, *Kirkus Reviews* 61 (May 15, 1993), 664.

7. Will Hobbs, *Bearstone* (New York: Atheneum, 1989; New York: Avon Camelot, 1991); hereafter referred to in text as *Bearstone* (page citations are to the reprint edition).

8. Will Hobbs, *Beardance* (New York: Bradbury Press, 1993; New York: Avon Camelot, 1995); hereafter referred to in text as *Beardance* (page citations are to the reprint edition).

9. Todd Morning, review of *Beardance* by Will Hobbs, *School Library Journal* 39, no. 12 (December 1993), 134.

10. Ben Mikaelsen, *Touching Spirit Bear* (New York: Scholastic, 2002); hereafter referred to in text as Mikaelsen.

11. Wendy Leopold, "Seeing beyond Tonto: How the News Media Perpetuate Indian Stereotypes." Available online at www.northwestern.edu/univ-relations/media/news-releases/*archives/*media-comm (accessed August 7, 2004); hearafter referred to in text as Leopold.

12. Joel Shoemaker, review of *Touching Spirit Bear* by Ben Mikaelsen, *School Library Journal* 47, no. 2 (February 2001), 122.

13. A. E. Cannon, *The Shadow Brothers* (New York: Delacorte, 1990; New York: Bantam Doubleday Dell Books for Young Readers, 1992); hereafter referred to in text as Cannon (page citations are to the reprint edition).

14. George Gleason, review of *The Shadow Brothers* by A. E. Cannon, *School Library Journal* 36, no. 6 (June 1990), 137.

15. George P. Lee, *Silent Courage, An Indian Story: The Autobiography of George P. Lee, A Navajo* (Salt Lake City, UT: Deseret Book Company, 1987).

16. James Bennett, *Dakota Dream* (New York: Scholastic, 1994); hereafter referred to in text as Bennett.

17. Rayna Green, "The Tribe Called Wannabee: Playing Indian in America and Europe," in *Aniyunwiya/Real Human Beings: An Anthology of Contemporary Cherokee Prose*, ed. Joseph Bruchac (Greenfield Center, NY: Greenfield Review Press, 1995), 117.

18. Vine Deloria Jr., "Secularism, Civil Religion, and the Religious Freedom of American Indians," *American Indian Culture and Research Journal* 16, no. 2 (1992), 19.

19. Tim Giago, "Indians Don't Rely on Gambling, Charity," *Daily Press*, January 22, 2004, A11.

20. Colin Kersey, *Soul Catcher* (New York: St. Martin's Press, 1995); hereafter referred to in text as Kersey.

21. Review of *Soul Catcher* by Colin Kersey, *Publishers Weekly* 242, no. 38 (September 18, 1995), 110.

22. MaryAnn Easley, *I Am the Ice Worm* (New York: Bantam Doubleday Dell Books for Young Readers, 1996); hereafter referred to in text as Easley.

23. Jon C. Stott, *Native Americans in Children's Literature* (Phoenix, AZ: Oryx Press, 1995), 161.

24. Cyrisse Jaffee, review of *I Am the Ice Worm* by MaryAnn Easley, *School Library Journal* 42, no. 11 (November 1996), 104.

25. Martha Brooks, *Bone Dance* (New York: Bantam Doubleday Dell Books for Young Readers, 1997); hereafter referred to in text as Brooks.

26. John Peters, review of *Bone Dance* by Martha Brooks, *Booklist* 94, no. 3 (October 1, 1997), 330.

27. Review of *Bone Dance* by Martha Brooks, *Kirkus Reviews* (September 15, 1997). Available online at www.kirkusreviews.com (accessed August 7, 2004). Subscription required.

28. "Martha Brooks," available online at www.stemnet.nf.ca/easternhorizons/presenters/martha_brooks.html (accessed August 7, 2004).

Chapter Two

The American Indian Renaissance and Contemporary Young Adult Literature

The owl's song. And he understood then what the people by the river's edge were saying. "The waterfalls," they were saying, "the waterfalls." They were warning him, look out for the falls. He was heading for the falls. He tried to move, to open his eyes.[1]

Author Janet Campbell Hale, Coeur d'Alene/Kootenai, wrote her first novel, *The Owl's Song*, when she was twenty-three years old. Published in 1974 and still in print some thirty years later, the groundbreaking work was hailed as "one of the few works about an adolescent urban Indian."[2] It is the coming-of-age story of protagonist Billy White Hawk, a teenager who struggles to find his way toward adulthood by leaving his home reservation for a stay in a Pacific Northwest city with an older half sister. White Hawk experiences the death of his mother, his father's alcoholism, the suicide of a beloved cousin, and the difficulties of coping in an urban environment. "Hale's groundbreaking exploration of race relations," Frederick Hale writes, "especially between urbanized Native Americans and African Americans, and her contrasting of two siblings who respond so differently to their immersion in ethnically plural city life, would in themselves make *The Owl's Song* a noteworthy early addition to Native American adolescent literature."[3] He adds that a mythic component, the use of dreams and visions, "anchors Hale's first novel culturally in the Native American Renaissance, in which indigenous spirituality has provided both substance and structure to fictional and other works" (F. Hale, *SAIL*, 74).

The renaissance referred to by Frederick Hale dates back to the late 1960s, a period marked by social activism across the country. Authors whose works serve as benchmarks for this resurgence of tribal literary output include N. Scott Momaday, Kiowa, who won the Pulitzer Prize for his novel *House Made of Dawn* in 1969, and Vine Deloria, Jr., Standing Rock Sioux, whose nonfiction manifesto *Custer Died for Your Sins*, was published the same year. "Both texts," one scholar has noted, "awakened the American public to the fact that Indians had not disappeared from the landscape and were indeed able to speak for themselves."[4] The era was characterized by revitalization in many areas of American Indian life, including ongoing efforts by tribal nations to achieve self-determination over their lives and resources. Other Native authors associated with the literary renaissance include Leslie Marmon Silko, James Welch, D'Arcy McNickle, Gerald Vizenor, Louise Erdrich, Michael Dorris, Linda Hogan, Elizabeth Cook-Lynn, Anna Lee Walters, Geary Hobson, Duane Niatum, Thomas King, Paula Gunn Allen, Simon Ortiz, Joy Harjo, Virginia Driving Hawk Sneve, and Ray Young Bear. Their voices are joined by First Nations writers in Canada, among them Markoosie, Jeannette Armstrong, Basil Johnston, Lee Maracle, and Maria Campbell. Native literary output continues to grow, with additional contributions from the writers first associated with the renaissance as well as the emergence of new voices such as Sherman Alexie, Susan Power, Leanne Howe, Taiaiake Alfred, David Treuer, Delphine Red Shirt, and Richard Van Camp. In fact, Returning the Gift, the first North American Native writer's festival held in 1992, was attended by hundreds of writers "from dozens of tribal nations, spanning the continent."[5] While most of the Native writers cited here create works for adult readers, a number of them have authored publications for children and teenagers. Besides Janet Campbell Hale, Native authors of young adult works include Joseph Bruchac, Louise Erdrich, Michael Dorris, Beatrice Culleton, Shirley Sterling, Don Sawyer, and Cynthia Leitich Smith. Among them are authors of "contemporary fiction, probably the most underrepresented type of Indian-themed book."[6]

Examining the historical and contemporary context of Native writers, including those who author books for young adults, is critical to a fuller understanding of their work. As Muskogee (Creek) author Craig Womack points out, "Tribal literatures are . . . the oldest literatures in the Americas, the most American of American literatures. We *are* the canon."[7] This legacy, transmitted orally for thousands of years, includes a rich array of knowledge. "In contrast to the inane stereotype of the Indian as soundless," writer Emma LaRocque notes, "we know from the vast storehouse of our oral traditions that Aboriginal peoples were peoples of words. Many words. Amazing words. Cultivated words. They were neither wordless nor illiterate in the context of their linguistic and cultural roots."[8] Besides millennia of oral literature, there is an extensive body of Native writings. "Indian people have authored a lot of books," Womack observes, "a history that reaches back to the 1770s in terms of writing in English, and hundreds of years before contact in terms of Mayan and Aztec pictoglyphic alphabets in which were written the vast libraries of Mesoamerica" (Womack, 2). He cites "Samson Occom, David Cusick, William Apess, George Copway, Elias Boudinot, John Rollin Ridge, Peter Dooyentate Clark, Elias Johnson, Sarah Winnemucca, William Warren, Alice Callahan, Simon Pokagon, and E. Pauline Johnson" as among the representatives of "a vast, and vastly understudied, written tradition" (Womack, 2–3). In Womack's estimation, "Not nearly enough of this intellectual history has been brought to bear on a study of contemporary Native writings. Most approaches to the 'Native American Literary Renaissance' have proceeded as if the Indian discovered the novel, the short story, and the poem only yesterday" (Womack, 3). Most approaches also fail to examine authors in the context of their specific literary traditions. Native writers represent richly diverse tribal backgrounds and experiences. One publication notes that while American Indians "represent less than one percent of the U.S. population, they have as much diversity as the other 99 percent put together."[9] This diversity is manifested in many ways, through the multitude of cultures, languages, histories, land bases, treaties, governments, populations, and other facets of tribal life.

Although referring to his own people, Inuit filmmaker Zacharias Kunuk could have been referring to other tribal groups when he wrote, "People in Igloolik learned through storytelling who we were and where we came from for 4000 years without a written language. Then foreign missionaries preached Paul's Epistles to my parents in Inuktitut saying, 'Turn away from your old way of life.' These days Igloolik young people are suiciding at a terrible rate. 4000 years of oral history silenced by fifty years of priests, schools and cable TV? This death of history is happening in my lifetime."[10] The impact of European colonization on indigenous peoples is an ongoing fact of life in tribal communities and lives. As novelist Louise Erdrich writes, "Many Native American cultures were annihilated more thoroughly than even a nuclear disaster might destroy ours, and others live on with the fallout of that destruction, effects as persistent as radiation—poverty, fetal alcohol syndrome, chronic despair."[11] Scholar Linda Tuhiwai Smith affirms that "imperialism and colonialism brought complete disorder to colonized peoples, disconnecting them from their histories, their landscapes, their languages, their social relations and their own ways of thinking, feeling and interacting with the world."[12] Indigenous peoples thus work to recover land, language, knowledge, sovereignty, voice, and indeed, entire peoples and nations. Native authors, including those who write for young adults, often incorporate themes from this struggle, conveying tribal presences and realities, presenting perspectives that have been devalued, misrepresented, or erased, and counteracting colonialist propaganda and myths. "To discuss Native literature," Emma LaRocque notes, "is to tangle with a myriad of issues: voicelessness, accessiblility, stereotypes, appropriation, ghettoization, linguistic, cultural, sexual, and colonial roots of experience, and, therefore, of self-expression—all issues that bang at the door of conventional notions about [the U.S. and] Canada and about literature" (LaRocque, xv). Erdrich contends that Native American writers have a task quite different than that of other writers. "In the light of enormous loss," she writes, "they must tell the stories of contemporary survivors while protecting and celebrating the cores of cultures left in the wake of the catastrophe" (Erdrich, 23).

In 1983, less than a decade after the publication of Hale's *The Owl's Song*, Beatrice Culleton's *In Search of April Raintree* appeared.[13] Published by Pemmican Publications in Winnipeg, the book is the story of two Métis "halfbreed" sisters, April and Cheryl, who suffer the breakdown of their family and are separated in different foster homes in rural Manitoba. Their voices reveal the multifaceted power of a racist society over their lives, manifested in cultural oppression and interwoven forms of abuse. April, removed from her parent's alcoholic home as a young child, eventually confronts her past. She explains: "I always felt most of my memories were better avoided, but now I think it's best to go back in my life before I go forward" (*Raintree* Critical Edition, 9). April serves as the narrator of the book, interpolating Cheryl's voice through letters, speeches, dialogue, and, ultimately, diary entries. The sisters have alternating, shifting takes on identity during the course of the narrative. April internalizes negative stereotypes about race and culture in foster care and school, eventually assuming a white identity and disavowing her family, but in the end emphatically reclaiming her own people. While Cheryl studies and embraces her Métis background during the course of the narrative, identity is neither clearcut nor static for either sister. As writer Margery Fee points out, "identification is a complicated and dangerous process for First Nations people, whatever their appearance, upbringing, or cultural background. Historical, legal, and political forces beyond any individual's control have meant that the category Aboriginal has become fluid and contested."[14] Whites, patronizing as well as racist, impose negative identifications on the Métis girls. "Vigilant against being named into Otherness," as writer Helen Hoy notes, "Cheryl multiplies identities" in the text.[15] She does so, for example, in the following interaction:

"Oh, I've read about Indians. Beautiful people they are. But you're not exactly Indians are you? What is the proper word for people like you?" one asked.
"Women," Cheryl replied instantly.
"No, no, I mean nationality?"
"Oh, I'm sorry. We're Canadians," Cheryl smiled sweetly. (*Raintree Critical Edition*, 107)

Although Culleton drew from her own life, including her experiences as a foster child, rape victim, and as the sibling of two sisters who committed suicide, *In Search of April Raintree* is a work of fiction. The author points out that when the novel first appeared, people treated it as autobiography and viewed her relatives and April's as one and the same. "That part really disturbed me," she wrote, "because unless I could explain what I meant by autobiographical, some would unfairly judge the people I admire and cherish."[16] The novel, which chronicles the lives of April and Cheryl from childhood to adulthood, includes a rape scene, "one of the most graphic . . . in English literature," as well as suicide.[17]

In Search of April Raintree, which sold over 82,000 copies in its first nine years of circulation, has continued to have broad appeal. Besides being translated into German, Dutch, and French, it has been anthologized in collections such as *Our Bit of Truth: An Anthology of Canadian Native Literature*.[18] The novel has also garnered a revised edition for younger readers as well as a recent edition incorporating ten essays by a range of scholars, becoming "the first critical edition of a Native Canadian text" (*Raintree* Critical Edition, 2). Emma LaRocque observes that Culleton's book and Maria Campbell's *Halfbreed* "have been reduced, at times, to grist for social workers rather than being treated as the powerful mirrors to Canadian society that they are" (LaRocque, xvii–xviii). Another writer, Jo-Ann Thom, asserts: "Steeped in the mythology that Canada was settled, for the most part, by peaceful negotiation and that Canadians are, as a whole, polite, considerate, and a trifle boring, my white students—and I think many white readers—are startled to see themselves through Métis eyes and to hear their behaviour analyzed from a Métis point of view."[19] Thom contends that "white readers learn that racism . . . is not just the practice of a few isolated individuals; it is a significant part of Canadian culture" (Thom, 298). Hoy, too, notes that "even to students versed in notions of hegemony and counter-discursive production, the presence of a book like *In Search of April Raintree* on the syllabus was fraught and disquieting" (Hoy, 274–275).

Joseph Bruchac, a prolific author of Abenaki descent, writes both fiction and nonfiction for a range of age groups. Among his extensive published works are contemporary offerings for young adults. *Skeleton Man*, a 2001 publication, is drawn from a traditional Mohawk story and recast as a contemporary novel.[20] Bruchac's protagonist Molly sets the stage for the narrative by recounting one of her favorite stories, that of a skeleton monster, who "was just a human being at first, a lazy, greedy uncle who hung around the longhouse and let everyone else hunt for him" (*Skeleton*, 3). After burning one of his fingers and sticking it into his mouth to cool down, "Lazy Uncle" cooks and devours the rest of his flesh before turning on relatives to do the same. A suspicious niece, assisted by a rabbit she had rescued from drowning, manages to escape the same fate by outwitting her uncle-turned-monster. After retelling the Mohawk story, Molly reveals her personal dilemma. Following the disappearance of her parents, local authorities placed her with an elderly man claiming to be a long lost great-uncle. This purported relative, who lived in a spooky house far from the center of town, had "a face that was so thin it looked like bone" (*Skeleton*, 14). Molly, believing her parents are alive, searches for a way out of her predicament and out of her "uncle's" oversight. While tying the story to the Mohawk oral tradition,

Bruchac incorporates other aspects of Molly's tribal heritage. Dreams, for instance, serve as a source of assistance and guidance for the protagonist throughout the narrative. Molly's name is taken from that of eighteenth-century Mohawk leader Molly Brant, hence a source of strength. In conjunction with creating a strong, smart girl for his protagonist, Bruchac acknowledges the lessons he has learned from a number of female "tradition bearers": "They have helped me understand even more deeply how different the strong women in our traditional American Indian stories are from the dependent damsels of European folktales who hope for a prince to rescue them. Not only do our Native American heroines take care of their own rescues, they often save the men, too!" (*Skeleton*, n.p.). The writing in *Skeleton Man* is spare, bare bones so to speak, with a quick pace and engaging suspense.

Eagle Song, another contemporary story by Joseph Bruchac, also centers on Mohawk characters.[21] Published in 1997, the book is about fourth grader Danny Bigtree, who lives with his parents Richard and Salli in a Brooklyn apartment. The family left their Akwesasne Mohawk homeland, located in New York state and Canada, for employment purposes. Danny's father is portrayed as an ironworker (work legendary among the Iroquois), often traveling to jobs away from home, while his mother Salli, possessing a degree in social work, works at the Indian Community House in Manhattan. Although his mother had promised life would be better for the family after the move, for Danny it is not. As he tells his father, he is taunted in school, saying of the kids at school: "They don't like me. They make fun of me and call me a chief and a redskin and they ask me where my headdress is and tell me to go home to my teepee" (*Eagle*, 21). Danny's father tells his son the story of the great Iroquois peacemaker Aionwahta (Hiawatha), later sharing the account with Danny's classmates as an invited guest speaker to the classroom. The episode of Richard Bigtree's school visit touches on the fact that American Indians are often sought after "to share their heritage" in schools, especially between Columbus Day and Thanksgiving. The underlying reality, not addressed in the book, is that schools too often fail to hire American Indians as full-fledged faculty or staff. Instead, school representatives typically arrange short-term visits from parents and others to make presentations. While the fictional classroom visit helps turn a negative situation around for Danny Bigtree, in reality a one-time appearance or visit, no fault of the speakers, has very real limitations. It relegates the treatment of tribal culture (including complex history) to an hour or so of classroom time, with children experiencing a Native adult in a peripheral (often unpaid) teaching role at best. The visit helps the protagonist in Bruchac's fiction, with Danny also obtaining a measure of peace from one of his worst tormentors after refusing to tattle on him.

One of the subplots of *Eagle Song* is a construction-site accident involving Richard Bigtree, emphasizing the danger of ironwork, "fifty stories or more above the earth" (*Eagle*, 11). Another subplot involves Will, Danny's Seminole friend, who attends school in the Bronx and joins a gang to gain a sense of family. Although the Bigtrees participate in events at the American Indian Community House and interact with other Indians there, the text conveys a sense of isolation and loneliness for the family. It is accentuated by Danny being a latchkey child, whose neighbor provided "a snack and kept an eye on him till his mom came home" (*Eagle*, 12). It is also underscored by the novel's portrayal of a small nuclear family, a contrast to the extended families typical of many Indian households and community networks, including those in cities. The black and white drawings illustrating the book contribute to the isolation, among them one that depicts Danny on the margins, excluded from a school basketball game in progress. Although the book's opening lines refer to Danny's "long black hair," the illustrations contradict the portrayal by showing a rather short hairstyle. One of the best drawings in the publication is an image of Danny and his father together, with Danny wearing his father's hardhat from work.

The Heart of a Chief, also by Joseph Bruchac, centers on eleven-year-old protagonist Chris Nicola, who lives on the fictional Penacook reservation.[22] Bruchac explains in an author's note that he decided against setting the novel on a real reservation because he deemed some of the book's issues, "such as casino gambling, leadership, and alcohol abuse . . . too sensitive" to do that. Instead, he "imagined a reservation where none currently exist . . . in New Hampshire" (*Heart*, n.p.). Although the Penacook do not exist today as a state or federally recognized community, the group flourished historically as a member nation of the Western Abenaki. While many of the contemporary issues raised in the book can be controversial, they pale in comparison to the underlying (and mostly unaddressed) reality of the erasure of groups such as the Penacook. In Bruchac's novel, the fictional Penacook survive European colonization and its aftermath with a land base (including an island) and tribal language intact. Chris and his seven-year-old sister Celeste, whose mother has died and whose father is in treatment for alcoholism, live with their grandfather Doda and their "auntie" on the reservation. Chris, just starting high school, is bused to a school off the reservation. Bruchac thus touches on a common experience for many reservation students, who are often transported to schools in towns bordering tribal communities, areas with some of the worst anti-Indian attitudes and behaviors. Chris reveals the fear and confusion of the first day in a new setting, noting: "Eyes ahead, I go into the classroom and quickly slide into the wrong seat—too close to the front. Big mistake. It's an unwritten rule that Indian kids who don't want to get in trouble sit in the back. All the Indian kids, from us lowly sixth graders on up to the three Penacooks who are in high school, know that" (*Heart*, 14).

Besides the border town school setting, Bruchac addresses Indian mascots, Indian alcoholism, and casino gambling in *The Heart of a Chief*. A number of these conflicts find easy resolution in the book, in fact, too easy. In the novel, Chris adjusts quickly to his new school setting, emerging as a leader with uncommon wisdom. In real life, Indian students generally suffer culture shock in circumstances such as that depicted in the book. The transition to a school in a hostile border town is often traumatic, resulting in a high dropout rate and low achievement for many Indian students. These students, including those who ultimately achieve academic and social success, often suffer difficult transitions in an unsupportive environment. In one of the best scenes of the book, Chris challenges the accuracy of *The Sign of the Beaver*, a Newberry Honor book by Elizabeth George Speare that is required reading in many schools.[23] During class discussion of the novel, Chris informs the teacher that the author was wrong to conclude that Indians just went away. "We didn't go away," he tells the class. "They tried to drive us off the land. They put bounties on our scalps. They burned our villages. But we didn't go away" (*Heart*, 20). The protagonist mirrors the assessment of Doris Seale, who deems *The Sign of the Beaver* a book to avoid. "In Speare's book," Seale comments, "the People have no name. But they did not go away. They are still here."[24]

The mascot issue, taken on by the protagonist as a small group class assignment, is easily resolved in Bruchac's novel. In contrast to actual cases, where the effort to eliminate Indian mascots is too often an ongoing

struggle against implacable opposition, Chris and his fellow students
get the school to reverse seventy years of mascot history with little effort. Bruchac similarly reconciles another controversial issue, the proposed building of a casino on tribal land, with fictional ease. The threat
of turning the Penacook tribal island into a casino project is conveniently averted through a gift, from Chris's father, of family land. The
Penacook can then have it both ways, maintain and protect their island
in its pristine state and build a casino for needed jobs in another location. Finally, Chris's father is depicted as making real progress in com-
bating the difficult disease of alcoholism in treatment. *The Heart of a
Chief* thus solves thorny problems in a flash, dispelling any controversy
in the process.

The Window, Michael Dorris's first novel for young readers with a
contemporary setting, centers on eleven-year-old protagonist Rayona
Taylor.[25] She first appeared as a teenager in the author's fiction, *A Yellow Raft in Blue Water*, written for adult readers and published in
1987.[26] A decade later, she reemerged in *Cloud Chamber*, another novel
for adults, and as a younger version of herself in *The Window*.[27] Rayona, a girl of tri-racial heritage, lives with her American Indian mother
in Seattle and has contact with her African American-Irish American father only on occasion. In *The Window*, Rayona is left home alone while
her mother goes out drinking, then placed in "under-the-table" foster
care settings arranged by her father. Those arrangements fall through,
and with her mother in treatment, Rayona travels to Louisville, Ken-
tucky to stay with paternal relatives. "Dad mentions his family so sel-
dom and then so vaguely that I have all but forgotten he has one," she
remarks. "I get cards, sometimes wrapped presents, clothes in the
wrong sizes—from his mother, his aunt, and his grandmother—but they
live far away back east somewhere. I've heard their voices on the phone
once or twice but I've never laid eyes on them" (*Window*, 36). En route
to Louisville, Rayona learns that this particular branch of the family is
white. She responds: "I have learned more about Dad's past in the last
two minutes than in all the years of my life so far and am speechless
with questions. The original one finally comes out first. '*White?*'" (*Window*, 43). The situation forces her to rethink what she knows about her
background. Dorris, of mixed Modoc and Euro-American ancestry, explores identity issues through Rayona's experiences with the people she
encounters. "The absence of fictional or biographical protagonists pos-

sessed of a bi- or tri-racial background is curious," Dorris has commented, "because by its very nature multiple relatedness is dramatic and interesting. A character with an insider's knowledge of more than one group is potentially an ideal guide, both objective and subjective, sufficiently well informed to know the right questions to ask but detached enough to still be surprised at the answers."[28] *The Window* provides more information on Rayona's African American and Irish American relatives, only passing references to the American Indian side of her family. "Mom's from Montana—'pure Indian,' [Rayona] brags—but Dad's more mysterious: dark complected, sharp cologne, sad pale-green eyes" (*Window*, 4). In another section, the protagonist voices worries that her Irish American relatives will suggest "we visit Aunt Ida on the reservation . . . and some friend of hers named Dayton" (*Window*, 80). Rayona's ties to tribal life, as revealed in *The Window*, are virtually nonexistent. Readers can learn more about Rayona and her family in *A Yellow Raft in Blue Water* and *Cloud Chamber*, where they also negotiate complicated boundaries of family, race, and culture. In Dorris's view: "Persons linked to a broad and disparate network of culture can match the solutions reached at one place to the problems faced by another. Their very marginality requires that they listen more sharply, use words with care and precision, watch closely in order to learn how to behave. They can easily stand as a metaphor for the dislocations of children in an adult world." ("Mixed Blood," 2–3).

Don Sawyer's *Where the Rivers Meet* centers on Shuswap protagonist Nancy Antoine, a senior three months short of graduating from high school in a small, rural community in British Columbia.[29] Seeing education as a way out, she is determined to endure the anti-Indian climate of the school and town until graduation. After a close friend commits suicide, Antoine has an altercation with a teacher and leaves school in despair. She eventually turns to a Shuswap elder for guidance, receiving assistance that helps turn her life around and contributes to a reawakening in her tribal community. Sawyer portrays the ongoing impact of colonization, the "death of history" referred to by Zacharias Kunuk. Tribal language and culture suppressed or erased, the existence of a culturally knowledgeable elder, such as Antoine's Shuswap teacher, survives by a thread. With the elder's help, Antoine is able to find her own strength and voice as well as the courage to stand up to those who oppress her. Sharing similarities with Hale and other contemporary

Native writers, Sawyer incorporates themes of identity, survival, and recovery. As author William Bevis points, "The hero comes home" in Native literary works. This "homing in" in Bevis's words, is in contrast to the American whites that keep leaving home in novels such as *Moby Dick, Huckleberry Finn,* and *The Great Gatsby.* In Native American fiction, Bevis writes, "coming home, staying put, contracting, even what we call 'regressing' to a place, a past where one has been before, is not only the primary story, it is a primary mode of knowledge and a primary good."[30] Although Nancy Antoine does not leave her community during the course of Sawyer's narrative, she does find her way home.

Set on a reservation in North Dakota, Susan Power's first novel *The Grass Dancer* is a series of stories of the lives of Dakota interconnected by relationship and community.[31] The story begins and ends with Harley Wind Soldier, a seventeen-year-old whose father and brother appear to him in dreams. Both of them had been killed in a car accident four weeks before Harley's birth, a loss that caused his mother Lydia to stop speaking. Her minimal expression left "an empty space between herself and her son, a deep cavity Harley had internalized" (Power, 25). A descendant of Ghost Horse, Harley's life intersects with that of Anna Thunder and her granddaughter, relatives of Red Dress, who flourished in the 1860s and lured enemies of her people to their death. The novel is alive with spirits who exert their will over the living. "You shouldn't ever be too arrogant or too loud about who you are." Pumpkin, a Menominee grass dancer, tells Harley. "I don't think I believe in God, but I believe in forces. And they're nosy. Don't tell them you're here. Don't light any bonfires. Walk in the shadows and you walk forever" (Power, 44). Indeed, spirits pervade the narrative, often angry, restless, playful, or just plain meddlesome.

Power, a member of the Standing Rock Sioux Tribe, has said "her inspiration comes from her mother's native influence, Louise Erdrich, Toni Morrison and Shakespeare, which stems from her memorizing *Romeo and Juliet* by the age of twelve."[32] *The Grass Dancer* shares similarities with Erdrich's work, especially in connection with the narrative structure. Each chapter could stand alone as a short story, but is also interlaced with the other stories in the novel to form a unified whole. The narrative, characterized by a nonlinear movement across time and generation, begins in 1981 and circles back to 1864. Power's distinctive voice centers on the Dakota, emphasizing the multilayered richness and complexity of the tribal nation and its people. As Jeannette McVay, a non-Indian character, admits: "I thought this was going to be a thing about death: dead culture, dead language, dead God. I came out here to record the funeral, so to speak. Collect data on how a people integrate this kind of loss into their souls. And you know what? I found all this activity and vitality and living mythology. I feel like I've stumbled upon a secret" (Power, 150). This character also tries to lead her classroom of Dakota students into areas they don't care to explore with her. A number of them "felt their teacher would never understand the intricacies of tribal relationships, how a woman could seem downtrodden, at the mercy of her husband's whims, yet turn around and join him in battle if she desired, tell him to vacate the lodge, which belonged solely to her. *It's complicated*, Harley Wind Soldier was thinking, unwilling to explain" (Power, 64). *The Grass Dancer*, which won the PEN/Hemingway Award for First Novel in 1995, is rich with such complications. Power is also the author of *Roofwalker*, an award-winning collection of short stories.[33]

Cynthia Leitich Smith, an enrolled member of the Muscogee (Creek) Nation, is the author of *Jingle Dancer*, *Rain Is Not My Indian Name*, and *Indian Shoes*, all published since 2001.[34] While *Jingle Dancer* is the author's first picture book, *Rain Is Not My Indian Name*, written for ages ten to fourteen, is her first novel. It is the story of fourteen-year-old protagonist Cassidy Rain Berghoff, a budding photojournalist who is one of the few Native Americans living in a small Kansas town. Her mother, of Muscogee Creek-Cherokee and Scots-Irish ancestry, died several years earlier and her father, Irish-German-Ojibway, is stationed in the military in Guam. During her father's temporary absence, Rain lives with her grandfather, brother, and her brother's fiancée. As the novel opens, Rain's best friend Galen is killed in a car accident, just after the two of them realized their friendship had blossomed into romance. Mourning her loss, Rain cannot bring herself to attend Galen's funeral and withdraws from her family and community. Six months later, she begins an assignment with the local newspaper to photograph a summer Indian camp run by her Aunt Georgia. Rain, who gets drawn into a local controversy over public funding for the youth program, reverses her decision against enrolling as a participant. She begins reconnecting with others, finding a way to honor Galen's memory in the process. Smith incorporates multiple plot lines, nonlinear storytelling techniques, and journal entries to tell the story.

Counteracting frozen-in-time ethnographic portrayals of Native life in *Rain Is Not My Indian Name*, Smith presents "a wry, sensitive girl who looks up to Aunt Georgia, who's protective of her brother Fynn and his fiancée Natalie, who enjoys powwows but is not herself a dancer, and who has practically memorized every episode of *The X-Files* in her DVD collection" (BookLinks/native, 3). Smith's protagonist is a mixed blood who lives off-reservation in a small town, one of many manifestations of tribal demographics across the country. Her interests and concerns are typical of young women her age, from any background. Smith comments on her writing, "it's important to me that none of my characters will ever be mistaken for guides on a Native American tour" (Book-Links/native, 2). Rain, definitely not a tour guide, does address some typical school fare concerning Native Americans during the course of the narrative. She comments, for example, on the period Michael Dorris referred to as "the annual twin peaks of Indian stereotyping," Halloween and Thanksgiving.[35] "At school," Rain says, "the subject of Native Americans pretty much comes up just around Turkey Day, like those cardboard cutouts of the Pilgrims and the pumpkins and the squash taped to the windows at McDonald's. And the so-called Indians always look like bogeymen on the prairie, windblown cover boys selling paperback romances, or baby-faced refugees from the world of Precious Moments. I usually get through it by reading sci-fi fanzines behind my textbooks until we move on to Kwanza" (*Rain*, 13).

Smith's book, *Indian Shoes*, is a collection of interrelated short stories aimed at younger readers. It features protagonist Ray and his grandfather, "Grampa Halfmoon," contemporary Cherokee-Seminole who live in Chicago, a city with one of the largest urban Indian populations in the country. Although little background information is provided about the family, readers learn that Ray's parents died in a tornado when he was just a baby. In the title story, Ray exchanges his hightop sneakers for a pair of antique shop moccasins that put Grampa Halfmoon "in the mind of bein' back home" in Oklahoma (*Indian Shoes*, 3). In other vignettes, Ray undergoes a last minute wardrobe change to serve as ring bearer in a family friend's wedding, cares for a houseful of pets during a Christmas power outage, and survives a haircut from his grandfather after Bud's Barbershop, the place they frequented, turned into Coiffures by Claudia. On a visit back home to rural Oklahoma, Ray goes on a predawn fishing excursion with Grampa Halfmoon, who reminisces about earlier trips with Ray's father. The book, which was named a "Notable Social Studies Trade Book for Young People for 2003," will appeal to a range of age groups, including young adults of any heritage. As one reviewer aptly concluded, "The stories' strength lies in their powerful, poignant evocation of a cross-generational bond and in the description of the simple pleasures two charming characters enjoy."[36] Leitich Smith is also the owner of a website devoted to children's and young adult books, www.cynthialeitichsmith.com, which was "named one of the top 10 writer sites by *Writer's Digest* in October 2001."[37] Regularly updated, the site features interviews, articles, and reading recommendations from a wide variety of literature. As Leitich Smith concludes of the contemporary Indian presence in her work, "Kids need to hear that we still exist, even occasionally prosper" (Book Flash article, 1).

NOTES

1. Janet Campbell Hale, *The Owl's Song* (New York: Doubleday, 1974; reprint, New York: HarperPerennial, 1995), 141 (page citations are to the reprint edition).
2. A. Lavonne Brown Ruoff, *Literatures of the American Indian* (New York: Chelsea House, 1991), 96.
3. Frederick Hale, "Dreams and Vision Quests in Janet Campbell Hale's *The Owl's Song*," *Studies in American Indian Literatures* 12, no. 1 (Spring 2000): 74; hereafter referred to as F. Hale, *SAIL*.
4. Kathryn Shanley, "The Lived Experience: American Indian Literature After Alcatraz," *Native Expressive Culture* XI, nos. 3 and 4 (Fall/Winter 1994): 120.
5. Joseph Bruchac, ed., *Returning the Gift: Poetry and Prose from the First North American Native Writers' Festival* (Tucson: University of Arizona Press, 1994), xx.
6. Cynthia Leitich Smith, "Native Now: Contemporary Indian Stories," American Library Book Association Book Links 10, no. 3 (December/January 2000–2001), 1. Available online at www.ala.org/BookLinks/native.html (accessed August 7, 2004); hereafter referred to in text as BookLinks/native.
7. Craig S. Womack, *Red on Red: Native American Literary Separatism* (Minneapolis: University of Minnesota Press, 1999), 7; hereafter referred to in text as Womack.
8. Emma LaRocque, "Here Are Our Voices—Who Will Hear?" in *Writing the Circle: Native Women of Western Canada*, comp. and ed. Jeanne Perreault

and Sylvia Vance (Norman: University of Oklahoma Press, 1993), xv; hereafter referred to in text as LaRocque.

9. Harold L. Hodgkinson et al., *The Demographics of American Indians: One Percent of the People; Fifty Percent of the Diversity* (Washington, DC: Institute for Education Leadership/Center for Demographic Policy, 1990), 1.

10. Zacharias Kunuk, "The Art of Inuit Storytelling," 1. Available online at www.isuma.ca/about_us/isuma/our_style/kunuk.html (accessed August 7, 2004).

11. Louise Erdrich, "Where I Ought to Be: A Writer's Sense of Place," *New York Times Book Review* (July 28, 1985), 23; hereafter referred to in text as Erdrich.

12. Linda Tuhiwai Smith, *Decolonizing Methodologies: Research and Indigenous Peoples* (London and New York: Zed Books, 1999), 28; hereafter referred to in text as Tuhiwai Smith.

13. Beatrice Culleton, *In Search of April Raintree* (Winnipeg, Manitoba: Pemmican Publications, 1983); also Beatrice Culleton Mosioner, *In Search of April Raintree,* Critical Edition, ed. Cheryl Suzack (Winnipeg, MB: Portage & Main Press, 1999); hereafter referred to in text as *Raintree* Critical Edition.

14. Margery Fee, "Deploying Identity in the Face of Racism," in *In Search of April Raintree*, Critical Edition, 217; hereafter referred to in text as Fee.

15. Helen Hoy, "'Nothing but the Truth': Discursive Transparency in Beatrice Culleton," in *In Search of April Raintree*, Critical Edition, 280; hereafter referred to in text as Hoy.

16. Beatrice Culleton Mosionier, "The Special Time," in *In Search of April Raintree*, Critical Edition, 248.

17. Agnes Grant, "Abuse and Violence: April Raintree's Human Rights (If She Had Any)," in *In Search of April Raintree*, Critical Edition, 244.

18. Agnes Grant, ed., *Our Bit of Truth: An Anthology of Canadian Native Literature* (Winnipeg, MB: Pemmican Publications, 1990).

19. Jo-Ann Thom, "The Effect of Readers' Responses on the Development of Aboriginal Literature in Canada: A Study of Maria Campbell's *Halfbreed*, Beatrice Culleton's *In Search of April Raintree*, and Richard Wagamese's *Keeper'n Me*," in *In Search of April Raintree*, Critical Edition, 296; hereafter referred to in text as Thom. See also Kateri Damm, "Dispelling and Telling: Speaking Native Realities in Maria Campbell's *Halfbreed* and Beatrice Culleton's *In Search of April Raintree*," in *Looking at the Words of Our People: First Nations Analysis of Literature*, ed. Jeannette Armstrong (Penticton, BC: Theytus Books, 1993).

20. Joseph Bruchac, *Skeleton Man* (New York: HarperCollins, 2001); hereafter referred to in text as *Skeleton.*

21. Joseph Bruchac, *Eagle Song* (New York: Dial Books, 1997); hereafter referred to in text as *Eagle.*

22. Joseph Bruchac, *The Heart of a Chief* (New York: Dial Books for Young Readers, 1998; New York: Puffin Books, 2001); hereafter referred to in text as *Heart* (page citations are to the reprint edition). For another young adult novel addressing the mascot issue, see Marlene Carvell's *Who Will Tell My Brother?* (New York: Hyperion Paperbacks for Children, 2002).

23. Elizabeth George Speare, *The Sign of the Beaver* (New York: Bantam Doubleday Dell Books for Young Readers, 1984).

24. Doris Seale, review of *The Sign of the Beaver* by Elizabeth George Speare, 3. Available online at http://oyate.org/books-to-avoid/signBeaver.html (accessed August 7, 2004).

25. Michael Dorris, *The Window* (New York: Hyperion Books, 1997); hereafter referred to in text as *Window*.

26. Michael Dorris, *A Yellow Raft in Blue Water* (New York: Henry Holt and Company, 1987).

27. Michael Dorris, *Cloud Chamber* (New York: Scribner, 1997).

28. Michael Dorris, "Mixed Blood," *Hungry Mind Review*, 2. Available online at www.angelfire.com/md/LittleFlute/narrative.html (accessed August 7, 2004); hereafter referred to in text as "Mixed Blood."

29. Don Sawyer, *Where the Rivers Meet* (Winnipeg, MB: Pemmican Publications, 1988); hereafter referred to in text as Sawyer.

30. William Bevis, "Native American Novels: Homing In," in *Recovering the Word: Essays on Native American Literature*, ed. Brian Swann and Arnold Krupat (Berkeley: University of California Press, 1987), 582.

31. Susan Power, *The Grass Dancer* (New York: G. P. Putnam's Sons, 1994); hereafter referred to in text as Power.

32. Susan Power, "Voices from the Gaps: Women Writers of Color," 3. Available online at http://voices.cla.umn.edu/newsite/authors/POWERsusan .htm (accessed August 7, 2004).

33. Susan Power, *Roofwalker* (Minneapolis: Milkweed Editions, 2002).

34. Cynthia Leitich Smith, *Jingle Dancer* (New York: Morrow, 2002); *Rain Is Not My Indian Name* (New York: HarperCollins, 2001); and *Indian Shoes* (New York: HarperCollins, 2002); the latter two books hereafter referred to in text as *Rain* or *Indian Shoes*.

35. Michael Dorris, "Why I'm Not Thankful for Thanksgiving," in *Through Indian Eyes: The Native Experience in Books for Children*, ed. Beverly Slapin and Doris Seale (1987; Philadelphia: New Society Publishers, 1992), 17.

36. Anne O'Malley, review of *Indian Shoes* by Cynthia Leitich Smith, *Booklist* 98, nos. 19 and 20 (1 and 15 June 2002): 1725.

37. "Native American Author Shows Off Indian Shoes," 1. Available online at www.bookflash.com/releases/100594.html (accessed August 7, 2004); hereafter referred to in text as Book Flash article.

Part Two

Historical Fiction

Chapter Three

Perils on the Frontier and Imaginary American Indian Protagonists in Young Adult Historical Fiction

An Indian stood on the cabin roof, clad only in breechcloth and leggings and carrying a hatchet. His lean body glistened in the glaring light.[1]

To Jimmy's horror, some held spears in the air, dangling scalps from a recent raid on a wagon train. Jimmy clamped his hand over his mouth and swallowed the bile rising in his throat. He had heard such things, but he hadn't thought friendly Indians killed people.[2]

These scenes, from *Danger Along the Ohio* by Patricia Willis and *The Legend of Jimmy Spoon* by Kristiana Gregory, are part and parcel of what author Mary Gloyne Byler characterizes as "too many books featuring painted, whooping, befeathered Indians closing in on too many forts, maliciously attacking 'peaceful' settlers or simply leering menacingly from the background."[3] Although one can expect to find such features in books published in the past, during periods now considered less than enlightened, recent works share the same characteristics. In a study of such novels for young adults published between 1995 and 2000, attorney-author Melissa Kay Thompson found that she could group them into three categories: "perils-on-the-frontier stories, captivity narratives, and tales narrated from the perspective of an imagined American Indian protagonist."[4] She examined writings by contemporary authors such as Patricia Willis, William Durbin, Ann Rinaldi, and Lynda Durrant, focusing her study "on the network of institutions (literary, educational, and legal) that enable conventional stereotypes to criss-cross White culture, linking these institutions" (Thompson, 354). These works overwhelmingly address the concerns, interests, and perspectives important to Euro-Americans and Euro-Canadians, while far fewer devote themselves to topics vital to the Native people at the center of their focus. Several such young adult historical novels are examined here, including separate chapters on captivity narratives and Ann Rinaldi's controversial novel *My Heart Is on the Ground, The Diary of Nannie Little Rose, A Sioux Girl.*

Danger Along the Ohio, published in 1997, is the story of three siblings (Amos, 13; Clara, 12; and Jonathan, 7) who become separated from their father during their journey down the Ohio River from their Pennsylvania home to resettle on the Ohio frontier in 1793. Stereotyping Indians as both beggarly drunks and terrifying threats, Willis writes of the children: "They'd seen Indians at Pittsburgh, shiftless, slouching men who loitered in doorways and begged money for whiskey. Their father had told them the whiskey lured the Indians away from their own people. It made them useless and dependent on the white men. The man looming over Amos was different. He had a power and command those begging Indians lacked, and a fierceness that scared Amos down to the ends of his toes" (Willis, 17). Following an Indian attack on the settlement where they had stopped, the three young Euro-Americans escape on a flatboat. Forced to swim to the north, or dangerous, Indian side of the river after the boat is torched, they set out on foot for Marietta, Ohio, where they hope to be reunited with their father. With few supplies and no means of transportation, the small party trudges on foot through the wilderness with their pet cow, Queen Anne, in tow. Following the river to avoid losing their way, the young travelers scavenge for food and struggle to reach their destination. In the middle of these quandaries, Amos spots a log floating in the river with someone clinging to it. He rescues the person, who turns out to be an "Indian boy" with a serious gunshot wound, and takes him to his siblings. His sister Clara, under protest, then uses her knowledge and experience in healing to nurse him back to health.

As Thompson points out, "the supposed moral and physical superiority of the White children is unmistakable throughout Willis's story, although Willis attempts to introduce some crosscultural camaraderie" (Thompson, 354). This camaraderie is primarily in the form of the siblings' interaction with the young Indian rescued from the river. Amos names him "Red Moccasin," an action that Thompson considers "on about the same level as naming the pet cow 'Queen Anne'" (Thompson, 355). Disregarding the Indian's own name and background, the white children also strip him of his knife. "Despite the look of outward calm," Willis writes, "the boy appeared to shrink back within himself. He was beaten. He had shown weakness. In some strange way Amos understood. The boy had willingly given up his weapon to the enemy and it shamed him" (Willis, 97). Physically and psychologically subjugating the young Indian at the individual level, the siblings mirror their society's treatment of entire groups. Hence, the depiction of the Shawnee nation in the novel is of the same variety. As Thompson concludes, Willis "does not even attempt to deal with important historical realities. She depicts frontier settlements, but seems uninterested in the reality of these settlements as the beginning of a land grab that would eventually mean the seizure of more than 90% of Native American homelands" (Thompson, 355). To *School Library Journal*'s reviewer, however, "Willis combines the suspense of a page-turner, the danger level of a thriller, the fascination of a survival story, and the ease of a hi/lo vocabulary."[5] Nonetheless, this novel's American Indian content is less than thrilling.

Kristiana Gregory's *The Legend of Jimmy Spoon*, set in the mid-nineteenth century in Utah territory, is another novel in a similar vein. This coming-of-age fiction centers on protagonist Jimmy Spoon, the twelve-year-old son of homesteaders who had followed Mormon leader Brigham Young to the Great Salt Lake of Utah's frontier. Gregory writes in a note that the account is "fiction inspired by *Among the Shoshones*, the memoirs of Elijah Nicholas Wilson" (Gregory, Note). Following his father's refusal to let him have a horse, Jimmy runs away from the home he shares with his parents and nine sisters. He joins two Shoshoni youngsters, tantalized by their promise of a pinto pony in exchange for accompanying them to their village. There, he is adopted as Dawii, "young brother," to Shoshoni leader Washakie. A white-turned-Shoshoni for over two years, Jimmy participates in daily activities and interprets tribal ways for the reader. While dispensing her protagonist's Euro-American perspectives throughout the text, Gregory renders Jimmy's adopted culture as simplistic and easy to acquire. "Although Shoshoni sounded strange on his tongue," she writes, Jimmy "was soon repeating short phrases. He felt like a real Indian. If only he could wear a feather in his hair" (Gregory, 25). In another passage, the author asserts: "Now he was like a real Indian" (Gregory, 40). Gregory thus generalizes and undercuts tribal identity and knowledge, a matter of merely learning some short phrases and wishing for a feather. Although adopted into a prominent Shoshoni family, Jimmy expresses little or no appreciation for his privileged position. Washakie, a busy leader with serious concerns, seems to exist merely to address little Jimmy's concerns and questions. In fact, the Shoshoni appear to become the special property of the Euro-American adoptee in the novel. "Even in the course of daily life Jimmy is portrayed as superior," author Donnarae MacCann writes, "as when he challenges an attacking bear, a selfless act on behalf of a friend. We are told that Shoshonis consider it proper and preferable to flee rather than help people in trouble."[6] Besides defeating a grizzly bear all by himself, the young man saves the life of his adopted parent, Old Mother, as well as that of a young female friend, Nahanee. Underscoring the boy's prowess, Gregory writes that Jimmy "was brave and twice saved Old Mother's life. He rescued Nahanee from the bear. He listened to his elders. He had taken the feather from an eagle without hurting the bird" (Gregory, 153).

Jimmy moralizes throughout the narrative, especially in connection with matters of war and peace. "No one wins if everyone keeps fighting. . . . Maybe if the chiefs put their pipes together they can agree to stop once and for all. You don't have to like each other. You just have to all want peace" (Gregory, 74). In another passage, Gregory's white-turned-Shoshoni-insider reiterates: "He wondered if people would ever stop enjoying a fight. *Would there ever be peace?*" (Gregory, 102). "War is not presented as a practice throughout the world," MacCann points out, "but as part of a fiercely aggressive Amerind temperament. We see a returning scalping party that has murdered white children traveling in a wagon train, but no context is provided for an understanding of this frontier war. Certainly it is never mentioned that whites initiated the war for the West" (MacCann, 141). Gregory also depicts several episodes of violence within the tribal community: "[Jimmy] ran for the lodge. As soon as he ducked inside, a squaw pushed her way past Old Mother, a knife in her hand. . . . The girl's mother slapped Old Mother across the cheek then reached for a chunk of firewood protruding from the snow" (Gregory, 52). As librarians Caldwell-Wood and Mitten comment:

"Several incidents of violence towards women and children have no basis in tribal cultures, and ring very false, as does much of the dialogue, which careens between 'noble savage' stereotypes and modern English. Guess who speaks which?"[7]

Gregory's novel is full of stereotypical words and phrases, among them papoose, squaw, brave, happy hunting ground, and "Chief With Many Squaws" (i.e., Brigham Young). "The women recognized their husbands' arrows and each one knew which *bojono* [buffalo] to work on," the author writes. "They laughed if their men had used too many arrows, planning to tease them later about being papooses, not mighty hunters" (Gregory, 27). While the protagonist's adoptive family and community members are described in demeaning terms, Jimmy is referred to as Dawii, a respectful Shoshoni family term. Although Gregory incorporates a number of Shoshoni words in the text, she takes them out of their cultural context and subverts them to serve Jimmy's purposes. While researching Shoshoni words, the author could have looked up this tribal nation's terms for men, women, and children. Instead, she selected terms such as "squaw" and "papoose" that reinforce the usual stereotypes. Caldwell-Wood and Mitten refer to *The Legend of Jimmy Spoon* as "a mixture of historical accuracy and silly stereotype and ignorance" (Caldwell-Wood and Mitten, 7). This novel would have readers believe that the Shoshoni were incapable of managing on their own, dependent on a twelve-year-old Euro-American boy who relinquished his own family for a pinto pony.

The Second Bend in the River by Ann Rinaldi, akin to Willis, features Shawnees and Ohio frontier settings.[8] Rinaldi's book is based on a romantic legend of the Shawnee leader Tecumseh's rumored love for Rebecca Galloway, the daughter of Indian fighter John Galloway who settled with his family in the Ohio territory in the late 1700s. Historian R. David Edmunds comments on this myth in his book, *Tecumseh and the Quest for Indian Leadership*: "Although there is not one fragment of evidence to support this 'romance,' local legends abound of Tecumseh sitting at the feet of the frontier maiden, receiving instructions in English and listening as she read extended passages from the Bible, Shakespeare, and world history. . . . Galloway family traditions assert that Tecumseh asked for her hand in marriage, and Rebecca agreed, on the condition that Tecumseh would give up his life as an Indian and 'adopt her people's mode of life and dress.'"[9] Following Tecumseh's refusal of

these terms, as the legend goes, the two parted ways and never met
again. "This story is so patently fictitious," Edmunds writes, "that it
taxes the credulity of all but the most gullible adherents of nineteenth-
century romanticism, but it has been included in several of the more
reputable Tecumseh biographies and even forms the basis for a historical drama performed each summer before large audiences of tourists
near Chillicothe, Ohio" (Edmunds, 218). Firmly within the ranks of
"the most gullible adherents" of the romance, Rinaldi adds her own
slant to the patently fictitious.

Protagonist Rebecca Galloway and her family are at the center of *The
Second Bend in the River* while Tecumseh's role is peripheral. In 1798,
then in his twenties, Tecumseh makes his first appearance at the Galloway homestead in this fiction. The novel opens with Rebecca, who is
nearly seven years old, ruminating: "I had a mother and two little brothers in the house, a father and four older brothers in the fields, a head
filled with tales of Indians swinging babies against trees and smashing
their brains out" (*Second Bend*, 1). This gruesome image, rooted in
colonialist propaganda, is repeated in the novel and reinforced as au-
thoritative by Rinaldi in a note at the end of the book. The author thus
sensationalizes notions of Indian savagery, with Rebecca emphasizing,
"*Wait until I tell Mrs. Maxwell* about this, I thought. She'll take to sleep-
ing in her loft again, like she used to do so the Indians wouldn't kill her
at night" (*Second Bend*, 13). This fiction then fosters the idea that a little girl with such beliefs would develop romantic feelings about a
Shawnee man. Rinaldi, though, has six-year-old Rebecca experience a
stir of attraction for Tecumseh. "I felt the touch of his hand on my head
long after he left," she reflects. "And the feeling was comforting. I knew
it shouldn't be, but it was. And it confused me" (*Second Bend*, 21). As
in Rinaldi's description of Waw-wil-a-way, another Shawnee figure in
the novel, the Shawnee leader is a "coming-and-going man" throughout
the narrative. He appears sporadically, primarily through visits to the
Galloway home, more object than person. Rinaldi dehumanizes Tecumseh in a number of ways, portraying him as animal-like and naturally
wild: "He ate ravenously, then bent to drink from the river. I watched
him bending over and thought how like a lean, healthy animal he is"
(*Second Bend*, 252). Tecumseh, in Rinaldi's words, "seemed part of the
trees, the undergrowth. Part of the landscape" (*Second Bend*, 3). She reiterates: "I felt as if I was looking at something wild. Something forgotten." (*Second Bend*, 12).

"I thought grown men are all like three-year-old little boys playing with tomahawks." Rebecca ponders. "Even Tecumseh" (*Second Bend*, 222). The young girl is portrayed as the knowledgeable teacher while Tecumseh, though a mature adult and respected leader, is presented as childlike and in need of instruction. At one point, Rebecca rebukes him: "Just because you've become an important chief invited here by the governor to speak to our people doesn't give you the right to chide me. . . . You'd best save your speechifying for those who want to hear it" (*Second Bend*, 104). Rebecca constantly corrects Tecumseh, as she would a young sibling under her care. She teaches the Shawnee leader English, observing: "Oh, he made such a fine figure on his horse! But, I thought, humble enough to submit to teaching by a ten-year-old girl. Even so" (*Second Bend*, 70). As depicted in the novel, Tecumseh's distorted language usage echoes that found in Rinaldi's book, *My Heart Is on the Ground: The Diary of Nannie Little Rose, A Sioux Girl*, although the two publications center on totally different tribal groups and time periods. Correcting Tecumseh again, Rebecca scolds: "But there *is* something I'm going to take you to task about. . . . Your letter to Governor Tiffin. Tecumtha, I taught you better English than that!" (*Second Bend*, 212).

In *The Second Bend in the River*, Rebecca is sexually attracted to Tecumseh, but also repelled by her feelings. As portrayed in the novel, she is drawn to Tecumseh's physical presence, observing: "Lord, he's beautiful, I thought. Lord, I must be coming on to be a woman. I never felt so in his presence before" (*Second Bend*, 106–107). In another passage, Rebecca swoons: "I could almost see the muscles in his arms through the deerhide shirt. The strength and dignity seeped out of him." (*Second Bend*, 166). She continues: "Everything about Tecumseh made my head addled. The graceful, sure moves of him, the sound of his voice as it echoed off the water, the thrust of his shoulders as he showed me the proper way to hold the paddle" (*Second Bend*, 168). Addled head or not, Rebecca's disdain for Tecumseh's culture permeates the text. "Indians don't visit," in her view. "They attack" (*Second Bend*, 5). Again, "I wished the Indian was real company" (*Second Bend*, 9). After Tecumseh proposed marriage, Rebecca shudders: "*Marry him?* Go and live in an Indian village? In a wigewa?" She also asks: "What of my children? Will they be raised as little savages?" (*Second Bend*, 241, 245). Discussing Tecumseh's marriage proposal with him, she agrees to marry him on the condition that they live among the whites. Conceding that his own people need him, she condescendingly agrees to let him visit. "You may go and travel among them," she allows, "even live among them, to do what you have to do. But come back to me. And our children. As my husband" (*Second Bend*, 254). Mercifully, actual history intervenes and Tecumseh does not marry Rebecca Galloway on these patronizing terms or any other.

Publishers Weekly described *The Second Bend in the River* as "elegant and moving," *School Library Journal* deemed it "well-written and carefully researched," and *Booklist* referred to the "careful separation of fact from fiction [strengthening] the credibility of the story without diminishing any of its appeal."[10] In contrast, *Kirkus Reviews* called the book "a disappointing historical offering," concluding that "Rinaldi never creates a clear picture of pioneer life or of Tecumseh's career, and his relationship with Rebecca is too sketchy to hold the foreground."[11] Melissa Kay Thompson finds that "stereotypes overwhelm nearly every page" of the novel (Thompson, 357). In her estimation, "White superiority is the underlying message" (Thompson, 358).

Many authors of young adult fiction cloak Euro-American perspectives in the guise of tribal identity and voice through imaginary American Indian protagonists. Narratives of this type include novels by Jan Hudson, Diane Matcheck, and Bebe Faas Rice. *Sweetgrass*, Jan Hudson's first novel, is the coming-of-age story of a young woman from the Blood Division of the Blackfeet Nation set in western Canada in the nineteenth century.[12] Although the author won the Canadian Library Association Book of the Year Award and other honors for this work, the book does not measure up to the accolades. The story, which centers on fifteen-year-old protagonist Sweetgrass, is essentially divided into two parts. In the first section, Hudson introduces her heroine in the context of her family and tribal society, presenting her as anxious to obtain parental consent to marry. The second section, actually a survival story, depicts Sweetgrass struggling to help save her family during a winter of smallpox, famine, and death. Hudson incorporates a substantial amount of ethnographic detail about the Blackfeet into the novel, including a bibliography of works about the tribal nation at the end of the novel. However, the out-of-context details do not add up to an accurate portrayal of Blackfeet family or community life. The young protagonist expresses resentment against her society's gender roles throughout the narrative, voicing perspectives that have more in common with contemporary Euro-Canadian or Euro-American viewpoints. Sweetgrass laments: "It was so unfair! I wished I were a man. I wished I had power with Sun or the spirits, then I would stop this [her friend's arranged marriage] from happening. But there was nothing I could do" (*Sweetgrass*, 19). As reviewers Beverly Slapin and Doris Seale point out, the protagonist "is self-absorbed to a degree that would be far more believable of a 20th century upper middle class American girl than of a young 19th century Blackfeet woman."[13] Hudson fails to take seriously the strict chaperoning of young women of the group, writing: "For one shy moment we leaned close together. For the first time I touched my face to his soft buckskin shirt. It was warm and clinging. Under my cheek I could feel his heart's movements. We listened to each other's rhythms. . . . Was he embarrassed by my shameful forwardness? I stood chilled by the thought. The old women would say I should not have let him touch me" (*Sweetgrass*, 106–107).

Family relations in the book also ring false. Sweetgrass behaves in ways that would be considered disrespectful within tribal society. Forward and ill-mannered, she makes negative comments about a number of family and tribal members, including elders. Of one of them, her "almost-mother," she remarks: "Bent-Over-Woman always walked like she was tired. And the baby in the back-carrier made her look humpbacked. With graying hair sticking out from her braids like dirty feathers, she looked just like a crow" (*Sweetgrass*, 30). In another instance, Sweetgrass muses: "Robe-Woman. She came to talk with my almost-mother, and they both looked at me and shook their heads. May her hair-grease stink!" (*Sweetgrass*, 78). Robe-Woman is not the only target; the protagonist also complains about her brother: "Everyone praises Otter for what he does. I could have killed that buffalo too if I had been up on a horse with a gun" (*Sweetgrass*, 97). Furthermore, Sweetgrass observes: "The babies were no company. They slept most of the time except when Little-Brother stayed awake to listen to Mother's lessons on the correct way to speak and act" (*Sweetgrass*, 111). As Slapin and Seale point out, Hudson's protagonist "says some truly extraordinary things" (Slapin and Seale, 173). Among them are these passages: "I will never comb his [Otter's] hair free of his fellow vermin again! And I will certainly never worry about him and his stupid warpath either. He is only a man! . . . But as I brewed the tea, I cried. All I wanted to do was leave all these sick people, go out on the clean snow and vomit them all

away" (*Sweetgrass*, 27, 130). In the second section of the novel, Sweetgrass is portrayed as being left alone with only members of her immediate family to stave off famine and smallpox in their tipi. With no other
tribal members nearby, she fights for survival on her own. This arrangement underscores the nuclear family configuration typical of the larger
society in modern times, rather than nineteenth-century Blackfeet kinship and dwelling patterns. "A masterpiece," *School Library Journal*'s
reviewer wrote in praise of Hudson's story, "combining elements of an
historical, a native American, a survival, and a coming-of-age novel set
in the 19th-Century western Canadian prairie."[14] On the contrary,
Slapin and Seale reached a different conclusion: "*Sweetgrass* may lack
the overt racism of the *Little House* books, say, or *The Matchlock Gun*,
but it is demeaning and inaccurate in so many ways that I would not
consider it, even as an alternative" (Slapin and Seale, 173).

Hudson's follow-up novel, *Dawn Rider*, also centers on a female protagonist of the Blackfeet Nation.[15] Set earlier in time than *Sweetgrass*,
the story focuses on Kit Fox, a sixteen-year-old in the early eighteenth
century. Hudson depicts the introduction of horses and guns to the tribal
group, portraying her protagonist as having a vision to ride a horse to
help save her people. The novel includes a buffalo hunt, a war party, a
young man's preparations to capture an eagle, a marriage ceremony, and
interactions with the Cree. Kit Fox shares similarities with Sweetgrass
in that she is self-absorbed and individualistic, rather than tribal. She
challenges gender restrictions, as when she wants to ride the horse new
to the Blackfeet. "Just because no warrior has ridden the horse," Kit Fox
asks, "why should I not try?" (*Dawn Rider*, 14) Failing to describe female and male roles in the context of tribal culture, where they complement each other, Hudson puts her protagonist at odds with males.
She depicts Kit Fox as taking risks with her reputation by having her
travel without a chaperone, in defiance of tribal ways, to spend time
with her male friend, Found Arrow. Hudson undercuts tribal custom and
her own statement that "once a girl became a woman, she would not be
trusted alone except with brothers and those who might as well be
brothers" (*Dawn Rider*, 53). Furthermore, the custom did not stem from
failing to trust a female child, but from childrearing practices designed
to provide care, instruction, and protection within the kinship system.

Another author, Diane Matcheck, imagines a female protagonist from
the Apsaalooka (Crow) nation in her first young adult novel, *The Sacri-*

fice.[16] Set in the mid-eighteenth century, the book centers on a fifteen-year-old living among her people on the Great Plains. Called Weak-one-who-does-not-last because she was not expected to live for long, she was the daughter of a woman who died giving birth to her and her twin brother, Born-great. Weak-one-who-does-not-last's father, Chews-the-bear, had been foretold in a dream that his wife would die bearing twins and one of the twins would die young while the surviving one "would become one of the greatest Apsaalooka ever to live" (Matcheck, 10). Chews-the-bear's assumption is that the female child would die young and her male twin would achieve greatness, but, instead, he dies at age four. Following the death of her father in a battle with the Lakota, Weak-one-who-does-not-last sets out to fulfill her destiny. Matcheck writes of her: "She was a starved-looking, long-limbed girl of fifteen winters, with eyes that smoldered from deep within, like a wildcat's eyes at night from within its den. The high cheekbones and fine, straight nose so common among her Apsaalooka people would have been beautiful on another girl, but her face was a hard mask, with a taut, thin line for a mouth. She wore crudely sewn boy's clothing: a plain buckskin shirt and leggings, gray with dirt from long wear, and a breechcloth that was now soaked with blood" (Matcheck, 4). Sharing similarities with Hudson, Matcheck portrays her protagonist as scornful of female roles, writing of her: "What would she do if she lived in Broken Branch's lodge? Just be a girl? She would not even be good at that; girls dug roots and cooked and sewed beadwork and did many other things of which she knew little. Also, girls courted and married" (Matcheck, 47). Matcheck also writes: "The girl had never cared much for others of her sex" (Matcheck, 121). In this novel, the underlying assumption is that female greatness is achieved in the male domain. This projection is false with respect to the roles of men and women in tribal cultures. The female role, as a matter of fact, possesses power and honor in and of itself. In this novel, Weak-one-who-does-not-last spats the assertion, "I am more of a man than you'll ever be," manifesting disrespect toward both Apsaalooka men and women (Matcheck, 34).

The protagonist's self-centeredness, especially prominent in the early section of the novel, soon wears thin. Her constant refrain is "I am the Great One!" Setting out on a solo quest across the plains to prove her greatness, Weak-one-who-does-not-last encounters a series of difficult obstacles and the novel veers into absurdity. She loses her horse and provisions and nearly starves to death, but manages to take down a powerful grizzly bear. "Alone, half-starved, half-crippled, with nothing but a knife," Matcheck writes, "she had killed it. No, she was not Weak-one-who-does-not-last. She could do anything now" (Matcheck, 84). The protagonist eventually tries to steal horses in a quest to achieve greater homecoming glory, but is taken captive by their Pawnee owners. "Their faces and shaved heads gleamed in the harsh yellow light." Matcheck writes of her captors. "In terror she remembered having heard from some Shoshone traders that the Pawnee cut out the hearts of captive girls" (Matcheck, 98). Telling herself that her fears were groundless and "just a tale to frighten children," Weak-one-who-does-not-last reiterates: "I am the Great One. I fear nothing" (Matcheck, 98). The protagonist is taken to a Pawnee village, where she is placed in the home of Wolfstar, the keeper of a sacred bundle, and treated with kindness. Wolfstar's name for the Apsaalooka captive becomes "Danger-with-snarled-hair," but, because she had defeated a powerful bear, she already thought of herself as Grizzly-fears-her (Matcheck, 131). After spending a great deal of time together, friendship, then love, blossoms between the keeper and the captive. By the end of the novel, the protagonist realizes that she is to be sacrificed to the Morning Star, an early ritual of the rich, complex religion of the Pawnee. Matcheck follows in the footsteps of countless other writers, who removed this aspect of religious belief from its cultural-historical foundations to sensationalize it. She also sets up the familiar duality of good Indian-bad Indian. Hence, Matcheck emphasizes notions of American Indian savagery, especially through the portrayal of enemy Pawnee. True to the heroics of the protagonist, she makes an escape in the nick of time, despite being surrounded by an entire village of Pawnees in their home territory. Calling herself Grizzlyfire, this imaginary Apsaalooka heroine heads for home. Consistent with the mainstream praise of the other books considered here, this novel was deemed a Booklist Top Ten First novel of 1998 and an ALA Best Book for Young Adults.

Another novel narrated from the perspective of an imagined American Indian protagonist is Bebe Faas Rice's *The Place at the Edge of the Earth*.[17] This ghost story is set at the fictional Fort Sayers, the author's thin disguise for the Carlisle Indian Industrial School, which operated from 1879 to 1918, in Carlisle, Pennsylvania. Two thirteen-year-old protagonists tell the story through alternating first-person narration,

Jenny Muldoon, a white eighth grader alive and well in the present, and Jonah Flying Cloud, a Lakota "unquiet spirit" who had died at the Fort Sayers Indian School in 1880. In this novel, Jenny is coping with her father's death, the remarriage of her mother to a U.S. Army officer, and a move to "Fort Sayers, a miserable little army post back East" (Rice, 20). Jonah, as imagined by Rice, says of himself: "I was the son of a Lakota chief, and the grandson of a great Lakota warrior. I was supposed to follow in their footsteps. I had a duty to grow up and lead my people. Instead, my Indian spirit was stolen from me, and I fell into a crack somewhere between the world of the white man and the world of my people" (Rice, 25). Both of Rice's main characters appear to one another in each other's time dimension, but only Jonah is trapped between two worlds.

As Carol A. Edwards, who reviewed *The Place at the Edge of the Earth* for *School Library Journal*, points out: "Logic is not the book's strong suit, as it is never clear why or how Jenny appears in the 1880s, except that time is a poorly understood continuum. This slipstream effect, however, doesn't seem to apply to Jonah, who is stuck until Jenny shares her philosophy of choice and comes up with an eagle memento for his grave."[18] At the bottom of this fiction is the notion that only Euro-Americans can rescue or save Indians, a cliché that Rice extends to the spirit world. Hence, Jenny comments: "Obviously there was a weird sort of spirit bond between us. What a scary thought! And now I was supposed to help him, to free him from those Wasichus—whoever they were—who were keeping him prisoner" (Rice, 97). Actually, the "scary thought" for Indians is the notion advanced by Rice that Euro-American cultural hegemony might extend to the afterlife.

Illogical though it is, the time-warp scenario helps the author play up another familiar theme, one that relegates Indians to the past. In Rice's version of this theme, the American Indian characters are part of history (having lived only briefly, at that), making it possible for her to present bogus Native perspectives without interference from authentic voices. Jonah, the fictional Lakota protagonist created by Rice, becomes the mouthpiece for words that pervert actual cultural knowledge and school history. All of Rice's primary Indian characters, who are portrayed as Lakota, die during the course of the narrative, while the Euro-American protagonist and her family and classmates flourish in the present. It is only in a note at the end of the book that the author acknowledges the survival of American Indians. Rice's novel fails to reflect the fact that tribal families, communities, and nations have ongoing ties with boarding school students, including those buried in school cemeteries. Furthermore, it fails to comprehend the profound, reverberating impact of this period of history on Native lives then and now. Worst of all, Rice exploits and sensationalizes student deaths at Indian boarding schools. Described as "inspired to write *The Place at the Edge of the Earth* after she visited the Indian children's cemetery at Carlisle Barracks," this author fictionalizes the most horrific dimension of Indian boarding school history (Rice, back cover). She misrepresents actual events, which are brutal in their own right, by concocting gruesome scenarios that have no basis in reality. One of them centers on Swift Running River ("His tongue, it was said, ran as swiftly as a river"), whose violence is as stereotypical as his name ("already his hatred of the Wasichus had set his feet on the snakepath of bitterness and violence") (Rice, 3, 24). In the novel, a town mob lynches this student as a "murdering heathen" for stabbing "Mr. Samuel, the chief of the school," to death. In Rice's portrayal, Running River dies slowly and torturously. "But he did not die. His neck did not break," she writes. "That would have been the quick, merciful thing. Instead, he spun first in one direction, then the other, his face darkening as he strangled slowly" (Rice, 82–83). Jonah, Running River's classmate, then runs through the crowd to assist him. "I pushed people roughly aside," he declares. "They stood like sheep, staring upward. They did not try to stop me. I reached the clearing beneath Swift Running River's feet. Taking hold of them in both hands I pulled down, swinging on them with my full weight. I felt his neck give. And then he was dead" (Rice, 83).

By the time of the "lynching" scene, Rice had already described the death of another student, a young child, who tried to cook a stolen potato in the school boiler room in an effort to assuage his hunger. "Little Fox lay in a small, bloody heap where he'd been thrown by the force of the blast," Jonah recalled of the explosion. "We did not have to go over to him to see that he was dead. His eyes were open, but they were staring and unseeing. His arms and legs were twisted and bent in the wrong directions. The smell of seared flesh was strong. And in one hand, one broken, scalded hand, Johnny Little Fox still clutched his potato" (Rice, 63). During the course of the narrative, Jonah also dies, his life slowly ebbing away in the school infirmary. Through these deaths, Rice evokes the horror of Indian children dying at boarding schools across the

United States and Canada, actual history. It should be needless to say, but for Native readers, Rice pours salt on open wounds. She is intrusive and disrespectful, misrepresenting lives and appropriating grief that does not belong to her. While purportedly speaking for dead students, Rice denies them their own names, identities, and stories. These school graves deserve to be treated with the utmost respect, with neither trespassing nor exploitation. These students also have the right to their own history, not some fraudulent version of it.

Adding insult to injury, Rice's depiction of Indian boarding school life and Lakota culture is dead wrong. A stabbing death of a boarding school administrator by a student during the period did not happen. If such an event had occurred, it would have likely shut down the fledgling experiment in schooling. There is no evidence to support the lynching of an American Indian student as depicted by Rice. Even presented fictionally, such a scenario has to be plausible. If a lynching had occurred, the town mob would not have let Jonah, who was in the company of the purported killer, get away. Furthermore, Jonah's role in hastening Running River's death is also farfetched, nowhere near the realm of possibility. In reality, early boarding school students were closely supervised, unlikely to be ambling around town on their own. The supervision was especially stringent in the founding years of the institution's history, the period depicted by Rice, because school officials did not want any incident, especially one with public ramifications, to derail their new school program. Even considering the possibility that Jonah and Running River wandered "free among the white people of Sayersville," the likelihood of them then encountering the "chief of the school" is remote. Indian students, far from home and family, knew they were at the mercy of strangers and would have acted accordingly.

Moreover, it is highly doubtful that an Indian boarding school student would possess a weapon, especially the same individual on two separate occasions. As Rice writes, however, Swift Running River had tangled with the school administrator in an earlier, separate incident before interrupting him in the middle of eating a sweet roll and stabbing him to death. "Whipping a knife from his waistband," as she describes that earlier scene, "he held it aloft and shouted: 'We will all soon be dead. They plan to kill us!'" (Rice, 43). Running River then cut off his own hair and slashed his arms before grabbing Mr. Samuel by the shirt and pushing him backward. Although children did indeed have their hair cut at boarding school, the haircutting scene concocted by Rice is preposterous. As Beverly Slapin and Doris Seale point out, "Children did not cut their own hair and mutilate themselves as a sign of rebellion."[19] In addition, Rice projects a cultural practice from the dominant society onto her "insider" protagnoist, who comments: "I knew Swift Running River was lying, because he did not look me in the eye when he spoke those words" (Rice, 74). As Slapin and Seale point out about this statement, "Lakota people do not look each other in the eye as a sign of telling the truth" (Slapin and Seale, 2). Furthermore, accounts of early Lakota students in boarding school history document their truthfulness. Rice is also wrong in writing that reservations are "tracts of land owned by the federal government" (Rice, 101). On the contrary, in the case of the Lakota and other federally recognized groups, lands are owned by the tribal nation. The federal government has a fiduciary responsibility, with duties that include holding land in trust through the Bureau of Indian Affairs. Rice's novel is permeated with errors. Substituting a patch from the 101st Airborne Division—the "Screaming Eagles"—for an eagle feather is no substitute, no matter how well intentioned, for actual Lakota religious practices. Similarly, *The Place at the Edge of the World*, which reflects the author's Euro-American perspectives, is no substitute for accurate history.

NOTES

1. Patricia Willis, *Danger Along the Ohio* (New York: Clarion Books, 1997), 17; hereafter referred to in text as Willis.
2. Kristiana Gregory, *The Legend of Jimmy Spoon* (New York: Harcourt Brace Jovanovich, 1990); hereafter referred to in text as Gregory.
3. Mary Gloyne Byler, "The Image of American Indians Projected by Non-Indian Writers," *Library Journal* (February 1974), 546.
4. Melissa Kay Thompson, "A Sea of Good Intentions: Native Americans in Books for Children," *The Lion and the Unicorn* 25, no. 3 (September 2001), 354; hereafter referred to in text as Thompson.
5. Liza Bliss, review of *Danger Along the Ohio*, by Patricia Willis, *School Library Journal* 43, no. 5 (May 1997), 140.
6. Donnarae MacCann, "Native Americans in Books for the Young," in *Teaching Multicultural Literature in Grades K–8*, ed. Violet J. Harris (Norwood, MA: Christopher-Gordon Publishers, 1993), 141; hereafter referred to in text as MacCann.
7. Naomi Caldwell-Wood and Lisa A. Mitten, comps., "Selective Bibliography and Guide for '*I' Is Not for Indian: The Portrayal of Native Americans in*

Books for Young People" (Program of the ALA/OLOS Subcommittee for Library Services to American Indian People, American Indian Library Association, 1991), 7. Available online at www.nativeculture.com/lisamitten/ailabib .htm (accessed August 7, 2004).; hereafter referred to in text as Caldwell-Wood and Mitten.

8. Ann Rinaldi, *The Second Bend in the River* (New York: Scholastic, 1997); hereafter referred to in text as *Second Bend.*

9. R. David Edmunds, *Tecumseh and the Quest for Indian Leadership* (New York: Addison Wesley Longman, 1984), 217–18; hereafter referred to in text as Edmunds.

10. Review of *The Second Bend in the River* by Ann Rinaldi, *Publishers Weekly* 244, no. 2 (January 13, 1997), 76–77; Carrie Schadle, review of *The Second Bend in the River*, *School Library Journal* 43, no. 6 (June 1997), 126; Kay Weisman, review of *The Second Bend in the River*, *Booklist* 93, no. 12 (February 15, 1997), 1016.

11. Review of the *Second Bend in the River* by Ann Rinaldi, *Kirkus Reviews* (March 15, 1997). Available online at www.kirkusreviews.com (accessed August 7, 2004). Subscription required.

12. Jan Hudson, *Sweetgrass* (Canada: Tree Frog Press, 1984; New York: Penguin Putnam Books for Young Readers, 1999); hereafter referred to in text as *Sweetgrass* (page citations are to the reprint edition).

13. Beverly Slapin and Doris Seale, eds., *Through Indian Eyes: The Native Experience in Books for Children* (Philadelphia: New Society Publishers, 1992 edition), 172; hereafter referred to in text by authors' surnames.

14. Yvonne A. Frey, review of *Sweetgrass* by Jan Hudson, *School Library Journal* 35, no. 8 (April 1989), 102.

15. Jan Hudson, *Dawn Rider* (New York: Philomel Books, 1990; New York: Puffin Books, 2000); hereafter referred to in text as *Dawn Rider* (page citations are to the reprint edition).

16. Diane Matcheck, *The Sacrifice* (New York: Farrar, Straus and Giroux, 1998; New York: Puffin Books, 1999); hereafter referred to in text as Matcheck (page citations are to the reprint edition).

17. Bebe Faas Rice, *The Place at the Edge of the Earth* (New York: Clarion Books, 2002); hereafter referred to in text as Rice.

18. Carol A. Edwards, review of *The Place at the Edge of the Earth*, by Bebe Faas Rice, *School Library Journal* 48, no. 12 (December 2002), 146.

19. Beverly Slapin and Doris Seale. Review of *The Place at the Edge of the Earth* by Bebe Faas Rice. Oyate—Avoid *The Place at the Edge of the Earth*. Available online at http://oyate.org/books-to-avoid/edgeEarth.html (accessed August 7, 2004).

Chapter Four

Running the Gauntlet

Fictional Captivity Narratives in Young Adult Literature

Dear Lord, prayed Mercy Carter, *do not let us be murdered in our beds tonight.*

Mercy tucked her brothers in, packing them close. *Or any night,* she told the Lord, shifting her weight from foot to foot.[1]

These opening lines from Caroline Cooney's *The Ransom of Mercy Carter* set the stage for the fear and violence to come at the hands of American Indians in her captivity novel. Based on the actual Deerfield, Massachusetts, captivities of 1704, this young adult fiction typifies central features of writings in this popular genre. The portrayal of the abduction and captivity of Euro-Americans by American Indians has a centuries-old literary history. Cooney's book is one of many fictional successors of historical captivities, such as that of Mary Rowlandson, the wife of a Puritan minister who was taken captive in 1676 during King Philip's War between Algonquian Indians and English colonists in New England. Rowlandson remained with Nipmuc and other Algonquian captors for some three months, until a twenty-pound ransom secured her release to family and friends. Rowlandson's account of her captivity, *The Soveraignty and Goodness of God*, was printed in Boston in March 1682.[2] A short time later, the work made its way into second and third editions in Cambridge as well as a London edition. As historian Jill Lepore points out, the publication "would become America's first best-seller."[3] "The scenes of horror or privation that Mary Rowlandson bequeathed to her successors," author Raymond Stedman observes, "rebound today from

printed page or theater screen or picture tube: A shrieking attack on an
anxious compound, terrified settlers dragged from their isolated cabins."[4]
Rowlandson's best seller was followed by hundreds of other captivity accounts, ongoing additions to a lucrative genre. Scholar Roy Harvey Pearce, who outlines the formulaic underpinnings of these accounts, identifies the first such narratives as religious documents. "They
are," he writes, "for the greater part Puritan; and their writers find in the
experience of captivity, 'removal,' hardships on the march to Canada
[during the French and Indian wars], adoption or torture or both, the life
in Canada which so often seemed to consist in nothing but resisting the
temptations set forth by Romish priests, and eventual return (this is the
classic pattern of the captivity), evidences of God's inscrutable wisdom."[5] Eventually, this approach gave way to other interests, especially
as "the propagandist value of the captivity narrative became more and
more apparent" (Pearce, 3). Religious concerns grew increasingly inci-
dental, with the typical writer focusing on registering "as much hatred
of the French and Indians as possible" and producing "a blood-and-
thunder shocker" to accomplish this (Pearce, 6). By the middle of the
eighteenth century, in Pearce's reckoning, "the captivity narrative had
become the American equivalent of the Grub street criminal biography"
(Pearce, 6–7). Adding more sensationalism, the creators of the narratives exhibited less concern about writing "accurate records of their (or
others') captivities, but with the salability of penny dreadfuls" (Pearce,
9). Among these accounts, Pearce notes, are "out-and-out fakes"
(Pearce, 13). Purportedly bona fide experiences, too, were heavily laced
with fiction and packaged for greater marketability. As scholar June
Namias writes, "Captivity materials, especially those from the late nineteenth century, are notorious for blending the real and the highly fic-
tive."[6] Unlike Rowlandson, who composed from her own experiences,
other authors produced "as told to" narratives with ensuing problems of
veracity. In addition, some accounts were altered or reinterpreted, with
material added or deleted in assorted editions. Captivities thus range
from "religious confessional" to "visceral thriller," serving "as a popular vehicle for various historically and culturally individuated purposes"
over time (Pearce, 1).

Besides Caroline Cooney's captivity fiction, other young adult novels in this genre include Lynda Durrant's *The Beaded Moccasins: The
Story of Mary Campbell*, Katherine Kirkpatrick's *Trouble's Daughter:*

The Story of Susanna Hutchinson, Indian Captive, Mary Pope Osborne's *Standing in the Light: The Captive Diary of Catherine Carey Logan*, Caroline Meyer's *Where the Broken Heart Still Beats: The Story of Cynthia Ann Parker*, Sally Keehn's *I am Regina*, Sollace Hotze's *A Circle Unbroken*, and Robin Moore's *Maggie Among the Seneca*.[7] These novels share similarities with earlier fictional narratives, such as Lois Lenski's *Indian Captive: The Story of Mary Jemison*, a Newbery Honor Book initially published in 1941, and Elizabeth George Speare's *Calico Captive*, published in 1957.[8] Following the well-worn path of past narratives, recent works tend to be recycled accounts of some of the best-known captives, among them Mary Campbell, Cynthia Ann Parker, and the individuals associated with the 1704 events in Deerfield, Massachusetts. This young adult fiction generally depicts Algonquian (typically, Delaware, Mohican, or Shawnee) or Iroquois (often, Seneca or Mohawk) abductions in the northeast during the colonial period. Other accounts, such as the Comanche in *Where the Broken Heart Still Beats* and "a band of renegade Sioux" in *A Circle Unbroken*, focus on Plains tribal groups and are set in the nineteenth century.

Captives in the young adult fiction considered here tend to include small groups of siblings and/or neighbors, but the central character is generally female. "[I]t is no coincidence," Lepore observes, "that the first and most popular captivity narrative was written by a woman. The tension between resistance and surrender was best managed by gendered explanations. Mary Rowlandson had already surrendered her will to her husband, and to God, and to surrender to Indians in God's name was consistent with what her culture expected of her" (Lepore, 134–135). Echoing Rowlandson's prototype, the young adult novels in this genre tend to be female-authored and, although they include both male and female captives, their protagonists are generally young females. In one exception, Lynda Durrant centers her first book, *Echohawk*, on a Euro-American boy captured and adopted by Mohicans (the novel also has a sequel, *Turtle Clan Journey*).[9] A short time later, however, Durrant returned to the fold (or more accurately, mold) with *The Beaded Moccasins*, her fictionalized version of the captivity of Mary Campbell, a young Euro-American female abducted by Delaware captors in the eighteenth century. The female voices of most of these books incorporate perceived roles for girls and women, adding themes of sexual tension crisscrossing forbidden (and alluring) boundaries of culture and race.

Paralleling the bulk of the historical narratives, young adult novels of this genre overwhelmingly fail to address the abduction and captivity of American Indians by Euro-Americans, although indigenous counterparts to Mary Rowlandson certainly existed. During King Philip's War, New England Algonquians suffered torture and captivity as well as the decimation of their communities, the loss of thousands of lives, imprisonment on barren islands, and permanent exile when they were sold into foreign slavery by English colonizers. In fact, Indian losses during the period were "far, far greater" than those sustained by the English (Lepore, xii). "The lasting legacy of Mary Rowlandson's dramatic, eloquent, and fantastically popular narrative of captivity and redemption," Lepore concludes, "is the nearly complete veil it has unwittingly placed over the experiences of bondage endured by Algonquian Indians during King Philip's War" (Lepore, 126).

The same holds true for the other wars that form the backdrop for many of the captivity narratives as well as the impact of European colonization on native groups generally. As Namias attests, "In the successive struggles for dominance on the North American continent, priests, soldiers, women, and children were held for ransom, adopted, or otherwise incorporated into the tribal life of an enemy. North American Indians were taken prisoner, enslaved, or forcibly taken on voyages to the other side of the Atlantic, where they were put on public display as showpieces of victory and novelty" (Namias, 2). Paul Fleischman's *Saturnalia* and Joseph Bruchac's *The Winter People*, discussed later in the chapter, offer perspectives on this dimension of captivity, with Fleischman focusing on a young Narragansett taken captive by the English during King Philip's War and Bruchac depicting a story of Abenaki captivity and rescue during the French and Indian Wars.[10] These works counter the one-sided literary focus on Euro-Americans held captive by American Indians, narratives with antecedents in the colonialist control of printing (and propaganda) that foster the overall perception of Indians as perpetrators of acts of violence. This emphasis obscures the fact that "the taking of captives was a centuries-old practice around the world" (Namias, 2). In fact, captivity has persisted into modern times with contemporary hostage situations, with what Namias notes, "we call the holding of prisoners of war (which sounds less 'savage')" (Namias, 4). Indeed, the rescue of Pfc. Jessica Lynch by American Special Forces from an Iraqi hospital in 2003 garnered an article by Melani McAlister in the *New York Times* drawing comparisons to "a classic American war fantasy: the captivity narrative." In McAlister's telling, Private Lynch is both victim and hero "in a way a man never could have been. She is tough, a soldier seized in the line of duty. Like Hannah Dunston [a Euro-American woman taken hostage by Abenaki captors in 1697], she was 'fighting to the death.' But she is also young, white and pretty. The focus of her injuries point up her vulnerability. Even her bravery is feminized."[11] In contrast, Lynch's tentmate, Lori Piestewa, a Hopi private who became the first American female soldier killed in Iraq, goes unmentioned in the article.[12]

In captivity fiction, the narrative progression generally includes brutal attacks, accompanied by scenes of torture, murder, and the destruction, often by fire, of the Euro-American family homestead. The captives then stumble forward on a danger-fraught journey through the wilderness. Along the way, they plot or attempt escape from captors, daydream of idyllic home and family scenes, express revulsion at all things Indian (people, language, food, clothing, customs), wear out "civilized" clothing (and Indian patience), finally arriving, exhausted and terrified, at the captors' destination. The captives ultimately encounter tests such as running the gauntlet, where weapon-wielding Indians arranged themselves in two lines facing each other and flogged the incoming hostages forced to run between them. As the captive's memories of pre-captivity life grow dimmer and adjustments to Indian life and tribal customs grow stronger, new attachments begin to form. These attachments often extend to liaisons (or thoughts thereof) with a member of the opposite sex and other culture. Finally, the captive faces an angst-ridden choice between returning home, via rescue, ransom, or treaty terms, or remaining with Indians. In a number of cases, a return to Euro-American life results in a traumatic readjustment, complete with the curiosity and racism of family and community members about captivity experiences and tribal customs. This situation generally intensified when a captive refused to relinquish his or her new Indian identity, had produced children with an Indian spouse, and/or spoke well of tribal life.

Historian James Axtell contends that Indians "wasted no time in beginning the educational process that would transform their hostile or fearful white captives into affectionate Indian relatives."[13] In fact, tribal groups were so successful that "even when the English held the upper hand militarily, they were often embarrassed by the Indians' educational power" (Axtell, 306). Axtell found that "the extraordinary drawing power of Indian culture" applied to children as well as adults, captive and non-captive, drawn into Indian societies (Axtell, 309). As he observes, "captives had been returned who . . . responded only to Indian names, spoke only Indian dialects, felt comfortable only in Indian clothes, and in general regarded their white saviors as barbarians and their deliverance as captivity" (Axtell, 306). Axtell reinforces this finding with the words and experiences of actual captives, including a released female hostage who defended the Indian practice of adopting outsiders: "'Those who have profited by refinement and education . . . ought to abate part of the prejudice, which prompts them to look with an eye of censure on this untutored race. . . . Do they ever adopt an enemy . . . and salute him with the tender name of brother?'" (Axtell, 316). "English captives," Lepore concurs, "were accepted by Algonquian communities in ways that Christian Indians were never accepted by the English" (Lepore, 296n16). Some of the authors of young adult captivity fiction attempt to depict the "drawing power of native culture." Cooney, for one, portrays captives who reject rigid Puritan ways in favor of tribal life and those who question, or backslide on, their protestant religious teachings when exposed to French Catholicism.

While a number of the authors of young adult captivity narratives, such as Katherine Kirkpatrick, show positive aspects of Indian life through the experiences of hostages, they are overshadowed by the Euro-American cultural and religious hegemony that permeates these works. "One would expect the captivity novel, in claiming to offer a perspective gained from close proximity with Amerind cultures," author Melissa Kay Thompson reasons, "to go beyond the superficialities of the frontier narrative. But in fact these two modes of storytelling are similar. They are still centered on justifying European conquest while failing to acknowledge the existence of conquest."[14] European aggression and colonization are ignored at the expense of American Indians, who continue to be presented in the context of systematic warfare. As Thompson asserts, "Today's captivity novels make this 'warfare' an ongoing phenomenon. They typically ignore the historical record because, consciously intended or not, their first aim is to produce for young White readers a laudable national heritage. Honest 'insider' viewpoints would tend to contradict that goal" (Thompson, 362).

The Indian violence pervading captivity fiction is especially disturbing and propagandistic when it is centered on young children. Keehn's

I am Regina, based on an episode near present-day Selinsgrove, Pennsylvania in 1755, is a case in point. Allegheny captors and villagers
force two- or three-year-old Sarah, strapped to the back of eleven-year-
old protagonist Regina, to run the gauntlet. Regina, fictionally based on
real-life Regina Leininger, laments: "The Indians emerge from their
huts. I shrink at the weapons they now brandish—sticks, axes, clubs.
Even the children carry them. They form two lines in front of me, one
line facing the other. . . . So this is our welcome. Our journey's end. We
are going to be beaten by these people. Sarah starts to cry" (Keehn, 65).
Regina's pleas for mercy fail and she and the toddler are pushed forward into the gauntlet: "Sarah squeals as a boy whips his branch across
our faces. I lift my arm, trying to protect us both. . . . Ahead, a lean man
raises his axe, waiting to cut us down. Sarah screams. I weave to the
other side and the old woman in the deerskin sacque clubs my arm and
then my shoulder. Three times she clubs me" (Keehn, 66). Refuting
stereotypes of Indian brutality, historians document American Indian
love of children and their kind treatment of them. Axtell relates a common story of how "'some of the children who were taken at Deerfield,
they drew upon slays; at other times they have been known to carry
them in their arms or upon their backs to Canada'" (Axtell, 311). Concerning the gauntlet, he writes that, "in most villages," only older captives were required to run it "or were rescued from any serious harm by
one or more villagers . . ." (Axtell, 312). Namias documents that among
the Iroquois only males were required to participate in the practice
(Namias, 3). Historically, the gauntlet served a number of purposes depending on tribal group and time period. It provided a means to ritually
avenge the deaths of slain relatives, but also served as "a purgative ceremony by which the bereaved Indians could exorcise their anger and
anguish, and the captives could begin their cultural transformation"
(Axtell, 313–314). The gauntlet was often followed by a cleansing ceremony to symbolically remove the captive's former life and make way
for his or her new identity, also as preparation for a formal adoption
ceremony.

Besides featuring Allegheny cruelty against a two-year-old, *I am
Regina* also portrays an attempted rape, with twelve-year-old protagonist Regina the victim and one of her captors, Tiger Claw, the perpetra-
tor. In this account, Keehn writes:

> Tiger Claw hits my face over and over again. Hot, bright pain sears my
> eyes, my mouth.

Suddenly, he stops. His breath is heavy, thick with the smell of rum. I
feel his body lower over mine. Now it pins me to the bed. "You be good
squaw," he mumbles.
    Blackness hovers over me. "No. No." I throw my aching head from
side to side. . . .
    Minutes pass. Long minutes filled with shadows and Tiger Claw's loud
breathing. Tiger Claw wants to possess me as . . . as a man does a woman.
I sense it now. I feel helpless and ashamed. (Keehn, 135–136)

Although Regina is saved in the nick of time by Tiger Claw's mother in
the novel, the damage has been done. While depicting an Indian man as
a brutal rapist, the author also adds drunkenness and stereotypical language to the portrayal. The desired female is depicted as Euro-American,
a child victim overpowered by a predatory Indian male.
    Similarly, Sollace Hotze's *A Circle Unbroken*, a novel centering on
the captivity of a ten-year-old protagonist, Rachel, in 1838, includes
two female characters "badly used" by Indian men (Hotze, 60). One of
them is Rachel herself, who was molested by one of her captors then
sold to a chief, who became her kind "Dakota father" and welcomed her
into "a family of the Teton tribe" (Hotze, 98). Following Rachel's return
home seven years after being captured, she eventually reveals details of
her molestation to Peter, a suitor who sought her hand in marriage:

"I have been taken by an Indian brave," she said and lifted her head
higher. "Not once but many times." She looked him full in the face and
spoke in a rush before he could respond. "On the journey north, after I
was taken from the fort, the brave who captured me . . . he lay with me,
Peter."
    The words seared her throat, burned her face. But she would not lose
courage now. "Can you think how it would be, Peter, to love a woman
who has been taken by an Indian brave, how it would feel to hold your
arms around my body that has been _____" (Hotze, 137–138).

Rachel then asked Peter whether he would "want a wife who has been in-
timate with an Indian in every way," reading his response on his face,
which registered "the horror, the pity, and, she could not pretend otherwise, the revulsion. It was fleeting perhaps, but there all the same, the
shadow in the eyes, the almost imperceptible drawing away" (Hotze, 138).
    The other white female "badly used" in Hotze's fictional captivity is
Rachel's aunt Sarah, who "was sold to the Comanche—to a brave who

needed a . . . a wife" (Hotze, 109). Sarah became a "slave," who was beaten and forced to do whatever her captor "brave" wished. In relating the seven-year captivity, a number of Sarah's comments defy credibility (as does the likelihood of both northern and southern plains tribal groups figuring in two female captivities and two rapes within one family): "Often I thought of ending my life, but he never let me out of his sight. When he went hunting, he tied me to a *tipi* pole" (Hotze, 110). During her captivity and presumably while untied from her pole, Sarah gave birth to a daughter who died at age two. Released from captivity (and without the burden of a child fathered by an Indian), she returned home to her Euro-American husband Nathan, who was unable to recapture his ardor for her. Sarah confided to her niece: "Since my return, he hasn't . . . Nathan can't . . . he hasn't lain with me as a husband. Oh, he shares my bed, for he would never be so unkind as to shame me, but he can't bring himself to—to love me in the way a husband should" (Hotze, 111). Sarah died an early death, broken by her captivity experiences and the loss of her husband's affection. Rachel's fate is not death, but she too is separated from her Euro-American life. After her "sweet and good" (i.e., virginal) sister becomes Peter's wife, Rachel leaves her home to look for her Dakota family. Although Hotze presents "good" Indians, such as a Dakota male who courts her protagonist, her novel underscores the message that being touched by Indians, especially sexually, is an act of defilement. The protagonists in this account are portrayed as martyrs, to their husbands and to their destinies. Unfit to live happy lives with the white men in their lives, these women suffer, die young, or leave their Euro-American families to rejoin Indians. Failing to take into account American Indian perspectives, the author just assumes that tribal societies would want these former captives to return to them.

Beginning with Mary Rowlandson, who wrote: "not one of them ever offered me the least abuse of unchastity to me, in word or action," redeemed captives did address fears or notions associated with American Indian sexuality.[15] According to historians, many captives "made a point of insisting that, although they had been completely powerless in captivity, the Indians had never affronted them sexually" (Axtell, 310). In her study of King Philip's War, Lepore found "very little evidence that Algonquians ever sexually abused their captives" (Lepore, 130). Axtell identifies several reasons for the Indians' lack of sexual interest in female captives, among them that "New England Indians, at least,

esteemed black the color of beauty" and that with "the Indians' strong in-
cest taboos, no warrior would attempt to violate his future sister or
cousin" (Axtell, 310). The existence of "a religious ethic of strict warrior
continence, the breaking of which was thought to bring misfortune or
death," was also part and parcel of proper conduct (Axtell, 310). Disregarding those historical realities, captivity fiction often incorporates fan-
ciful interracial relationships. "The observations and fantasies of Anglo-
American men and women between 1607 and 1870," to Namias, "had to
do with ideology, politics, and culture. To cross these boundaries was to
enter into a world of forbidden intimacies, whether in fact or in the imag-
ination of the reader or viewer" (Namias, 109). She notes: "The first
signs of relationship, both threatening and companionate, for Anglo-
American women date to the early Indian wars in New England. . . .
Overt brutality and sexuality of Indian men toward white women in captivity literature first appeared in the seventeenth century but became
more common in the late eighteenth century" (Namias, 109). It continues to flourish in captivity narratives in young adult fiction.

Besides the portrayal of Indian males as "badly using" white females,
tribal societies are presented as childlike and primitive. Algonquian
housing appears as windowless and smoky "huts," reflecting the attitudes of the colonists, who "refused to consider Indian settlements . . .
real 'towns,' or their wigwams true 'houses'" (Lepore, 87). In one of
many examples from these novels, Osborne writes in *Standing in the
Light*: "For three days I have sat in the old woman's cold, smoky hut,
dressed like an Indian, stinking of bear grease" (Osborne, 46). In contrast, Lepore points out: "Algonquian settlements were generally small,
and consisted of a group of wigwams, sturdy buildings constructed of
woven mats that could be easily disassembled and transported (and quite
similar to the 'English wigwams' the colonists had lived in when they
first arrived)" (Lepore, 86). Historical evidence aside, American Indians
continue to be described as nomads, wandering or "rambling" over the
land (temporary), and Euro-Americans as "settlers" in fixed communities (permanent). Refuting this notion, Lepore writes of seventeenth-
century New England Algonquians: "They lived for most of the year in
regular, settled communities, one in summer, one in winter. In summer,
families gathered to live in villages near fertile agricultural lands; in
winter, they moved closer to hunting grounds, returning to the same
place for as many years as the lands could sustain them" (Lepore, 86).

In a refreshing change of pace, Paul Fleischman's *Saturnalia*, set in Boston in 1681, centers on Weetasket, a fourteen-year-old Narragansett male taken captive by the English during King Philip's War. He was taken into captivity following the annihilating Puritan strike against the Narragansett known as the Great Swamp Massacre of 1675, when most of his family perished. One of Weetasket's brothers was shipped to the West Indies as a slave, another was hanged for taking up arms against the English, and still another escaped westward among the Niantics. Weetasket, called William by the English, was sent to Boston and apprenticed to a printer, Mr. Currie. By 1681, the Narragansett was six years into his apprenticeship and a gifted student of the classics. "The English were greedy, ruthless, self-righteous, fearfully serving a god who was as cruel a master as the worst who walked Boston," Fleischman writes. "Yet [William] now spoke, wrote, thought, and dreamed in their language. . . . He was held up as a shining example of hard work and quick wits—a model for the very people who'd murdered his family" (Fleischman, 54). The protagonist William has parallels to highly skilled Algonquian translators, such as Cockenoe, John Sassomon, Job Nesutan, and James Printer, whose linguistic work with missionary John Eliot made possible the creation of *Mamusee Wunneetu-panatamwe Up-Biblum God*, the first Bible published in North America.[16] William is also reminiscent of Caleb Cheeshahteaumuck, who became known as the first Native American graduate of Harvard University (class of 1665), and other early indigenous scholars. In Fleischman's novel, the tithingman, Mr. Baggot, asks: "What had inspired Mr. Currie [the printer] to send the tawny to school, to hire tutors, to read to him from Homer and Plato until his learning surpassed Mr. Baggot's own?" (Fleischman, 7). William searches for a brother by night while evading his tithingman adversary, eventually finding a great-uncle and a cousin. He interacts with them as well as Fleischman's array of colorful Puritan characters around the period of the Saturnalia, the Roman holiday when masters and slaves exchanged places. "Offering lyrical prose, resonant themes and a tragicomic tone," *Publishers Weekly* incisively notes, "this story will captivate those who seek a challenging and enlightening read."[17]

In *The Winter People*, Joseph Bruchac also shifts the usual emphasis on Euro-American damsels in distress to an American Indian-centered account of captivity. The novel is based on the events surrounding the

British attack led by Major Robert Rogers, of Rogers Rangers fame, that decimated the Abenaki village of St. Francis in 1759. Bruchac's young male protagonist Saxso tells the story of the act of war that destroyed his family's home, carried his mother and two sisters into captivity, and devastated his people. Bruchac incorporates tribal sources to present a pivotal event from untold perspectives. He also interweaves in details that convey the influence of the French, allies in the struggle against the British. Countering the usual static, anachronistic portrayal of tribal communities in captivity fiction and other accounts, Bruchac describes how Abenaki homes in the village of St. Francis looked in the mid-eighteenth century, his protagonist commenting: "Mrs. Johnson [a white captive] had told me of the great surprise she felt when she saw our mission village for the first time, its sixty or so neatly built houses arranged in a horseshoe with the steeple of the church rising up from among them. There were log cabins and homes made of squared timbers covered with boards. There were also four houses made of stone" (Bruchac, 25–26). Bruchac notes that the Abenaki continued to use wigwams to some extent, but mainly for hunting camps and similar purposes.

While refuting English claims that the St. Francis villagers were completely wiped out during the 1759 strike, Bruchac delineates the tribal group's struggle to survive and rebuild. "Some Abenakis quietly returned to parts of their homelands in New England," Bruchac writes, "or remained in relatively isolated communities in northern Vermont, New Hampshire, and New York. They lived peacefully, but it was painful to hear the way their history was recorded" (Bruchac, 163). Bruchac further notes that he still finds recently published works deeming the Abenakis "an extinct tribe" (Bruchac, 163). This in turn has present-day implications for Abenaki, including efforts to attain government recognition in the United States. In her review of *The Winter People* for *School Library Journal*, Rita Soltan astutely comments: "An excellent complement to Native American or French and Indian War units with high discussion potential."[18] Other readers agree. "I've been told by some of my Abenaki friends who've read this story in manuscript," Bruchac notes, "that it is the most important thing I've ever written" (Bruchac, 165).

While fictional captivities written for young adults vary in quality, with some authors adhering more closely to the historical record and portraying diverse communities in a more responsible manner, the inescapable conclusion is that most of these accounts predictably reinforce cherished Euro-American myths. As historian Arlene Hirschfelder points out: "In contemporary society, those children socialized to believe kidnapping and killing are wrong become conditioned to consider Indians as 'savages,' given their predilection to kidnap and kill in so many juvenile novels."[19] She contends that "since captivity-and-kidnapping books, as well as a disproportionate number of other novels about Indians, are set in the past, non-Indian children today struggle with the idea that Indians are contemporary human beings" (Hirschfelder, 431). The captivity narratives are primarily about Euro-American figures and their perceptions of Indians, not about Indian people themselves (or Indian perceptions of themselves). In fact, tribal peoples and cultures generally appear as stock props, exotic others, and convenient backdrops to Euro-Americans. Pearce observes that the captivity narrative has interest and value to us, "not because it can tell us a great deal about the Indian or even about immediate frontier attitudes towards the Indian, but rather because it enables us to see more deeply and more clearly into popular American culture, popular American issues, and popular American tastes" (Pearce, 20). He concludes: "As religious confessional, as propaganda, and as pulp thriller, the captivity narrative gives us sharp insight into various segments of popular American culture. Only a properly historical view, a consideration of form, impact, and milieu as well as of content, will enable us to see what the captivity narrative really was and came to be" (Pearce, 20). In other words, the fictional captivities written for young adults provide us with "sharp insight" about the authors themselves and the dominant culture. Until such views are informed by American Indian perspectives and the "properly historical view" of the genre, such narratives will continue running the gauntlet through Eurocentric, colonialist plots.

NOTES

1. Caroline B. Cooney, *The Ransom of Mercy Carter* (New York: Delacorte, 2001).

2. Mary Rowlandson, *The Soveraignty & Goodness of God, Together, With the Faithfulness of His Promises Displayed; Being a Narrative of the Captivity and Restauration of Mrs. Mary Rowlandson* in *So Dreadfull a Judgment: Puritan Responses to King Philip's War, 1676–1677*, eds. Richard Slotkin and James Folsom (Middletown, CT: Wesleyan University Press, 1978).

3. Jill Lepore, *The Name of War: King Philip's War and the Origins of American Identity* (New York: Vintage Books, 1999), 125; hereafter referred to in text as Lepore.

4. Raymond William Stedman, *Shadows of the Indian: Stereotypes in American Culture* (Norman: University of Oklahoma, 1982), 75–76.

5. Roy Harvey Pearce, "The Significance of the Captivity Narrative," *American Literature* 19 (March 1949), 2; hereafter referred to in text as Pearce.

6. June Namias, *White Captives: Gender and Ethnicity on the American Frontier* (Chapel Hill: University of North Carolina, 1993), 23; hereafter referred to in text as Namias.

7. Lynda Durrant, *The Beaded Moccasins: The Story of Mary Campbell* (New York: Clarion Books, 1998); Katherine Kirkpatrick, *Trouble's Daughter: The Story of Susanna Hutchinson, Indian Captive* (New York: Delacorte Press, 1998); Mary Pope Osborne, *Standing in the Light: The Captive Diary of Catherine Carey Logan* (New York: Scholastic, 2000); Caroline Meyer, *Where the Broken Heart Still Beats: The Story of Cynthia Ann Parker* (New York: Harcourt Brace, 1992); Sally Keehn, *I Am Regina* (New York: Philomel Books, 1991); Sollace Hotze, *A Circle Unbroken* (New York: Clarion Books, 1988), and Robin Moore, *Maggie among the Seneca* (New York: J. B. Lippincott, 1987); hereafter referred to in text by the surname of each author.

8. Lois Lenski, *Indian Captive: The Story of Mary Jemison* (1941, New York: First Harper Trophy edition, 1995) and Elizabeth George Speare, *Calico Captive* (1957, New York: Bantam Doubleday Dell Books for Young Readers, 1989).

9. Lynda Durrant, *Echohawk* (New York: Clarion Books, 1996) and *Turtle Clan Journey* (New York: Clarion Books, 1999).

10. Paul Fleischman, *Saturnalia* (New York: Harper & Row, 1990); Joseph Bruchac, *The Winter People* (New York: Dial Books, 2002); hereafter referred to in text by the surname of each author.

11. Melani McAlister, "Saving Private Lynch," *New York Times*, April 6, 2003, Section 4, Col. 2 p. 13. Available online at www.nytimes.com/2003/04/06/opinion/06MCAL.html (accessed August 7, 2004).

12. See Gary Younge, "What about Private Lori?" *The Guardian* (April 10, 2003). Available online at www.guardian.co.uk/print/0,3858,4644802-103550,00.html (accessed August 7, 2004).

13. James Axtell, *The Invasion Within: The Contest of Cultures in Colonial North America* (New York: Oxford University Press, 1985), 309; hereafter referred to in text as Axtell.

14. Melissa Kay Thompson, "A Sea of Good Intentions: Native Americans in Books for Children," *The Lion and the Unicorn* 25, no. 3 (September 2001), 361; hereafter referred to in text as Thompson.

15. "Narrative of the Captivity of Mrs. Mary Rowlandson, 1682," in *Narratives of the Indian Wars, 1675–1699*, ed. Charles H. Lincoln (1913; reprint, New York: Barnes & Noble, 1959), 161.

16. As Jill Lepore writes in *The Name of War: King Philip's War and the Origins of American Identity*, "in one of the most sublime ironies of King Philip's War, James Printer set the type for *The Soveraignty and Goodness of God*," Mary Rowlandson's captivity account (Lepore, 127). Printer, a Nipmuck convert who had worked with John Eliot at Cambridge Press before the war and resumed the work after surviving bondage at the hands of the English, also served as a scribe during the negotiations for Rowlandson's release.

17. Diane Roback, review of *Saturnalia*, by Paul Fleischman, *Publishers Weekly* 237, no. 11 (March 16, 1990), 72.

18. Rita Soltan, review of *The Winter People* by Joseph Bruchac, *School Library Journal* 48, no. 11 (November 2002), 158.

19. Arlene B. Hirschfelder, "Native American Literature for Children and Young Adults," *Library Trends* 41, no. 3 (Winter 1993), 430; hereafter referred to in text as Hirschfelder.

Chapter Five

Historical Fiction

The Controversy over
My Heart Is on the Ground

> There I found the Indian burial ground, with dozens of white head-
> stones bearing the names of the Native American children from all
> tribes who had died while at the school. The names, with the tribes
> inscribed underneath, were so lyrical that they leapt out at me and
> took on instant personalities. Although many of these children at-
> tended Carlisle at dates later than that of my story, I used some of
> their names for classmates of Nannie Little Rose.[1]

These words, from Ann Rinaldi's *My Heart Is on the Ground: The Diary of Nannie Little Rose, A Sioux Girl*, are part of the "flash point, or
focus point, for many native critics" of this work of historical fiction.[2]
Published in 1999 as one of the fictional diaries of Scholastic's popular
Dear America series, the novel generated a firestorm of criticism, especially from Native Americans. The setting of Rinaldi's fictional diary is
the Carlisle Indian Industrial School in Carlisle, Pennsylvania. Founded
by military officer Richard Henry Pratt in 1879, the school became part
of the extensive network of mission and federal boarding schools established by American and Canadian authorities.[3] During the thirty-
nine-year period of Carlisle's existence, American Indian students were
separated both physically and culturally from their families and communities to undergo assimilationist indoctrination in the "white man's
road," immersion in English, Christianity, and manual labor-intensive
training. This instructional package, typified by Pratt's motto, "Kill the
Indian, and Save the Man," was designed to eradicate American Indian

languages and customs and dismantle tribal cultures and land bases.[4] Carlisle's program, famed for athletes such as Olympic medallist Jim Thorpe, became one of the best-known boarding schools in the country. The school site, part of a military installation, continues to draw visitors, including descendants of early students, scholars, filmmakers, and assorted curiosity-seekers. Attracted by Carlisle's fame, writers and producers often venture no further than that institution when considering a print or film treatment of American Indian boarding school history. At Carlisle, they can see the site of the historic campus, consult archival collections, and find, as Rinaldi did, the student burial ground.[5] Rinaldi, however, went beyond visiting the site. She took names from the headstones and fictionalized the lives associated with them in her novel.

"Like Lucy Pretty Eagle, not all the children in the book were at Carlisle that first year," Rinaldi writes. "But like Lucy Pretty Eagle, their personalities came through to me with such force and inspiration, I had to use them. I am sure that in whatever Happy Hunting Ground they now reside, they will forgive this artistic license, and even smile upon it" (MHIOTG, 196). Scholar K. Tsianina Lomawaima, far from alone in reacting to *My Heart Is on the Ground* with shocked disbelief, commented on Rinaldi's words in a letter to Scholastic editor Tracy Mack:

> Two aspects of this statement make me cringe. "Happy Hunting Ground" is an anachronistic and patronizing phrase used only by non-natives ignorant of native cultures. It is an immediate tip-off that no native person was ever consulted, or taken seriously if they were. Second, the assumption that no living native person, let alone representatives of the Lakota tribe, or any descendants of Carlisle students, needed to be consulted comes perfectly clear here. The arrogance of the author, to assume that dead Indian children would approve of her appropriation of their lives, is one of the clearest contemporary examples of the paternalistic, colonial, "we know what is best for Indian people or Indian history" attitude of (some) non-native scholars that I have ever seen. It staggers me to read such a comment written in 1999. I don't even want to believe it is possible, but it sits here before me. (Lomawaima, 3)

Rinaldi's fictional diary garnered an eighteen-page collaborative review from nine native and nonnative educators and parents objecting to the book's lack of historical accuracy, lack of cultural authenticity, and stereotypical language and treatment.[6] At least one of the reviewers deemed *My Heart Is on the Ground* the "worst book she had ever read"

(Oyate, 1). In a separate review, writer MariJo Moore commented: "This book is a slam to the non-Indians who have written quality books about Native peoples."[7] Genevieve Bell, the novel's fact-checker, concurred: "I completely sympathize with the critical review of Rinaldi's work that has proliferated both on the Internet and off it. There is much in the book that is offensive, and I did say so to Scholastic. Indeed, there is much more in this book that is offensive that I missed, which is why I urged [Assistant Editor] Melissa Jenkins to get a Lakota person to read it. She knew that I was not Native American."[8] This contested work points to the gaping divide that often exists between American Indians and the mostly non-Indian authors, publishers, and reviewers of Indian-themed books. The controversy, briefly recounted by Jeanne M. McGlinn in her biography of Ann Rinaldi, has important implications, especially for young readers.[9]

My Heart Is on the Ground is centered on protagonist Nannie Little Rose, a "Lakota Sioux girl, daughter of White Thunder and Goodbird," who is recruited to Carlisle at age twelve by Richard Henry Pratt (MHIOTG, 6). Little Rose, given a "die-eerie" by teacher "Missus Camp Bell," describes her first year of schooling at Carlisle, from December 1879 to October 1880, in the fictional journal while also providing descriptions of family and tribal life at home. She writes of the changes required of her by school officials, everything from having her outward appearance transformed via a haircut and "citizens' clothes" to learning English and interacting with teachers and students. Other characters in the book include students such as Lucy Pretty Eagle, a Lakota student who is buried alive in the course of the novel (hence, "die-eerie"), and Belle Rain Water, a Hopi student described in the text as Nannie's enemy.

Rinaldi's fictional diary received positive reviews in leading journals, such as *School Library Journal*, whose reviewer wrote: "Rinaldi depicts widely divergent cultures with clarity and compassion. . . . The period, the setting, and Nannie herself all come to life. An excellent addition to a popular series."[10] *Booklist* commented: "The entries are a poignant mix of past and present—Nannie's life with her family, encounters with other students, the horrific death of a friend, the efforts of both well-meaning and misguided adults. They burst with details about culture and custom, adding wonderful texture to this thought-provoking book, which raises numerous questions as it depicts the frustration, the joy, and the confusion of one of yesterday's children growing up in two cultures. A solid addition to the Dear America series."[11] *Kirkus Reviews* found: "This is a strong addition to Rinaldi's ongoing historical explorations; it builds slowly to a terrifying climax that will linger long in readers' emotions, and offers genuine insight into the courage, weaknesses, and essential humanity of Native American children who made the painful transition from old ways to new ones."[12]

In a 2001 interview conducted by Elizabeth Bush, who had earlier given *My Heart Is on the Ground* a positive review in the *Bulletin of the Center for Children's Books*, Ann Rinaldi attributed the furor over *My Heart Is on the Ground* to "political correctness" and "just something that started on the Internet, and everybody had to jump on the bandwagon and have their say."[13] She commented: "I did not know as a white person, you're really asking for it, doing a book on Native Americans. I did not know that! But it's a touchy thing. And I grant them all their feelings. . . . But my book, I didn't intend to do anything but enhance them and honor them" (Bush, 319). Rinaldi placed the blame on a "Native American woman, very intelligent, very educated" for starting the controversy. As far as taking names from Carlisle's cemetery, she said of her critics: "They objected to the fact that I used the names of the children in the graveyard, whose names I found on the tombstones, who had died while at the school. Well, I was so moved; the names were so beautiful, and I wanted it to have a taste of reality. And I thought I was honoring these children, but it was taken wrong" (Bush, 319). These statements indicate a continuing failure to understand why Native Americans would find her deed "the coldest kind of appropriation" and an act of desecration (Oyate, 7). Scholastic defended the author's use of these names by way of a comparison: "Louise Erdrich in the acknowledgments for her book *Birchbark House* (Hyperion, 1999) says, 'The name Omakayas (main character) appears on a Turtle Mountain census. I am using it because I've been told those old names should be given life.'"[14] In the passage, Erdrich actually refers to using the name "in the original translation," an important distinction. She reclaimed a name from the Ojibwe language, knowing the cultural and historical context of her choice. The word she selected has other uses within the tribal culture, including myriad naming associations over time. In addition, Erdrich chose a name, but created a new and separate identity for it in her work. In contrast, Rinaldi appropriated the names as well as other aspects of the students' identities for her own use. As scholar Debbie Reese, one of the Oyate reviewers of the fictional diary, points out: "We viewed this use of names as a violation of the respect due to those children and their families, and we were struck by the utter lack of sensitivity extended to them. We doubt that a similar story would have been created using names taken from another tragic episode in history—the names on the Vietnam Memorial come to mind."[15] Clearly, the names, identities, and personal histories appropriated by Rinaldi belong to the respective students.

Although Rinaldi attributes the criticism of *My Heart Is on the Ground* in part to "political correctness," she does not say what the term means or who gets to define it. Depending on perspective, the label could just as easily refer to business-as-usual hegemonic white cultural dominance or serve as the latest smokescreen to deflect legitimate criticism. "Correctness" or accuracy is certainly a desired quality, especially in a book marketed to young people. As a matter of fact, Oyate and other reviewers found factual errors "on nearly every page" of the book (Oyate, 8). Perhaps one could get away with cloaking criticism of historical inaccuracies under the cover of "political correctness" if the errors were few, minor, or inconsequential. The truth is, however, there are too many to overlook or dismiss. Rinaldi's mistakes include misrepresenting treaties, especially with respect to "Sioux" (Dakota, Lakota, Nakota) lands. Her protagonist voices misinformation, such as the following: "At one time my people ruled much good land—all the Black Hills, which the whites give us in a treaty in the year They-Killed-One-Wearing-A-Striped-War-Bonnet, 1868" (MHIOTG, 12). In fact, the tribal nation already owned the Black Hills; furthermore, the whites could not "give" land they did not own. As authors Mario Gonzalez and Elizabeth Cook-Lynn point out:

> When gold was discovered in the Black Hills in 1874, white miners and settlers began pouring into Sioux territory. When the Sioux refused to negotiate a sale or lease of the Black Hills, President Grant ordered the Army not to enforce the provision of the 1868 Treaty prohibiting non-Indians from entering Sioux territory. Congress then declared a halt to treaty-guaranteed rations until the Sioux agreed to sell. An "agreement" to sell was reached in 1876 with less than 10% of the Sioux consenting. Ignoring the fact that the provision in the 1868 Treaty requiring the consent of three-fourths of the adult males to any land cession was clearly violated, Congress implemented the terms of the agreement in the Act of February 28, 1877 and the Black Hills were lost.[16]

The tribal nation continues its longstanding struggle to regain the Black Hills in the present, refusing to relinquish its moral and legal rights to this sacred area of their homelands. Rinaldi's words constitute serious errors, counteracting the effort to provide accurate information essential to the understanding of the historical, legal, and contemporary status of American Indian nations. As Debbie Reese comments, "Authors insist on creative license, but that license cannot be taken with known facts" (Reese, 2).

Rinaldi's errors are also evident in her depiction of a Hopi student, Belle Rain Water. K. Tsianina Lomawaima and her husband, who is Hopi and serves as Director of Arizona State Museum, find this character "highly improbable" in several important ways. One of them is the scenario of Belle drawing a "scalping party" to fulfill an art class assignment (MHIOTG, 61). Lomawaima comments: "No such thing in Hopi life; they are rather renowned pacifists. Why in heaven's name would she pick such a topic, and how would she know what it might look like? . . . the notion of a 'scalping party' is part of white America's fantasy about Indians" (Lomawaima, 1). In another part of the narrative, Belle declares of Nannie, "She is a witch! My people know there are witches" (MHIOTG, 87). Refuting the likelihood of such an exchange between these students, Lomawaima explains: "Witchcraft is a reality in Hopi life, but one that is extremely dangerous and destructive, and therefore a reality which is taken very seriously. Any Hopi with any sense would never discuss a thing so lightly, and would never accuse someone face-to-face like this. It would be the height of idiocy" (Lomawaima, 1). In another passage involving female students swimming in "bathe dresses," Rinaldi writes: "Belle Rain Water took off her dress and bathed with no clothes on" (MHIOTG, 114). Addressing the problems with this scenario, Lomawaima observes: "Hopi notions of maidenly modesty in the 19th century did not include girls swimming nude; the whole notion of swimming, in fact, is very problematic for girls for philosophical reasons. . . . Consider the practical problems: where would she have learned to swim? Not at Hopi—no suitable water courses or lakes or reservoirs or swimming pools" (Lomawaima, 1).

Perhaps reviewers who lauded *My Heart Is on the Ground* would fail to see the absurdity of a fictional scenario featuring a nineteenth-century female student from the desert Southwest swimming nude at Carlisle, but they should be able to recognize stereotypical language by now. Rinaldi's contrived compound words and convoluted phrases strung together with hyphens, "ed-u-cat-ed," "The-Time-That-Was-Before," and "A-Friend-To-Go-Between-Us" pervade the text. The language conveys to the reader the author's idea of Indian speech, rather than actual speaking patterns of Native Americans.[17] Flowery wording abounds, with phrasing such as "let fly at me words like poison arrows," "his face full of storm," and "the council fire burns bright between Maggie and Missus Mary now" (MHIOTG, 27, 21). As reading specialist Jan LaBonty notes, "To write a language that one has never spoken, very likely, never even heard, and furthermore is not written, may be impossible. Representing a language the way white people may think it sounds is not acceptable and using movies and television as linguistic models is a mistake."[18] Nonetheless, Rinaldi's text is permeated with such representations, reinforcing stereotypical perspectives of American Indians. In one of many examples, Belle says to Nannie, "We must light the council fire" (MHIOTG, 144).[19] As Lomawaima notes, "'Council fire' is another generic white stereotype about Indians; it has nothing to do with Hopi cultural or political life" (Lomawaima, 1–2). Other such phrases include: "This is my worth if our ways were not done," "But the old ways are done," "the Sioux people have been conquered," Carlisle was the students' "only chance for a future" (MHIOTG, 6, 24, 63, 177). Lomawaima concludes: "Carlisle was not their only chance for a future, as all the non-Carlisle students and their lives attest. The cumulative effect of these statements portrays Indians as backward, defeated victims. It is also clear that the author envisions all Indians as 'Plains Indians,' who all hunted buffalo" (Lomawaima, 2).

Besides Rinaldi's use of the names of Indian children from Carlisle gravestones, there are other issues of appropriation. Rinaldi takes the title of her book from a Cheyenne proverb, translated: "A nation is not conquered until the hearts of its women are on the ground. Then it is done, no matter how brave its warriors nor how strong their weapons" (Oyate, 7). The proverb speaks of an entire nation, not one individual. As the Oyate reviewers explain: "In its original form, this statement is about the strength and courage of Indian women. In its original form, the phrase suggests total defeat, the conquering of a nation, the death of a way of life. Throughout this book, the child protagonist, Nannie Little Rose, uses the phrase 'my heart is on the ground' whenever she happens to feel sad or upset" (Oyate, 7). Furthermore, Rinaldi appropriates textual material from a number of classic Indian boarding school

sources, including Pratt's memoir, *Battlefield and Classroom.*[20] Among
the examples are these:

> Pratt: "Spotted Tail, you are a remarkable man. Your name has gone all
> over the United States. It has even gone across the great water." (*Battle-
> field and Classroom,* 222)

> Rinaldi: "Then Mister Captain Pratt tell Spotted Tail he is re-mark-able
> man. His name has gone all over Unit-ed States and even across the great
> waters." (MHIOTG, 25)

> Pratt: "Captain, thee is undertaking a great work here. Thee will need
> many things. Thee must remember if thee would receive thee must ask.
> Will thee take thy pencil and put down some of the things thee needs very
> much just now and the cost?" (*Battlefield and Classroom,* 235)

> Rinaldi: "Thee is undertaking a great work here. Thee will need many
> things. If thee would receive, thee must ask. Will thee take thy pencil and
> put down some of the things thee needs very much and the cost?"
> (MHIOTG, 45)

These examples illustrate Rinaldi's use of source materials, which
she altered in many cases by turning them into stereotypical Indian-
speak. Although historical fiction by its very nature requires research
into primary and secondary sources, the sentence-by-sentence replica-
tion demonstrated above is at best questionable. Besides text appropriation, characters and scenarios that appear in Carlisle source materials
are flimsily fictionalized. Historical figures, among them students,
change identities or other characteristics in ways that distort reality and
deny history. Historic speeches, taken out of context, are improbably incorporated into the narrative. This pattern is intensified by the confus-
ing format of the Dear America series. It is difficult to tell whether these
books are fiction or nonfiction, as their appearance leads one to believe
they are diaries of actual historical figures. The format's incorporation
of epilogues and historic photographs at the end of each "diary" contributes to the puzzle, leaving viewers to ponder whose words appear on
the pages. As Lomawaima asserts, "It is depressing that this kind of
white fantasy can be passed off as 'impeccable and sensitive' native history, in a format that most people cannot distinguish as fiction, because

it is so carefully packaged and presented as autobiographical 'fact'" (Lomawaima, 3). In fact, Rinaldi's historical note section compounds the problems with the fictional diary. Incredibly, she claims "education could not be accomplished without taking away [Indian] identity" (MHIOTG, 175).

In response to some of the format problems with the "diaries," the publisher wrote: "A stumbling block for some people about Dear America has been the epilogues. Many have commented that the epilogues are too realistic-seeming, and therefore mislead readers into thinking the books are about a real, not fictional, person. In response to these comments, we have announced that in future books and in all reprints, we will strengthen the disclaimer stating that the entire book is a work of fiction, and specifically mention the epilogues in the disclaimer" (Feiwel, 2). While future books and reprints benefit from the criticisms voiced about this aspect of the publications, *My Heart Is on the Ground* and other early novels from this series are still on the market with these problems. Disturbingly, the harm associated with marketing a book full of racist stereotypes and historical inaccuracies to young readers has not been addressed by those responsible. Oyate reviewers commented: "Given the marketing and distribution forces behind *My Heart Is On the Ground*, we know that it will probably be more widely read than any other book about the boarding school experience. The book adds to the great body of misinformation about Native life and struggle in the United States and Canada" (Oyate, 17). In her *New Advocate* interview with Elizabeth Bush, Rinaldi inadvertently confirmed the predictions of these reviewers: "But I have to tell you, that book is selling like crazy, not because of the controversy." She reiterated: "That book was my biggest wage earner" (Bush, 319). Valid criticisms addressing serious matters of cultural authenticity, historical accuracy, and ethical principle have been marginalized, dismissed, or attacked by the parties who sanctioned the publication. The author deflected attention from these issues, in part by blaming others, while also maintaining that she "didn't intend to do anything" but enhance and honor Native Americans. As attorney Melissa Kay Thompson observes, however, "Good intentions, whether from Justice Marshall or Ann Rinaldi, and artistic license, whether from writers or their critics, will not suffice as excuses for abusive treatment of the young."[21]

NOTES

1. Ann Rinaldi, *My Heart Is on the Ground: The Diary of Nannie Little Rose, A Sioux Girl* (New York: Scholastic, 1999), 195; hereafter referred to in text as MHIOTG.

2. K. Tsianina Lomawaima to Tracy Mack, Editor, Scholastic, June 14, 1999, 2. Available online at http://home.epix.net/~landis/lomawaima.html (accessed August 7, 2004); hereafter referred to in text as Lomawaima. Professor Lomawaima is also the author of *They Called It Prairie Light: The Story of the Chilocco Indian School* (Lincoln: University of Nebraska Press, 1994).

3. See Richard Henry Pratt, *Battlefield and Classroom: Four Decades with the American Indian, 1867–1904*, ed. Robert M. Utley (Lincoln: University of Nebraska Press, 1964); hereafter referred to in text as *Battlefield and Classroom*.

4. See "'Kill the Indian, and Save the Man': Capt. Richard H. Pratt on the Education of Native Americans." Available online at http://historymatters.gmu.edu/d/4929 (accessed August 7, 2004).

5. There are numerous publications about the Carlisle Indian School. Besides Pratt's memoir, they include Luther Standing Bear's account of his student days at Carlisle in his book, *My People the Sioux* (Lincoln: University of Nebraska Press, 1975); Linda F. Witmer, *The Indian Industrial School, Carlisle, Pennsylvania, 1879–1918* (Carlisle, PA: Cumberland County Historical Society, 1993); and dissertations such as that of Genevieve Bell, "Telling Stories Out of School: Remembering the Carlisle Indian Industrial School, 1879–1918" (Ph.D. diss., Stanford University, 1998). See the Carlisle Indian Industrial School Research Pages, available online at http://home.epix.net/~landis/index.html for other sources (accessed August 7, 2004). Furthermore, there are an extensive number of works devoted to boarding schools besides Carlisle, among them Margaret L. Archuleta et al., eds., *Away from Home: American Indian Boarding School Experiences, 1879–2000* (Phoenix, AZ: The Heard Museum, 2000); Basil Johnston, *Indian School Days* (Norman: University of Oklahoma Press, 1989); and Francis La Flesche, *The Middle Five: Indian Schoolboys of the Omaha Tribe* (1900; Lincoln: University of Nebraska Press, 1963).

6. Marlene Atleo et al., "A Critical Review of Ann Rinaldi's *My Heart Is on the Ground: The Diary of Nannie Little Rose, A Sioux Girl.*" Available online at www.oyate.org/books-to-avoid/myHeart.html (accessed August 7, 2004); hereafter referred to in text as Oyate. See also the following articles by these authors: "*My Heart Is on the Ground* and the Boarding School Experience," *Multicultural Review* 8 (September 1999), 41–46; and "Fiction Posing as Truth: A Critical Review of Ann Rinaldi's *My Heart Is on the Ground: The Diary of*

Nannie Little Rose, A Sioux Girl" in *Rethinking Schools* (Summer 1999), 14–16.

7. MariJo Moore, "'Artistic License' Should Be Revoked If It Involves the Re-writing of History: *My Heart Is on the Ground: The Diary of Nannie Little Rose* by Ann Rinaldi," review of *My Heart Is on the Ground* by Ann Rinaldi, *Studies in American Indian Literature* 12, no. 1 (Spring 2000), 84. Also expressing opposition to the book, singer Arigon Starr has composed a song, "My Heart Is on the Ground," recorded on her audio CD, *Wind-Up*. See www.arigonstarr.com/lyrics_all/wind-up/myheart.html.

8. Genevieve Bell, "The Politics of Representation: A Response to the Publication of Ann Rinaldi's *My Heart Is on the Ground*" (May 1999), 5. Available online at http://home.epix.net/~landis/review.html (accessed August 7, 2004).

9. Jeanne M. McGlinn, *Ann Rinaldi: Historian & Storyteller* (Lanham, MD: Scarecrow Press, 2000).

10. Faith Brautigam, review of *My Heart Is on the Ground: The Diary of Nannie Little Rose, A Sioux Girl* by Ann Rinaldi, *School Library Journal* 45, no. 4 (April 1999), 141.

11. Stephanie Zvirin, review of *My Heart Is on the Ground: The Diary of Nannie Little Rose, A Sioux Girl* by Ann Rinaldi, *Booklist* 95, no. 15 (April 1, 1999), 1428.

12. Review of *My Heart Is on the Ground: The Diary of Nannie Little Rose, A Sioux Girl* by Ann Rinaldi, *Kirkus Review* 67 (February 1, 1999), 228.

13. Elizabeth Bush, "A Conversation with Ann Rinaldi, Author," *The New Advocate* 14, no. 4 (2001), 319; hereafter referred to in text as Bush. See also Elizabeth Bush, review of *My Heart Is on the Ground: The Diary of Nannie Little Rose, A Sioux Girl* by Ann Rinaldi, *Bulletin of the Center for Children's Books* 52, no. 6 (February 1999), 215.

14. Jean Feiwel, Publisher, Scholastic, letter to author, June 9, 1999, 2; hereafter referred to in text as Feiwel.

15. Debbie Reese, "Authenticity & Sensitivity: Goals for Writing and Reviewing Books with Native American Themes." *School Library Journal* (1 December 1999), 1. Available online at www.schoollibraryjournal.com/article/CA153126.html (accessed August 7, 2004); hereafter referred to in text as Reese.

16. Mario Gonzalez and Elizabeth Cook-Lynn, *The Politics of Hallowed Ground: Wounded Knee and the Struggle for Indian Sovereignty* (Urbana: University of Illinois Press, 1999), 260.

17. Examples of writings by boarding school students are included in publications such as Brenda Child's *Boarding School Seasons: American Indian Families, 1900–1940* (Lincoln: University of Nebraska Press, 1998).

18. Jan LaBonty, "A Demand for Excellence in Books for Children," *Journal of American Indian Education* (Winter 1995), 6.

19. This phrasing also appears in other books by Ann Rinaldi, including *The Quilt Trilogy*, where a "half-Shawnee" character comments, "But I couldn't put out the council fire between us, by talking out of turn" (*The Blue Door*, Scholastic Press, 1996, 225).

20. For other discussions of text appropriation, see Paulette F. Molin, "Dear Diary, Dear America: Commentary on Ann Rinaldi's *My Heart Is on the Ground*," *HONOR Digest* 10, no. 3 (May/June 1999), 4. A longer version of her commentary appears in *They Taught You Wrong: Raising Cultural Consciousness of Stereotypes and Misconceptions about American Indians* by Kathy Kerner (Lynchburg, VA: O. L. and Carole Durham Publishers, 2000 edition). In addition, Beverly Slapin's "'Literary License' or 'Mutated Plagiarism'? Additional Comments about Ann Rinaldi's *My Heart Is on the Ground*" examines this issue, Available online at http://oyate.org/books-to-avoid/myHeartMore .html (accessed 2004 August 7, 2004).

21. Melissa Kay Thompson, "A Sea of Good Intentions: Native Americans in Books for Children." *The Lion and the Unicorn* 25, no. 3 (September 2001), 371.

Chapter Six

"The Best Teller of Stories"

American Indian-Themed Historical Fiction for Young Adults

There was no denying Woyaka's gift as a storyteller and historian. How he became that, he told his youthful audiences. "Regard me, my grandchildren, and observe that I am very old. I have passed more than eighty winters. Many a man of lesser years finds his eyesight fading, his hearing gone, his memory faulty, while I retain all my powers and remember everything I hear. That is because my grandfather had a plan for me and he never rested in carrying it out. The day I was born he looked on me and vowed to make of me the best teller of stories that ever lived among the Tetons."[1]

In this passage from her historical novel *Waterlily*, author Ella Cara Deloria portrays one of many dimensions of Dakota life, the training of a historian and storyteller within her culture. Set in the 1800s, the book is "a unique portrayal of nineteenth-century Sioux Indian life, unequaled for its interpretation of Plains Indian culture from the perspectives of women."[2] Deloria, recognized "as the leading authority on the Sioux" by the 1940s, follows her protagonist Waterlily from birth to adulthood during the course of the narrative. Born into a prominent Dakota family in 1889, Deloria worked to counteract "the assumption that the Dakotas had *nothing*, no rules of life, no social organization, no ideals" (De-Mallie, 237–238). Deloria's extensive writings include *Dakota Texts*, *Dakota Grammar* (a collaboration with ethnologist Franz Boas), and *Speaking of Indians*. She wrote *Waterlily* in the 1940s, but it was not published until decades later, in 1988. The novel "represents a blurring of categories: in conception it is fundamentally a work of ethnographic description, but in its method it is narrative fiction, a plot invented to provide a plausible range of situations that reveal how cultural ideals shaped the behavior of individual Sioux people in social interactions" (DeMallie, 241). The book is excellent for a range of audiences, including young adults.

While depicting another tribal group, *Night Flying Woman: An Ojibway Narrative*, written by Anishinaabe (also Ojibwe and Chippewa) writer and community activist Ignatia Broker, shares a number of similarities with *Waterlily*.[3] Both Deloria and Broker wrote as insiders, knowledgeable of their respective cultures and languages. Their narratives center on female protagonists and provide perspectives largely absent in other accounts of tribal life. *Night Flying Woman*, set in the nineteenth century, is the story of a young girl, Ni-bo-wi-se-gwe (Night Flying Woman) or Oona, as she was called, and her journey from birth to death. The text encompasses changes wrought by "a strange people whose skins were as pale as the winter white and whose eyes were blue or green or gray" (Broker, 18). Like Deloria, Broker blurs categories, incorporating both fiction and nonfiction in her book. These authors struggled to get their manuscripts published, eventually achieving publication via regional presses. Deloria, with the longer wait, did not live to see her book in print. *Night Flying Woman*, published by the Minnesota Historical Society Press, made its way into publication a few years before Broker's death in 1987. In their novels, Deloria and Broker both emphasize the importance of history. In *Waterlily*, Woyaka's grandfather tells him, "'Grandson, speech is holy; it was not intended to be set free only to be wasted. It is for hearing and remembering'" (Deloria, 50). "'You owe it to our people,'" he teaches Woyaka, "'If you fail them, there might be nobody else to remind them of their tribal history'" (Deloria, 50–51). In *Night Flying Woman*, too, the narrator informs the young, "it has always been the custom for us to tell what must be passed on so that our ways will be known to the Ojibway children of the future" (Broker, 8).

In a 2001 article, author Nora Murphy analyzed the treatment of American Indians in historical fiction for young people, looking at the availability of books such as *Waterlily* and *Night Flying Woman* in collections in the Twin Cities.[4] She writes that *Waterlily* "remains in print but is mostly available through academic and research libraries" (Murphy, 292). Murphy found that the St. Paul Public Library held one copy and Minneapolis four copies of the novel. Although Broker's book was more readily available, by Murphy's count "there are still four times as many copies of [Laura Ingalls Wilder's] *Little House in the Big Woods* as of *Night Flying Woman* in the St. Paul library system" (Murphy, 292). While she does not attempt to separate out Native American audiences or libraries in the region, it is likely they constitute a significant segment of the books' readers. Such individuals and groups, largely overlooked by mainstream publishers, accord these works the status they deserve, as must-read classics. Oyate, an organization that endeavors to see that Native lives and histories are portrayed honestly, comments on *Waterlily*: "Told from a woman's viewpoint, it emphasizes the traditional network of obligations and relationships that formed cultural unity. Woven into it are the solidly-based facts of actual plains life."[5] Oyate's review of *Night Flying Woman* reads in part: "This beautiful book is a blessing, a gift, an antidote for all the poisonous lies about our past that we have had to endure. It is full of courage, and love. This is how it *really* was."[6] In 2004, *Night Flying Woman* was honored by the St. Paul Reads One Book program, a partnership between St. Paul's city and school system, as its reading selection for the year. The three-year-old program's goal is to encourage high school students and adults to read a book in common and discuss it together. For the program, *Night Flying Woman* was the first selection written by a Minnesotan, the first by a woman, and the first published by a local press. "Thanks to St. Paul Reads One Book," writer Mary Ann Grossman notes, "a new generation is going to read [Broker's] great-great-grandmother's story."[7]

Nonetheless, as Murphy points out, "publishers and educators have preferred Wilder's version of our past" (Murphy, 286). Her books "have been staples of American literature since the 1930s," even with passages that deny the presence of entire groups of people (Murphy, 284). Wilder, in fact, writes in *Little House in the Big Woods*:

Once upon a time, sixty years ago, a little girl lived in the Big Woods of Wisconsin, in a little gray house made of logs. The great, dark trees of the Big Woods stood all around the house, and beyond them were other trees and beyond them were more trees. As far as a man could go to the north in a day, or a week, or a whole month, there was nothing but woods. There were no houses. There were no roads. There were no people. There were only trees and the wild animals who had their homes among them.[8]

"Today I cringe," Murphy writes, "because I know that there *were* people who lived in and near Wilder's woods 100 miles south of St. Paul" (Murphy, 287). Besides Dakota and Ojibwe, other tribal groups such as Menominee, Ho-Chunk, Potawatomi, and Odawa call the region home. Both Deloria and Broker hailed from tribal groups erased, or disparaged, in Wilder's books.

Louise Erdrich, a member of the Turtle Mountain Chippewa Tribe in North Dakota, writes of the same region as these authors. She is best known for her adult fiction, but is also the author of *The Birchbark House*, a National Book Award finalist in 1999 and her first novel for young readers.[9] Erdrich wrote the book to chronicle the history of her Anishinaabe ancestors, creating a young female protagonist, Omakayas, to tell the story. Omakayas, translated Little Frog, lives with her family on their people's sacred Moningwanaykaning, the Island of the Golden-Breasted Woodpecker (Madeline Island) on Lake Superior in the 1840s. Reviewers have compared *The Birchbark House*, the first of a planned series of historical novels, to Wilder's books. "Why has no one written this story before?" Hazel Rochman asks. "Why are there so few good children's books about the people displaced by the little house in the big woods?"[10] Erdrich herself has said: "I loved the 'Little House' books and the specificity of daily detail, the earthy substance of the food, work, the repetitions, and growth that make family . . . [but] I get crazy when I read about pioneers moving into 'empty' territory. They were moving into somebody else's house, home, hearth, and beloved yard" (Murphy, 287). Erdrich incorporates Anishinaabe words, including place names that were obliterated through European colonization. Commenting on this aspect of *The Birchbark House*, she noted: "The characters . . . did not speak English and I really wanted the reader to know something about the way they sounded" (Murphy, 288). Erdrich also illustrated the book herself, to "convey the humor of Ojibwe life and draw the very things in my house that are authentic to Ojibwe life, like makakoon and makazinan" (Murphy, 288). In this novel, as in *Waterlily* and *Night Flying Woman*, the protagonist is center stage, a refreshing change from books that relegate Native American characters to the margins or as sidekicks to Euro-American heroes or heroines. "The combined collections of the Minneapolis and St. Paul public libraries," Murphy writes, "house more than 70 copies of *Little House in the Big Woods* but only 11 copies of [Charles Alexander Eastman's] *Indian Boyhood*.

The prognosis for *The Birchbark House*, with about 35 copies in the combined collections, and its series successors is a little better, especially since it was nominated for a National Book Award in 1999" (Murphy, 288–289).[11] As Rochman commented on this book, "Little House readers will discover a new world, a different version of a story they thought they knew" (Rochman, 1427).

While these books address nineteenth-century tribal life through the perspectives of female protagonists from Dakota and Ojibwe tribal cultures, historical novels for young adults also center on a wide range of other American Indian-themed subjects and settings. One of the most popular topics is the colonial encounter, often starting with accounts of Columbus and his journey to the "New World." The annual holidays of Columbus Day and Thanksgiving Day generally prompt cycles of new or revised publications each year, too often reinforcing deeply engrained national myths. In Joel Taxel's words, many of the Columbus books "suffer from . . . [historical] amnesia, more precisely, a troubling inability to deal forthrightly with the catastrophic impact Columbus's arrival in the western hemisphere had on native cultures."[12] A notable exception is the publication *Rethinking Columbus: The Next 500 years*, which was first published in 1991, a year before the Columbus Quincentenary.[13] This publication, which was revised and expanded in 1998, provides resources for teaching about the impact of the arrival of Columbus in the Americas, incorporating essays, poems, short stories, interviews, and historical vignettes by a host of contributors. One of them, Bill Bigelow, examines books devoted to the Columbus-Taíno encounter, including works authored by Michael Dorris, Jean Fritz, and Jane Yolen. Bigelow writes that Dorris, in his young adult novella *Morning Girl*, "effectively re-centered attention on the people who were here first, those so thoroughly neglected in the traditional Columbus canon."[14]

Published in 1992, *Morning Girl* is the story of Taíno siblings and their lives on their Bahamian island homeland shortly before the Spanish arrived in 1492.[15] Twelve-year-old protagonist Morning Girl and her younger brother, Star Boy, narrate alternating chapters of the book. Their names and characterization, as well as the novella's narrative structure, have multifaceted associations with daytime and nighttime. Reflecting this theme, Morning Girl comments: "I don't know how my brother came to see everything so upside down from me. For him, night

is day, sleep is awake. It's as though time is split between us, and we only
pass by each other as the sun rises or sets. Usually, for me, that's enough"
(*Morning Girl*, 3). This metaphor is at play throughout the book, form-
ing alternating patterns of daytime-nighttime, female-male, and sister-
brother dualities. The book focuses on the inner lives of Morning Girl
and Star Boy, their interactions with each other as well as other family
members. Dorris situates the story before the Spanish invasion, subtly
foreshadowing the events to come. While pointing out "it's worth remembering that to capture the experiences and worldview of the Taínos
500 years past is almost purely speculative, as they left no written
records," author Bill Bigelow criticizes *Morning Girl* for its "checkered
success in abandoning the assumptions absorbed from life in contemporary U.S. society" (Bigelow, 66). One of Bigelow's criticisms is that the
book focuses on a nuclear-family structure, with little or no attention
given to the Taíno organization of family and community. Another is that
Dorris "leaves readers ill-equipped to reflect on the full range of social
consequences initiated by Columbus's arrival" on the island, among
them a legacy of resistance (Bigelow, 66). For some readers, though, the
invasion may be perceived as even more horrific and brutal, especially
in contrast to the everyday normalcy depicted in the novella. Dorris ends
Morning Girl with an epilogue, incorporating words directly from
Christopher Columbus: "They should be good and intelligent servants,
for I see that they say very quickly everything that is said to them. . . .
Our Lord pleasing, at the time of my departure I will take six of them
from here to Your Highnesses in order that they may learn to speak"
(*Morning Girl*, 74). This concluding passage, using Columbus's own
statements, sets the stage for what is to follow.

Another book, Joyce Rockwood's young adult fiction, *To Spoil the
Sun*, is "a story of invasion, of Spanish ships, of smallpox" and the ensuing devastation on Cherokee life.[16] Joel Taxel describes the book,
which was originally published in 1976 and reissued in 2003, as a "mas-
terful and strangely neglected account of the catastrophic effects the arrival of the Spanish had on a vibrant Cherokee culture" (Taxel, 6). Set
in the sixteenth century, the novel follows protagonist Rain Dove from
her girlhood among family and clan relatives into adulthood as a wife
and mother. Forewarned by omens that presage devastation, her Cherokee village in the southern Appalachians is struck by an epidemic disease of cataclysmic proportions. "You cannot imagine what it [small-

pox] is like," a hunter observes in the book. "It falls on everyone and soon there is no one who can stand, no one who can give water to the dying. It is like a fire that sweeps through the town, an invisible fire. People begin to fall with fever, and blisters rise on their skin and turn to running sores, and there is no way to give them comfort" (Rockwood, 129–130). Rockwood, who studied anthropology at the University of Georgia, is also the author of *Long Man's Song* and *Groundhog's Horse* for young readers and *Apalachee*, an adult novel.[17] She has said of her work: "I write primarily about the American Indians, setting my stories in the cultures of the past, relying heavily on anthropological and historical research in order to recreate the reality that has since been shattered by the European invasion. . . . My purpose is not to teach, but to offer a powerful human experience."[18] In Rockwood's words, *To Spoil the Sun* is a book "about a people who lived and died on the other side of history, just beyond our view" (Rockwood, 180).

First published in 1966, Canadian author Christie Harris's young adult novel, *Raven's Cry*, also concerns itself with "the other side of history."[19] The book focuses on the near annihilation of the Haida Nation of Haida Gwaii (the Queen Charlotte Islands), located off the coast of Northern British Columbia, following the arrival of Europeans to their homelands in 1775. Artist Bill Reid, a descendant of the family depicted by Harris, illustrated the novel. A 1992 reprint edition of the novel features a discussion between artist Robert Davidson and anthropologist Margaret Blackman in the book's foreword. Their comments address a number of issues concerning publications centered on American Indians. "In school," Davidson remembered, "we talked about Hannibal, we talked about Cleopatra, Alexander the Great, and all the romanticism that went with those people" (Harris, ix). In contrast, he was unable to find his own people, the Haida, represented in texts, realizing only later that "we had our own culture and our own heroes such as Albert Edward Edenshaw, Charles Edenshaw—but there was no information anywhere so that I could relate to them" (Harris, ix). In Davidson's estimation, *Raven's Cry* had a significant impact on his search for information about the Haida, helping to fill the gap that existed for him. Deeming the illustrations in this novel "ahead of their time," he emphasized the importance of getting them right. Davidson observed: "When I first saw the illustrations, I was impressed by the emotions that Bill Reid put into them. You could feel the smallpox epidemic. You could feel the storm"

(Harris, x). Author Alexandra West agrees: "That Reid agreed to be the illustrator for the white author's *Raven's Cry* speaks to the high regard in which Harris was held by her Haida friends."[20] Davidson, echoing comments by Deloria and Broker, emphasized: "We have to know our history before we can move on" (Harris, xi).

Blackman attributes *Raven's Cry* with launching her career as a student of Haida history, commenting that the book "can also be read as a children's story. I've read it to my daughter" (Harris, ix). Like Davidson, she considered the publication ahead of its time, particularly "because the Haida people . . . are not the 'Other' encountered by the maritime traders and explorers. Rather, the Haida people are the central actors in this book; the story revolves around them. And that makes a real difference" (Harris, x). Her cautionary note to readers is also telling, an important consideration:

> I do think the book has to be read as one *family's* perspective on Haida history, because it's very much the story of the Edenshaw lineage. Chief 7idansuu's [sic] rivals . . . are not portrayed particularly favorably in this book because events are seen through the eyes of the Edenshaw family. Probably Haida history was always viewed through the eyes of particular actors and their respective lineages." (Harris, xi)

Both Davidson and Blackman address the importance of quality research to books such as *Raven's Cry*. Besides studying in archives, Harris had the opportunity "to achieve a level of authentic knowledge not generally accorded . . . to non-natives" (West, 16). She "learned from descendants of Charles Edenshaw, the Eagle Chief Edinsa, who had become a great artist in order to preserve" disappearing tribal history (West, 16). By the time she wrote *Raven's Cry*, Harris was "very much aware both of the responsibilities that went with her task and of the need to educate herself as best she could about native culture before she ever wrote a word of the retellings. She knew that the great tales, the histories, of those called by her the Lords of the Coast were the possessions of individual families and thus needed to be treated with respect. She knew, too, that her versions of these tales should be regarded as no more than mediations between their native origins and a white audience and never as replacements" (West, 1). *Raven's Cry* needs to be examined in the context within which it was created, a period when the Native presence was mostly excluded from classroom instruction and book publishing. Of Irish heritage, Harris, who was born in New Jersey and grew up in British Columbia, also possessed a unique set of personal circumstances. She wrote for over seventy years, learning during that time to overcome the erroneous information and negative viewpoints she had been taught about Native people in society. *Raven's Cry* "is permeated with admiration for the old Haida society, for its art . . . and way of life, and Harris makes short work of most of the white characters who are seen as grasping and ignorant villains for the most part" (West, 18). As West points out, "the moral outrage that drove it in 1966 has come to be the common public response" (West, 18). Harris, who died in 2002 at the age of 94, is the recipient of numerous awards, including the Canadian Library Association Book of the Year for Children Award. "Storytellers," she has said, "have always been my kind of people" (West, 2).

Another topic of American Indian-themed fiction is the Trail of Tears, the removal of Southeastern tribal peoples to Indian Territory, or present-day Oklahoma, in the nineteenth century. The Cherokee Nation has received the most attention on this event, including an entry in Scholastic's Dear America series, Joseph Bruchac's *The Journal of Jesse Smoke, A Cherokee Boy, Trail of Tears, 1838*.[21] The fictional diary, dating from 1837 to 1838, is told from the perspective of sixteen-year-old Jesse Smoke (Gogisgi). Introducing himself first by clan and family, he continues: "My Cherokee name is Gogisgi, which means 'Smoke.' At the Mission School they gave me the name of Jesse. Jesse Smoke, I became, and was so recorded in the Mission records" (*Jesse Smoke*, 8–9). Jesse and his two sisters initially lived with their parents on "a modest plantation" in Georgia near New Echota, the Cherokee capitol, but were forced to relocate to a small farm in Tennessee after being threatened by white intruders intent on seizing tribal property. While returning to Georgia to attend to family belongings still on the original site, Jesse's father was murdered by a gang of white men. Jesse, then thirteen, took over his father's duties on the family's farm until capitulating to his mother's insistence that he return to his studies. When the school closed in order to be converted into a fort, he made his way back home to help out. By 1838, Jesse's family was forced to relocate yet again, this time all the way to Indian Territory. Jesse then tells of his experiences and observations "on the bitter road the Cherokees call Nunda'utsun'yi, 'the Place Where the People Cried,' or 'the Trail of Tears'" (*Jesse Smoke*, 178).

Bruchac weaves historical information into the fictional diary, incorporating facts about the Cherokee Nation and the events that propelled federal and state forces to drive the tribal group out of their southern Appalachian homeland. Unlike Dear America books published earlier, this novel includes an introductory page clearly identifying the author and citing the text as a work of fiction. Bruchac's preparation for writing about the Cherokee and this pivotal period of their history included extensive study. He writes: "to do justice to this story I had to spend years in the process of learning with the help of many Cherokee people. That kind of learning teaches you patience. I would not have been able to write this story twenty years ago, even though I thought of doing such a novel more than once. I am glad that I waited" (*Jesse Smoke*, 201). Readers reap benefits from these preparations, which included consultations with contemporary Cherokee, such as author Robert Conley, artist Murv Jacob, and storyteller-author Gayle Ross, and Bruchac's work on related books, among them his nonfiction *Trail of Tears, Paths of Beauty: The Story of the Navajos and the Cherokees*.[22] This book, with illustrations by Murv Jacob, would serve as an excellent companion work to *The Journal of Jesse Smoke*. Robert Conley's writings on Cherokee life, including his novel on the Trail of Tears, *Mountain Windsong*, would also serve this purpose.[23] A related publication, Beatrice Orcutt Harrell's young adult novel, *Longwalker's Journey*, centers on the Choctaw Trail of Tears.[24]

Besides imagined American Indian protagonists such as Jesse Smoke, young adult fiction centers on actual historical figures. The majority of these include treatments of the famous, especially those known for providing assistance to Europeans or Euro-Americans. Sacajawea and Pocahontas, the focus of nationwide attention, are among the many examples. Renewed interest in such figures tends to intensify during commemorative periods, generating an even greater flurry of programs and publications. A case in point is the bicentennial of the Lewis and Clark Expedition, which refocuses attention on Sacajawea, the famed Shoshone guide of the 1804–1806 "Corps of Discovery." Besides gracing a recent United States coin, she is immortalized in a bronze statue installed in the U.S. Statuary Hall in the Capitol in Washington, DC, in 2003. New publications depicting her life have also emerged. One of them is Joseph Bruchac's young adult novel, *Sacajawea: The Story of Bird Woman and the Lewis and Clark Expedition*.[25] Bruchac begins his account with a prologue dated 1833 in the voice of Sacajawea's by then grown son, Jean Baptiste Charbonneau, who sets the stage for the story:

"Those two voices who told that tale to me, my mother's and my uncle's, will now tell it to you. It is the shared telling of this story that is the beginning of my life. Now, brought back to life and breath are those voices, as I remember them in my heart. Here is my mother, Sacajawea. Here is my adopted uncle, Captain William Clark. Listen. Here is our story" (*Sacajawea*, 2). Bruchac then tells of the historic journey, alternating the voices and viewpoints of Sacajawea and Clark.

As in *The Journal of Jesse Smoke*, Bruchac provides information about his methods and sources. He writes: "One of the questions asked of writers of historical novels is this: How much of your story is history and how much is fiction? The answer depends not only on the research done (or not done) by the writer, but also on what sources are available" (*Sacajawea*, 195). Bruchac then provides an overview of the sources he consulted, indicating that there was "no shortage of firsthand testimony about the Lewis and Clark expedition" (*Sacajawea*, 195). Besides attempting "to be absolutely true" to the explorers' journals, he also "turned to the history, stories, and traditions of the Shoshone for more information about the character of Sacajawea, to gain insight into what she might have thought or said about her experience" (*Sacajawea*, 198). Furthermore, Bruchac consulted Wayland Large, the Tribal Historian of the Wind River Shoshones, acknowledging "his helpful comments on [Sacajawea's] story, her 'Hidatsa' name, and the Shoshone language" (*Sacajawea*, 198). In addition, Eileen Charbonneau, a contemporary descendant of Sacajawea and author of young adult fiction in her own right, read and commented on the manuscript.[26] Bruchac does what he implores readers to do: "Imagine yourself to be Sacajawea, a teenage mother in the company of men traveling rivers and mountains without end, enduring hunger and pain and danger, and not only doing it without complaint but contributing on numerous occasions to the success and well-being of the company" (*Sacajawea*, 199). He imagines the life of the unique young guide in her multiple roles serving as an invaluable member of the Corps of Discovery.

Patricia Clark Smith's *Weetamoo, Heart of the Pocassets*, is another work of fiction based on an actual historical figure.[27] Weetamoo, translated Sweet Heart, flourished in New England during the seventeenth century. Born in about 1640, she was the daughter of Corbitant, sachem, or leader, of the Pocasset band of Wampanoag in New England. As Smith acknowledges, Weetamoo entered history in adulthood, primarily in connection with the events of King Philip's War between 1675 and 1676. Hence, she writes, "this story is almost entirely fictional, though grounded as solidly as possible in what we do know: the places where her father's Pocassets tended to make their homes; what daily life among the Wampanoag people entailed; and the strains between the Wampanoags and Plimoth Colony" (Smith, 193). Published as part of Scholastic's Royal Diaries series, the book opens in the fall of 1653, when Weetamoo was about fourteen years old. She later succeeded her father as sachem of the Pocassets, providing leadership during a pivotal period of history. In writing her fictional account, Smith had to try to overcome significant drawbacks, including the lack of information about Weetamoo's early life and the fact that she "did not read or write, and would not have kept a diary in the traditional sense of written accounts of her daily life" (Smith, iii). Known biographical details appear in the book's epilogue, among them firsthand observations gleaned from the captivity narrative of Mary Rowlandson, who was held hostage by Weetamoo and her family in 1676. "A severe and proud dame was she," Rowlandson wrote, "bestowing every day in dressing herself neat as much time as any gentry of the land. . . . When she had dressed herself, her work was to make wampum and beads" (Smith, 154–155). During her lifetime, Weetamoo was married to Wamsutta, one of the sons of the prominent leader Massasoit. This marriage, as well as that of her sister Wootonekanuske into the same family, "strengthened the ties between their two bands of Wampanoag people, the Pocasset and the Pokanoket" (Smith, 148).

Colonial military leader Benjamin Church deemed Weetamoo "next after Philip in the making of [King Philip's] war" against the English (Smith, 154). She drowned on August 6, 1676, while attempting to cross a river on a raft. "The colonists cut off her head," Smith writes, "as was the European custom when dealing with dead enemies, and displayed it on a pole in Taunton, Massachusetts" (Smith, 156–157). The fictional diary includes information on Weetamoo's family tree, illustrations, a map of southern New England, a glossary, and historical notes. In a note about the author, Smith writes: "The Native women whom most people in the United States tend to honor are those such as Pocahontas and Sacajawea, who were helpful to the European newcomers. But there were many other brave women like Weetamoo who fought to preserve their own land and culture and gave their lives to that cause" (Smith, 196). Smith covers much of the same ground about Weetamoo in a nonfiction book, *As Long as the River Flows: The Stories of Nine Native Americans*, she coauthored with Paula Gunn Allen.[28] The novel, less successful, is strongest when it sticks to the facts of Weetamoo's life. The section on the leader's childhood is especially problematic, with implausible language, scenarios, and interpretations.

Shirley Sterling, a member of the interior Salish Nation of British Columbia, is the author of *My Name Is Seepeetza*, a book that portrays the experiences of twelve-year-old Seepeetza at a residential school.[29] The novel, which author Melissa Kay Thompson refers to as "a quantum leap beyond *My Heart Is on the Ground*" in terms of boarding school stories, is set at the Kalamak Indian Residential School (K.I.R.S. or "curse" to students) in British Columbia in the late 1950s.[30] Called Seepeetza, Tootie, or McSpoot at home, the protagonist is known as Martha Stone at school. Basing the novel, her first, on her own experiences, the author tells the story through a secret journal kept by Seepeetza between September 1958 and August 1959. Sterling captures experiences, familiar to American Indians caught up in the network of mission and boarding schools, in deceptively simple, disarming prose. She reveals the myriad emotions of a student, an insider who details aspects of everyday life in the residential school, including loneliness and terror. Seepeetza writes: "That night, just before she turned the lights off, Sister Maura taught us how to pray on our knees with our hands folded. Then she told us about devils. She said they were waiting with chains under our beds to drag us into the fires of hell if we got up and left our beds during the night. When she turned the lights off I was scared to move, even to breathe" (Sterling, 19). Seepeetza was so frightened that she did not leave her bed, even to use the bathroom, suffering the following consequences: "In the morning my bed was wet and Sister Superior strapped me. I had to wear a sign to the dining room saying, I am a dirty wetbed" (Sterling, 19). Residential school experiences are juxtaposed with Seepeetza's memories and experiences at home on a ranch with her parents and siblings. "When we're at home," she notes in her journal, "we can ride horses, go swimming at the river, run in the hills, climb trees and laugh out loud and holler yahoo anytime we like and we won't get in trouble. At school we get punished for talking, looking at boys in church, even stepping out of line" (Sterling, 13–14).

While "stepping out of line" and punishments pervade daily life at K.I.R.S., Sterling provides a balanced account of the book's characters and their experiences. The individuals depicted are complex, manifesting a range of human traits and behaviors recognizable to readers. Both Indians and non-Indians possess good qualities as well as bad and are shown in diverse activities and situations. Seepeetza's father, for instance, is portrayed as a man who serves as a court interpreter because of his knowledge of "lots of Indian languages," but is also shown as a family man who bestows the playful nickname "McSpoot" on Seepeetza, works to support the household, goes deer hunting, and does ranch chores. He also drinks on occasion, his behavior literally driving other family members out of the house to sojourn with relatives. The K.I.R.S. students, too, behave in various ways. Some of them become members of gangs, fighting with rival groups. "The girls in a gang stuck up for each other," Seepeetza writes.

> They got mad at girls from other towns. They said, what are you staring at, or liar liar pants on fire. . . . Sometimes when Sister was out of the rec they used to fight with other gangs. They used to roll on the floor with everybody cheering. When the lookout girl said, "Sister's coming," everybody would jump up and pretend nothing happened, because the worst thing you can be in this school is a snitch. You don't ever tell on anyone here. (Sterling, 21)

An older student physically threatens Seepeetza and ridicules her: "You dirty shamah. How does it feel to look like a white?" (Sterling, 20). She learns to defend herself, fighting back in a number of ways to stay safe.

Seepeetza detests K.I.R.S., but writes of her older sister, "Dorothy doesn't mind Kalamak School but the rest of us hate it. She likes classes. Her marks are in the nineties. I think she got tired of babysitting Benny and Missy and me when we were little. Maybe that's why she likes school" (Sterling, 30). Seepeetza also observes dimensions of the school's personnel, nuns and priests, in ways that extend beyond their harsh treatment of the students. She recounts kindnesses, as when a nun helped make it possible for her sister Dorothy to study at night. In another journal entry, Seepeetza notices a nun's hurt feelings at being mistaken for a witch by a young child. Sterling's words, sometimes too adult for a twelve-year-old, nonetheless ring true. They authentically portray an insider's view of a system of schooling with a profound, ongoing impact on the lives of the students and their families. Readers will feel the hardships of a young girl forced to live away from her family, caught up in powerful forces difficult for her to understand.

They will experience Seepeetza's loneliness, sadness, hunger, and loss at the school, but also her fortitude and moments of joy.

NOTES

1. Ella Cara Deloria, *Waterlily* (Lincoln: University of Nebraska, 1988), 50; hereafter referred to in text as Deloria.
2. Raymond J. DeMallie, "Afterword," *Waterlily* (Lincoln: University of Nebraska Press, 1988), 233; hereafter referred to in text as DeMallie.
3. Ignatia Broker, *Night Flying Woman: An Ojibway Narrative* (St. Paul: Minnesota Historical Society Press, 1983); hereafter referred to in text as Broker.
4. Nora Murphy, "Starting Children on the Path to the Past: American Indians in Children's Historical Fiction," *Minnesota History* 57, no. 6 (Summer 2001), 284–95; hereafter referred to in text as Murphy.
5. Oyate Catalog 2003/04 (Berkeley, Ca.: Oyate, 2003), 25.
6. Beverly Slapin and Doris Seale, eds., *Through Indian Eyes: The Native Experience in Books for Children* (1987; Philadelphia: New Society Publishers, 1992), 133.
7. Mary Ann Grossman, "Ojibwe Tale Is 2004 Book Selection," *Twin Cities.com*, Pioneer Press (February, 10 2004). Available online at www.twincities.com/mld/twincities/news/local/7915097.htm (August 7, 2004).
8. Laura Ingalls Wilder, *Little House in the Big Woods* (1932; reprint, New York: Harper Trophy Edition, 1971), 1–2. See Michael Dorris's discussion of the Little House novels in his article "Trusting the Words," *Booklist* 89, no. 19–20 (1 June 1993), 1820–22.
9. Louise Erdrich, *The Birchbark House* (New York: Hyperion Books for Children, 1999).
10. Hazel Rochman, review of *The Birchbark House* by Louise Erdrich, *Booklist* 95, no. 15 (April 1, 1999), 1427; hereafter referred to in text as Rochman.
11. Charles Alexander Eastman, *Indian Boyhood* (1902; reprint, New York: Dover Publications, 1971).
12. Joel Taxel, "The Politics of Children's Literature: Reflections on Multiculturalism and Christopher Columbus" in *Teaching Multicultural Literature in Grades K–8*, ed. Violet J. Harris (Norwood, MA: Christopher-Gordon Publishers, 1993), 8; hereafter referred to in text as Taxel.
13. Bill Bigelow and Bob Peterson, eds. *Rethinking Columbus: The Next 500 Years*, 2nd edition (Milwaukee: Rethinking Schools, 1998).
14. Bill Bigelow, "Good Intentions Are Not Enough: Recent Children's Books on the Columbus-Taino Encounter," in *Rethinking Columbus: The Next*

500 Years, 2nd edition, eds. Bill Bigelow and Bob Peterson (Milwaukee: Rethinking Schools, 1998), 65; hereafter referred to in text as Bigelow.

15. Michael Dorris, *Morning Girl* (New York: Hyperion Books for Children, 1992); hereafter referred to in text as *Morning Girl*.

16. Joyce Rockwood, *To Spoil the Sun* (New York: Holt, Rinehart and Winston, 1976), book jacket; hereafter referred to in text as Rockwood.

17. Joyce Rockwood, *Long Man's Song* (New York: Henry Holt and Company, 1975), *Groundhog's Horse* (New York: Holt, Rinehart and Winston, 1978), and *Apalachee* (Athens: University of Georgia Press, 2000).

18. Anne Commire, ed., *Something about the Author: Facts and Pictures about Authors and Illustrators of Books for Young People*, Vol. 39 (Detroit: Gale Research Company, 1985), 185.

19. Christie Harris, *Raven's Cry* (New York: Atheneum, 1966; Seattle: University of Washington, reprint, 1992); hereafter referred to in text as Harris (page citations are to the reprint edition).

20. Alexandra West, "Christie Harris: Biocritical Essay," University of Calgary Library, 2000, revised 2002, 17. Available online at www.ucalgary.ca/library/SpecColl/harrisbio.htm (accessed August 7, 2004); hereafter referred to in text as West.

21. Joseph Bruchac, *The Journal of Jesse Smoke: A Cherokee Boy, Trail of Tears, 1838* (New York: Scholastic Press, 2001); hereafter referred to in text as *Jesse Smoke*.

22. Joseph Bruchac, *Trails of Tears, Paths of Beauty: The Story of the Navajos and the Cherokees* (Washington, DC: National Geographic Society, 2000).

23. Robert Conley, *Mountain Windsong: A Novel of the Trail of Tears* (Norman: University of Oklahoma Press, 1992).

24. Beatrice Orcutt Harrell, *Longwalker's Journey: A Novel of the Choctaw Trail of Tears* (New York: Dial Books for Young Readers, 1999).

25. Joseph Bruchac, *Sacajawea* (New York: Silver Whistle, Harcourt, 2000); hereafter referred to in text as *Sacajawea*.

26. Titles by Eileen Charbonneau include *The Ghosts of Stony Clove* (New York: Scholastic, 1988), *In the Time of the Wolves* (New York: Tor, 1994), *Honor to the Hills* (New York: Tor, 1996), and *Rachel LeMoyne* (New York: Forge, 1998).

27. Patricia Clark Smith, *Weetamoo: Heart of the Pocassets* (New York: Scholastic, 2003); hereafter referred to in text as Smith.

28. Paula Gunn Allen and Patricia Clark Smith, *As Long as the Rivers Flow: The Stories of Nine Native Americans* (New York: Scholastic, 1996).

29. Shirley Sterling, *My Name Is Seepeetza* (Toronto: Douglas & McIntyre, 1992); hereafter referred to in text as Sterling.

30. Melissa Kay Thompson, "A Sea of Good Intentions: Native Americans in Books for Children," *The Lion and the Unicorn* 25, no. 3 (September 2001), 370.

Part Three

Nonfiction

Chapter Seven

American Indian Topics in Young Adult Nonfiction

> We live with contradictions, which make up the gulf between the
> ideal world we are led to believe in and the real world we live in.
> This gulf has prevented us from breaking the great cycle of pain—
> the generations of poverty, alcoholism, drug use, violence, and var-
> ious forms of physical, emotional, and sexual abuse.[1]

These words by educator Thomas D. Peacock appear in *The Seventh Generation: Native Students Speak about Finding the Good Path*, a book he coauthored with Amy Bergstrom and Linda Miller Cleary. This publication, based on interviews with 120 Native youth from a range of tribal groups across North America, is one of a number of recent nonfiction books devoted to Native Americans. Among them are titles by Tricia Brown, Roger and Walter Echo-Hawk, Jim Hubbard, Bruce Hucko, Kenji Kawano, and Herman Viola as well as poetry anthologies. Many of these works incorporate the voices of Native people themselves through interview material, artwork, photography, and creative writing on a variety of topics in a range of settings. The majority of the publications selected here are devoted to contemporary Native Americans, an area that tends to be underrepresented or problematic in young adult fiction. Other nonfiction includes autobiography and biography, books that are addressed in a separate chapter.

Amy Bergstrom, Linda Miller Cleary, and Thomas D. Peacock collected stories from Ojibwe youth in the Midwest for *The Seventh Generation*, but also traveled to other communities to interview Abenaki,

Aleut, Choctaw, Cree, Dakota, Hoopa, Inuit, Karuk, Lakota, Mohawk, Navajo, Oneida, Penobscot, Seneca, Ute, Wampanoag, and Yurok students in a variety of school settings. The authors requested that administrators or guidance counselors "select students who were doing well, doing average work, and struggling in equal numbers" (Bergstrom, 178). The authors then placed the students' accounts in the context of the very real challenges they face, including overt racism and internalized racism as well as collective trauma stemming from colonization. The school experiences of students are often part of the "great cycle of pain" referred to by Peacock. "What's a typical day like?" one student asks. "We all have to walk to the end of our road and stand there early, by the highway, until the bus picks us up. It's almost an hour bus ride. I don't like high school that much. When the kids from the reservation get off, the teachers watch us when we walk in. It's like, 'What are you watching us for?' and we get treated differently" (Bergstrom, 6).

While *The Seventh Generation* focuses on student voices that "relate the joys, frustrations, and dreams of their generation," it is also interspersed with teaching stories, research methodology, and a section written specifically for educators. The book uses the Ojibway code for long life and wisdom, delineated by author Basil Johnston, as a framework to help students find their own path to follow. An earlier book by Cleary and Peacock, *Collected Wisdom: American Indian Education*, is an excellent companion work for teachers.[2] These publications, based on facts and research concerning the actual experiences of students and teachers, are critically important. "To continue educating our children and grandchildren in schools that relegate our histories, cultures, and language to an occasional sideshow (under the guise of 'diversity') and that ignore the presence of institutional, overt, and covert racism," the authors point out, "is to doom another generation of Native young people to educational failure" (Bergstrom, 173). Their work is a badly needed antidote to that ongoing failure.

In *Battlefields and Burial Grounds: The Indian Struggle to Protect Ancestral Graves in the United States*, Roger C. Echo-Hawk and Walter R. Echo-Hawk focus on a modern-day issue deeply rooted in history.[3] They trace the desecration of Native human remains back to the earliest days of European colonization, recounting the rise of scientific racism as well as the development of the contemporary repatriation movement. "When the Pilgrims first landed in New England in 1620," they write, "they sent out exploring parties to see what the new land had to offer. The scouts returned to the *Mayflower* with corn taken from Indian storage pits and articles removed from a burial. One scout reported, 'We brought sundry of the prettiest things away with us, and covered up the corpse again'" (Echo-Hawk, 12). Grave robbers such as this, often acting in the name of science, eventually took Native corpses as well. As the authors point out, collecting Indian remains also became part of official government policy, with the U.S. Surgeon General issuing orders to army personnel to obtain American Indian skulls for study at the Army Medical Museum in Washington, DC, in 1867 and 1868. Archeologists and anthropologists sought remains and burial goods for museum research and collections. In contrast, the authors write, "Most Native Americans believe that respect for the dead is more important than any knowledge of the past that might be gained by digging up graves" (Echo-Hawk, 21).

The Echo-Hawks focus on the repatriation struggles of the Pawnee Tribe, a tribal nation now located in present-day Oklahoma, but with roots in the Central Great Plains, a region encompassing today's states of Kansas and Nebraska. These authors trace Pawnee history, including the treatment of tribal remains as spoils of conquest. "During the 1860s and 1870s," they comment, "various Pawnee skeletal remains were sent to the Army Medical Museum in Washington, DC. In 1869, acting under the orders issued by the Surgeon General, the army obtained the heads of six Pawnees slain in western Kansas. These Pawnees, who were veterans of the U.S. Pawnee Scouts, were killed in a fight with an army unit and beheaded" (Echo-Hawk, 51). The authors recount several aspects of the repatriation movement, including a bitter struggle with the Nebraska State Historical Society over that agency's "ownership" of over 400 Pawnee dead in their museum holdings, the effort to close the "Indian Burial Pit" tourist attraction near Salinas, Kansas, and negotiations to have the remains of over 18,500 individuals held by federal agencies repatriated to their respective tribal nations. "The Pawnee efforts to redress these injustices required an enormous amount of tribal resources and extensive lobbying campaigns," the Echo-Hawks note. "In the end, it took attorney general orders and opinions, negotiated agreements, several pieces of state legislation, court cases, administrative proceedings, and two acts of Congress to win justice for the Pawnee cause" (Echo-Hawk, 71).

The authors, both citizens of the Pawnee Tribe of Oklahoma, are uniquely qualified to write this book. Walter R. Echo-Hawk serves as a senior staff attorney for the Native American Rights Fund in Boulder, Colorado, and was involved in legislative efforts on behalf of the Pawnee Tribe leading to passage of burial protection and reburial laws in Nebraska and Kansas, the Smithsonian Institution's repatriation provisions of the National Museum of the American Indian Act, and the Native American Graves Protection and Repatriation Act of 1990. Roger C. Echo-Hawk is a historian specializing in the study of ancient Indian history. "Rarely are the topics of history, ethics, and current events combined in such a readable format," M. Colleen McDougall keenly observes in *School Library Journal.* "This volume is a suitable resource for students of social studies, history, ethics, Native American, cross-cultural, and multicultural studies due to its high readability, excellent graphic and pictorial qualities, and discussion-sparking style and subject matter. All in all, an excellent examination of a complex topic."[4] The publication has won numerous awards, among them the Carter G. Woodson Secondary Outstanding Merit Book, and named A New York Public Library Book for the Teen Age, A Public Library Association Distinguished Title for Adult New Readers, and A Society of School Librarians International Outstanding Secondary Social Studies Book. For a biographical account related to repatriation issues, readers can turn to *Give Me My Father's Body: The Life of Minik, The New York Eskimo* by Kenn Harper.[5]

It Is a Good Day to Die: Indian Eyewitnesses Tell the Story of the Battle of the Little Bighorn by Herman J. Viola focuses on one of the most famous events in American history.[6] The author, the former director of the National Anthropological Archives, assembled accounts of Native participants or observers of the historic battle known as the Greasy Grass to Plains Indians and as Custer's Last Stand to whites. "Many years passed before the Indian side of the story began to be told," Viola writes. "Even then, many Indians present that day in 1876 were fearful of telling what they knew. They thought the government would arrest them and put them in jail or even execute them. By then Custer had become an American legend, and no one wished to believe he had behaved improperly or recklessly" (Viola, 93). Viola gleaned firsthand vignettes from source materials, especially the writings of Thomas Marquis, a medical doctor who worked on the Northern

Cheyenne and Crow reservations in Montana during the first part of the twentieth century. Marquis, who interviewed elderly veterans from the tribal nations involved, had published a number of articles and books on the Indian side of the battle by the time he died in 1935.

The book features eleven eyewitnesses, among them Sitting Bull (Hunkpapa), Low Dog (Oglala), Black Elk (Oglala), Red Horse (Miniconjou), Iron Hawk (Hunkpapa), and Standing Bear (Miniconjou) from Lakota bands as well as Antelope Woman, Wooden Leg, and Two Moon of the Cheyenne. Two others, Young Hawk (Arikara) and White Man Runs Him (Crow), served as scouts for Custer's Seventh Cavalry. The first vignette begins with the perspectives of renowned leader Sitting Bull: "The white man came here to take the country from us by force. He brought misery and wretchedness into our country. We were here killing game and eating, and all of a sudden we were attacked by white men. We were not out there to fight; we had to fight because we were attacked" (Viola, 19). The narratives, and Viola's arrangement of them, provide immediacy to the escalating events during the period as well as capture the great confusion of the battle itself. Antelope Woman, providing an important female perspective, details the excitement and hurried preparations. "Old men," she said, "were helping the young warriors in dressing and painting themselves for battle. Some women were bringing horses from the horse herd. Other women were working fast taking down their tepees" (Viola, 40).

Viola provides contextual information about the Battle of the Little Bighorn in the book's introduction and epilogue. He also incorporates illustrations, such as photographs of some of the eyewitnesses, maps, a copy of Custer's last note, and paintings by Lakota artist Amos Bad Heart Bull, including an image on the book jacket showing Crazy Horse charging Custer and his troops. Viola concludes the book with biographical notes about each eyewitness, a chronology, notes on sources, and an index. This brief, 101-page book packs in a great deal of history, dramatizing the victory of the Lakota and Cheyenne over Custer and the Seventh Cavalry at the Battle of the Little Bighorn and the reverberating impact of that pivotal event.

Another book, *Warriors: Navajo Code Talkers*, by photographer Kenji Kawano, focuses on wartime activity of a later period, World War II.[7] Kawano, a native-born Japanese, came to the United States in 1973 and visited the Navajo Reservation a year later. There, he met Carl

Gorman, one of the leaders of the Navajo Code Talkers Association, who introduced him to other members of the group. These men had served in the U.S. Marine Corps, where they created a secret code in the Navajo language and transmitted radio communications between the front lines and headquarters during pivotal battles during the war. "I didn't know this kind of Indian veteran existed or that America's victory in the South Pacific was aided by an Indian language," Kawano writes. "These were the Indians America ignored!" (Kawano, XIV). Kawano began photographing the veterans and, in 1982, the Navajo Code Talkers Association named him an honorary member and appointed him as the organization's official photographer. Kawano's book includes some seventy-five black and white photographs of the code talkers, a foreword by Carl Gorman, and an introduction by Benis M. Frank, Head, Marine Corps Oral History Program, Marine Corps History and Museums Division. At the time Kawano wrote the book, there were some 200 to 250 surviving Navajo code talkers.

"When I was going to boarding school," code talker Teddy Draper, Sr. recalled in the book, "the U.S. government told us not to speak Navajo, but during the war, they *wanted* us to speak it!" (Kawano, XVI). Kawano notes that these Native servicemen were sometimes mistaken for Japanese, intensifying the dangerous conditions under which they served. "By the end of the war," Frank explains in his introduction, "code talkers had been assigned to all six Marine divisions in the Pacific and to Marine Raider and parachute units as well. They took part in every Marine assault, from Guadalcanal in 1942 to Okinawa in 1945" (Kawano, 11). It was not until 1969 that the Navajo code talkers were nationally recognized for their service to the country. At that time, the Fourth Marine Division Association invited them to a reunion, where they were honored with a specially designed commemorative medallion in recognition of their wartime heroism. In 2001, President George W. Bush presented Presidential medals to Navajo code talkers at a ceremony held in the nation's capitol.[8] The contributions of these veterans are finally becoming better known, with media coverage as well as print and film treatments about their service. Code talkers Carl Gorman and Peter MacDonald both have book length books devoted to their lives.[9] Other authors have also written about the Navajo code talkers, among them Doris A. Paul, Sally McClain, Nathan Aaseng, Margaret T. Bixler, and Deanne Durrett. *The Comanche Code Talkers of World War II*, by

William C. Meadows, a related work, features another group of tribal servicemen using their Native language during wartime.[10] Publications such as these will lead readers to additional information about code talkers, including those from other tribal groups, but also to American Indian service in the military generally.

In *Children of the Midnight Sun: Young Native Voices of Alaska*, Tricia Brown presents a range of contrasts while profiling eight of today's Yup'ik, Iñupiat, Aleut, Athabascan, Tlingit, Tsimshian, and Haida youngsters in Alaska.[11] "Asked about their favorite foods," she writes, "the kids listed tacos and french fries right along with moosehead soup and muktuk. They play computer games and basketball as well as compete in the two-foot kick, an Eskimo game of old. They can tell us about today's news or a story from long, long ago" (Brown, 11). Ranging in age from nine to thirteen, the four boys and four girls profiled live in locales that stretch from northernmost Barrow to the Aleutian Islands and the Southeast Panhandle of the state. As Randy Meyer wrote in his review for *Booklist*, "The violet-and-crimson photo of a sunset on the jacket immediately dispels the narrow image of Alaska as a stark, uninviting place. Inside are more excellent photos, all taken by Roy Corral, which show Alaska's vibrant contrasts—snow-swept villages and manicured city gardens, native dances and trips to the mall."[12]

The book also dispels myths about Native Alaskans through its depiction of each young person profiled, enhanced by images illustrating a range of activities and settings. Even with limitations posed by number and space (eight subjects with three to four pages each), the author and photographer succeed in capturing an impressive measure of the diversity of the people and land. Change is reflected in a number of ways, with attention to the impact of historical forces. Katiana Bourdukofsky, one of the young people profiled, lives on St. Paul Island, where nearly everyone is Aleut and "like Katiana, nearly everyone has a Russian name and attends the Russian Orthodox church. . . . Today, to be Aleut is to be Russian Orthodox. Parts of the two cultures have become inseparably entwined" (Brown, 22). As Brown points out, "With the Russians came Western-style clothing, above-ground frame houses, and Christian beliefs. Also war and disease. Aleut numbers plummeted from 10,000 in the late 1700s to about 4,000 a century later. Now there are about 2,000 Aleuts" (Brown, 22). Brown takes into account the devastation of colonization on Native populations and cultures, but also writes of an indigenous cultural rebirth that began toward the end of the twentieth century. The text is further enlivened with the viewpoints and images of the young people profiled. Related titles include *The Winter Walk: A Century-Old Survival Story from the Arctic* by Loretta Outwater Cox and *Aleutian Sparrow*, a novel written in unrhymed verse about the Aleutian Islands during World War II, by Karen Hesse.[13]

Earth Always Endures: Native American Poems is a compilation of historical writings selected by Neil Philip, who drew from early anthropological sources and paired chants, prayers, and songs from a variety of tribal groups with duotone photographs by Edward S. Curtis (1868–1952).[14] "The eloquent words of the Sioux, Chippewa, Zuni, Navajo, and other native nations echo throughout this powerful collection of Native American poetry," reviewer Sharon Korbeck notes in *School Library Journal*. "Many of the poems are prayers to the heavens and gods, lullabies, or ceremonial dances."[15] The content is indeed eloquent. However, the translated words have been divorced from their original tribal contexts, including religious ceremonies. Compounding that problem, the writings have been paired with photographs that are often mismatched. On one page, for example, "My Words Are Tied in One," stanzas from a Yokuts prayer, appear with a photograph of Hollow Horn Bear, Brulé Sioux (Philip, 30–31). In another selection, there are several translations of Chippewa songs by Frances Densmore, paired with a photograph of Apaches posed by Curtis (Philip, 34–35). In still another, two songs (one Chiricahua Apache and one Chippewa) are paired with a photograph of Nez Perce leader Chief Joseph (Philip, 68–69). The book includes a preface, sources, and suggestions for further reading, but little information about the translators and none on the native contributors and their tribal nations. The cultural and religious context of the words is missing and subverted to an unintended purpose and audience.

Works devoted specifically to the creativity of contemporary American Indian young people include titles such as *Shooting Back from the Reservation: A Photographic View of Life by Native American Youth*, *Where There Is No Name for Art: The Art of Tewa Pueblo Children*, *When the Rain Sings: Poems by Young Native Americans*, and *Night Is Gone, Day Is Still Coming: Stories and Poems by American Indian Teens and Young Adults*. In *Shooting Back from the Reservation: A Photographic View of Life by Native American Youth*, Jim Hubbard selected black and white photographs taken by children and young adults from Pine Ridge and Rapid City in South Dakota, the Twin Cities in Minnesota, and locales in Arizona, New Mexico, and Wisconsin.[16] In 1989, Hubbard, a former staff photographer for the Detroit News and United Press International, created Shooting Back, an education and media center devoted to teaching photography and writing to homeless and other at-risk youth. The center's first project resulted in a traveling exhibition and publication, *Shooting Back: A Photographic View of Life by Homeless Children*.[17] "Millions of people have seen these photographs," Hubbard writes, "and many have pondered how they too might help relieve human suffering. Not only did people witness these children's visions, these children found a new freedom—the freedom to express themselves, to learn a creative skill, to join forces with others and nourish a growing feeling of pride" (Hubbard, xi). In 1991, committed to reaching Native American young people, he started a second Shooting Back center in Minneapolis. "When I opened the *New York Times* on December 28, 1993, to the Op-Ed page and saw the entire page of photographs by Native American youth that we had recently gathered from around the country," Hubbard observed, "I realized our work had not been in vain" (Hubbard, xiv). In his estimation, the photographs, "from one of the most silenced groups in America . . . reveal a world most of us know only through hackneyed media images" (Hubbard, back cover). After appearing at the Washington Project for the Arts, the exhibition later traveled to other venues in the nation.

Shooting Back from the Reservation offers audiences the opportunity of seeing aspects of Native life from the perspectives of young people who live that life. The book incorporates over 125 black and white photographs that explore family and friends, community activities, plants and animals, abstract portraits, and the diverse landscapes of home. "Some of the kids in the workshops take pictures of their friends and then give them to their friends," Hubbard notes. "On more than one occasion we have found that these kids carry the photographs of themselves every day to show others. Though they didn't take the pictures, the photos are important nonetheless. They proclaim: 'Here I am, I am real, I am of value' to the rest of the world" (Hubbard, xiii). The book also incorporates prose and poetry written by the young photographers, moving words that complement their visionary images. One of the students, Ronald Lewis, Jr., from the Hualapai Reservation in Arizona, comments, "When I pick up a camera, it feels like I'm going to a different dimension. I like to take pictures of good things, in all kinds of ways" (Hubbard, 21). Another young photographer, eighteen-year-old

Davidica Little Spotted Horse from the Pine Ridge Reservation in South Dakota, observes: "I think one of the things that makes our community unique from other places is that everyone knows everyone. So if a family or a person needs help there's always someone around to lend a hand. Being close isn't all that great either 'cause everyone knows your business" (Hubbard, 95). As activist Dennis Banks writes in his foreword to the book, "Keep up the shooting! Never let up! Never leave it to others to represent you, photographically or otherwise. Hang on to those dreams and visions. They may come true! Shoot the truth. It's a good story" (Hubbard, ix).

Another book centered on the work and voices of young people is *Where There Is No Name for Art: The Art of Tewa Pueblo Children.*[18] Bruce Hucko, who wrote the text and took the photographs, has served as an "art coach" at Santa Clara, San Ildefonso, and San Juan Pueblo Day Schools since 1991. Named as one of the country's leading art educators by the Rockefeller Brothers Fund for Excellence in Arts Education, he collaborated with Tewa Pueblo students as well as their families and communities to complete the publication. Hucko writes that the students "were involved in every step of the publishing process, from artwork and interviews to book design and marketing" (Hucko, n.p.). The result is a book with vibrant artwork, compelling photographic images, and remarkable commentary by the young people and members of their families. Hucko provides background information about the pueblos of the Rio Grande, including a map pinpointing the six Tewa-speaking Pueblos in New Mexico. "In their own language," he writes, "Tewa Pueblo people have no word for art. Pottery, painting, embroidery, dance, and other 'art' forms are not considered separate from life. On the contrary, art is seen as synonymous with work, thoughts, and expressions" (Hucko, 4).

Providing insider perspectives on what it means to grow up Pueblo in today's world, the young people talk about their lives among extended family and community as well as their activities and interests. "It is important that children have the opportunity to recognize and express the whole of who they are," Hucko writes. "To limit Pueblo children to drawing only Indian designs would be like allowing people of English descent to perform only Morris dancing. Such an attitude is ultimately patronizing; besides, the children would never stand for it. When youngsters are encouraged to explore a variety of art forms and expressions, their own culture takes on greater personal value" (Hucko, 104). The young artists encounter patronizing ideas enough, especially from tourists who visit the pueblos each year. "They ask you the dumbest questions that you'll ever hear!" one student exclaimed (Hucko, 111). "Pueblo children and adults alike find themselves bombarded with questions," Hucko points out. "Dealing with curious and well-intentioned visitor questions can be a test of patience. Each visitor asks a question only once, but residents must answer repeatedly. There are also times, especially during a dance, when *any* talk borders on rudeness" (Hucko, 111). These students, akin to others, reflect contemporary features of daily life, such as watching television and playing video games, but they also carry on the cultural ways of their people. "Well, the first thing is that it's not how it's usually mentioned in books or TV," one young artist comments. "We're modern people. We don't do anything different but our Indian ways" (Hucko, 113).

When the Rain Sings: Poems by Young Native Americans is the first collaboration between the Smithsonian Institution's National Museum of the American Indian (NMAI) and Wordcraft Circle of Native Writers and Storytellers.[19] The poets, ranging in age from seven to seventeen, created poems in response to objects from the museum's collections. W. Richard West, Director of NMAI, writes in his foreword to the book: "Perhaps drawing inspiration from the influential and compelling example of Native American oral tradition, contemporary Indian writers have made an increasingly significant place for themselves in the current literary landscape. This anthology indicates that those advances show no signs of letting up" (*Rain*, viii–ix). The Indian nations represented include Cochiti, Hopi, Kiowa, Lakota, Navajo, Ojibwe, Omaha, Tohono O'odham, and Ute. Lee Francis, the National Director of Wordcraft Circle, and Elizabeth Woody, poet from the Confederated Tribes of the Warm Springs Reservation of Oregon, provide contextual information about the anthology.[20] "The student writing that came out of this collaboration was marked by notable talent and ambition," Francis notes. "Those of us involved in the project thought that these young and gifted voices needed to be heard far and wide. The only question was how to make that need become reality. *When the Rain Sings* became one of the answers to our question" (*Rain*, xi). Woody, too, observes, "The strongest voices in contemporary Native poetry are those rooted in community. Neither the difficult landscape of the reservation nor the impact of urban relocation has diluted the strength of oral literature, which endures through new forms" (*Rain*, xiv). Young Lakota poet Cokata Aupi/Quinton Jack-Maldonado is one of the many young writers affirming this observation, writing in his poem, "Ration Day": "But someday our children will carry on, / Pine Ridge / And our beautiful culture will never be gone / *Ma Lakhóta!* ["I am a proud Lakota!"] (*Rain*, 15).

Similarly, *Night Is Gone, Day Is Still Coming: Stories and Poems by American Indian Teens and Young Adults*, edited by Annette Piña Ochoa, Betsy Franco, and Traci L. Gourdine, incorporates poetry and prose from contemporary tribal youth.[21] With close to eighty selections from some fifty-eight contributors ranging in age from eleven to twenty-two, this collection encompasses a wide representation. Acclaimed Acoma poet Simon Ortiz writes in his introduction to this anthology, "when I see, hear, and read poetry and stories by Native youth speaking strongly, wonderfully, and honestly about land, culture, community, I cannot help but feel the hope and courage with which they sing, dance, shout, and speak" (Ochoa, xiii). These young authors give voice to a range of emotions in a range of circumstances, sharing aspects of their lives on reservations, in small towns, and in large urban areas. Nineteen-year-old Vena A-dae laments her separation from home, "I am the Cochiti carrot in the huge ethnic salad," in her poem "Subway Mourning," centered in New York City. Twenty-one-year old Thomas M. Yeahpau created "My Favorite Runner" to portray a Kiowa figure named Tricky Heights. "Finally, I found two thin branches, about a foot long apiece, and sculpted his hair with them," Yeahpau writes in the prose selection. "He just sat there as I tossed his greasy hair around like a salad. I didn't waste too much time with his grooming and finished as fast as I could. 'He looks like an Indian Elvis Presley, don't he?' I asked" (Ochoa, 78). Writing anonymously, another young writer pours out her heart to her mother in a letter documenting sexual abuse, but also her strength and determination to work toward a promising future.

NOTES

1. Amy Bergstrom, Linda Miller Cleary, and Thomas D. Peacock, *The Seventh Generation: Native Students Speak about Finding the Good Path* (Charleston, WV: ERIC Clearinghouse on Rural Education and Small Schools, 2003), 48; hereafter referred to in text as Bergstrom.

2. Linda Miller Cleary and Thomas D. Peacock, *Collected Wisdom: American Indian Education* (Boston: Allyn and Bacon, 1998).

3. Roger C. Echo-Hawk and Walter R. Echo-Hawk, *Battlefields and Burial Grounds: The Indian Struggle to Protect Ancestral Graves in the United States* (Minneapolis, MN: Lerner Publications Company, 1994); hereafter referred to in text as Echo-Hawk.

4. M. Colleen McDougall, review of *Battlefields and Burial Grounds: The Indian Struggle to Protect Ancestral Graves in the United States*, by Roger C. Echo-Hawk and Walter R. Echo-Hawk, *School Library Journal* 40, no. 7 (July 1994), 122.

5. Kenn Harper, *Give Me My Father's Body: The Life of Minik, The New York Eskimo* (1986; South Royalton, VT: Steerforth Press, 2000).

6. Herman J. Viola, *It Is a Good Day to Die: Indian Eyewitnesses Tell the Story of the Battle of the Little Bighorn* (New York: Crown Publishers, 1998); hereafter referred to in text as Viola.

7. Kenji Kawano, *Warriors: Navajo Code Talkers* (Flagstaff, AZ: Northland Publishing Company, 1990); hereafter referred to in text as Kawano.

8. "President Bush Honors Navajo Code Talkers" (July, 26 2001). Available online at www.whitehouse.gov/news/releases/2001/07/print/20010726-5.html (accessed August 7, 2004).

9. Henry Greenberg and Georgia Greenberg, *Power of a Navajo: Carl Gorman: The Man and His Life* (Santa Fe, NM: Clear Light Publishers, 1996); Peter MacDonald, *The Last Warrior: Peter MacDonald and the Navajo Nation* (New York: Crown Publishers, 1993).

10. William C. Meadows, *The Comanche Code Talkers of World War II* (Austin: University of Texas Press, 2003).

11. Tricia Brown and Roy Corral (Photographer), *Children of the Midnight Sun: Young Native Voices of Alaska* (Portland, OR: Alaska Northwest Books, 1998); hereafter referred to in text as Brown.

12. Randy Meyer, review of *Children of the Midnight Sun: Young Native Voices of Alaska* by Tricia Brown, *Booklist* 94, no. 21 (July 1998), 1874.

13. Karen Hesse, *Aleutian Sparrow* (New York: Simon & Schuster, 2003); Loretta Outwater Cox, *The Winter Walk: A Century-Old Survival Story from the Arctic* (Anchorage: Alaska Northwest Books, 2003).

14. Neil Philip, selector, *Earth Always Endures: Native American Poems* (New York: Viking, 1996); hereafter referred to in text as Philip.

15. Sharon Korbeck, review of *Earth Always Endures: Native American Poems* by Neil Philip, *School Library Journal* 42, no. 11 (November 1996), 130.

16. Jim Hubbard, ed., *Shooting Back from the Reservation: A Photographic View of Life by Native American Youth* (New York: The New Press, 1994); hereafter referred to in text as Hubbard.

17. Jim Hubbard, ed., *Shooting Back: A Photographic View of Life by Homeless Children* (San Francisco: Chronicle Books, 1991).

18. Bruce Hucko, *Where There Is No Name for Art: The Art of Tewa Pueblo Children* (Santa Fe, NM: School of American Research, 1996); hereafter referred to in text as Hucko.

19. Lee Francis et al., *When the Rain Sings: Poems by Young Native Americans* (New York: Simon & Schuster Books for Young Readers, 1999); hereafter referred to in text as *Rain*.

20. For more information on Wordcraft Circle of Native Writers and Storytellers, an organization that "seeks to ensure that Native voices—past, present, and future—are heard throughout the world," see http://wordcraftcircle.org (accessed August 7, 2004). See also Lee Francis and James Bruchac, eds. *Reclaiming the Vision: Native Voices for the Eighth Generation* (New York: Greenfield Review Press, 1996).

21. Annette Piña Ochoa, Betsy Franco, and Traci L. Gourdine, *Night Is Gone, Day Is Still Coming: Stories and Poems by American Indian Teens and Young Adults* (Cambridge, MA: Candlewick Press, 2003); hereafter referred to in text as Ochoa.

Chapter Eight

Nonfiction

American Indian Life Stories

What does it mean to grow up Native American? There are as many answers to that question as there are Native American people. Certainly, there are as many stories. Stories of oppression and survival, of people who grew up surrounded by tradition, and people who did not. Stories of the pressures of forced assimilation and stories of resistance, of heritage denied and of heritage reclaimed. A multiplicity of stories.[1]

These words by Patricia Riley appear in *Growing Up Native American: An Anthology*, a collection of life stories she edited. This anthology incorporates writings from twenty-two Native American writers from fifteen tribal nations in the United States and Canada, encompassing a time range extending from the nineteenth century to the 1990s. Besides autobiographical accounts, the collection also features short stories and excerpts from novels. Black Elk, Sara Winnemucca Hopkins, and Luther Standing Bear are among the early writers represented, followed by selections from Louise Erdrich, Linda Hogan, N. Scott Momaday, Leslie Marmon Silko, and other contemporary authors. With its focus on growing up, the anthology incorporates stories that will appeal to diverse audiences, including young adults. The selected writings address a range of experiences, among them schooling in several settings in the United States and Canada. Excerpts from Francis La Flesche's *The Middle Five: Indian Schoolboys of the Omaha Tribe* and Basil H. Johnston's *Indian School Days* provide compelling firsthand accounts of boarding school life.[2] These excerpts, along with the others on the topic, offer readers exemplary alternatives over young adult fiction such as Ann Rinaldi's *My Heart Is on the Ground: The Diary of Nannie Little Rose, A Sioux Girl* and Bebe Faas Rice's *The Place at the Edge of the Earth* in their treatment of Native schooling.[3] *Growing Up Native American* also introduces readers to a range of other coming-of-age experiences through the diverse lives portrayed in the collection.

Riley writes that in the books available to her as a child, Native Americans were generally portrayed as static cultural artifacts from history. She explains that she put together *Growing Up Native American* "as a chance to rectify, in some small way, the situation of my childhood, not only for myself and my own children, but for anyone, Indian or non-Indian, interested in the real-life experiences of Native American people" (Riley, 23). The number of Native American biographies and autobiographies has grown, ranging in scope from brief sketches to full-length works.[4] In too many instances, the quality of biographies remains a throwback to earlier times, with an overemphasis on a narrow selection of famous historical figures. Relieving this, however, are high quality works that offer new perspectives on such figures and others that stand out for their timeliness and quality. There are also growing numbers of critical works examining aspects of this genre, including as-told-to accounts.[5] The life stories considered here, drawn from an extensive list of available possibilities, range from historical personages to contemporary figures. The first section emphasizes books written specifically for young adults, followed by other biographies and autobiographies appropriate for this audience.

Two biographies written by Albert Marrin center on two famous tribal leaders, Quanah Parker, Comanche, and Sitting Bull, Lakota.[6] Although written fairly recently, these books reflect characteristics that Riley and other authors strive to counteract. Marrin's *Plains Warrior: Chief Quanah Parker and the Comanches* is, as librarian Lisa Mitten writes in *School Library Journal*, "a throwback to the sensationalistic dime novel Westerns of the turn of the century."[7] The stereotypical language is one characteristic, with Indian men appearing as "braves," "warriors," or "chiefs," and women as "squaws" on nearly every page of the book. Another feature is the constant portrayal of Plains Indians, in general, and Comanches, in particular, with biased, inflammatory, and inaccurate information. Marrin permeates his text with statements such as "War paint . . . gave the brave a fiendish appearance," "Indians believed that the dead went to the Happy Hunting Ground," and "Women captives were usually raped" (*Plains Warrior*, 32, 33, 46). In Marrin's telling, the Plains Indians lived for war. In one of many such passages, he writes: "Comanche braves, like the men of all Plains tribes, were above all, warriors. They hunted to live, but they lived to fight. War was their passion, at once a pleasure and a necessity, essential to their entire way of life" (*Plains Warrior*, 28). In his estimation, "the idea of 'pleasurable' war seems weird; twentieth-century Americans have had a bellyful of fighting in every corner of the globe. We see war as a calamity to be avoided at almost any cost. Yet The People's world was not ours, and they saw things differently. The idea that humans should always live in peace seems never to have entered their minds" (*Plains Warrior*, 28). Marrin clearly underscores notions of white superiority, sidestepping the historical realities of European conquest and America's record of engagement in war.

In a book purported to be about Quanah Parker and the Comanches, there is remarkably little information about either, most of it based on dated sources. Instead, there are lengthy accounts of Texas Rangers, centered on the bravado of "that brotherhood of fighting men" and other Indian fighters (*Plains Warrior*, 73). "There was another reason for killing Comanche women and, yes, children," Marrin writes. "War is always brutalizing. Yet nothing is so brutalizing as fighting an enemy who is very different from yourself and who fights by different rules. Indians ignored the rules of 'civilized' warfare; that is, they did not follow the rules as laid down by whites. As a result, rangers saw nothing wrong in paying them back in kind" (*Plains Warrior*, 77). As evidenced by these statements, Marrin attributes uncivilized brutality to American Indians and holds them responsible for the behavior of their attackers.

Marrin's treatment of treaties is likewise irresponsible, conveying problematic misinformation. "In short," he contends, "treaties were made to be broken at a future time, when convenient. Even had the authorities been sincere, they could not have enforced the treaties. The United States really is a democracy, and democracy is government by the people through their elected representatives. Unpopular treaties could not be enforced without the people's consent. Any treaty that gave the Indians territory would have to be broken when enough white voters set their sights on the same land" (*Plains Warrior*, 95). As a matter of record, treaties provided the United States with territory from tribal nations. Marrin overlooks centuries of federal Indian law as well as the U.S. Constitution, including Article VI, Clause 2, which states in part: "Treaties made, or which shall be made, under the Authority of the United States, shall be the supreme Law of the Land." Treaties are a fundamental component of federal Indian law, the body of law regulating the legal relationships between American Indian nations and the United States. Like the U.S. Constitution, clearly an instrument of American democracy, treaties (including those deemed "unpopular") are an ongoing reality.

Concerning tribal religious beliefs, Marrin comments: "Quanah, like all Comanches, explained strange happenings in terms of magic, not science" (*Plains Warrior*, 143). Furthermore, the author declares: "Indeed, buffalo chips were sacred in themselves; braves swore they were telling the truth on a pile of manure" (*Plains Warrior*, 25). Gender roles do not fare any better. "Naduah's [captive Cynthia Parker's] mother taught her all she needed to know to be a wife, or 'squaw,'" he writes. "Main rule: daily tasks were strictly separated according to sex. There was no such thing as a man helping a woman with the housework. Men hunted, fought, and protected their families, as the Great Spirit intended. A squaw would not allow her husband to do anything for himself; serving him was a matter of her womanly pride" (*Plains Warrior*, 53). In Marrin's interpretation, "Naduah was a prize catch for any brave. Being white was a real advantage in winning a mate" (*Plains Warrior*, 58).

Unfortunately, Marrin's biography, *Sitting Bull and His World*, is just as flawed as *Plains Warrior*. The author turns his attention to Tatan'ka Iyota'ke or Sitting Bull, the nineteenth-century Hunkpapa Lakota spiritual leader, emphasizing many of the same themes that appear in the Quanah Parker book. "If Plains Indians hunted to live," he reiterates, "they lived to fight. War was part of Slow's [young Sitting Bull's] mindset, his expectations of life, ingrained in him from infancy. The idea that people should prefer peace to war would have struck him as strange. Peace, to him, was merely a time between wars. Fighting was natural" (*Sitting Bull*, 40). In Marrin's telling, there is only war. "Successful warriors," he maintains, "were the village darlings" (*Sitting Bull*, 41). "Plains Indians," according to this perspective, "also killed, scalped, and mutilated women and children for the sake of honor. That made sense to them. Since men fought desperately to defend their families, warriors believed that killing loved ones in front of their defender showed courage" (*Sitting Bull*, 45). These statements, which underscore notions of American Indian savagery, defy common sense. Certainly, nineteenth-century Lakota had a rich cultural life that encompassed other activities besides war. Marrin defines government policy toward the Lakota and "all Native Americans" as "ethnocide," which "was not a war waged by brutal enemies, but by white people with good intentions" (*Sitting Bull*, 195). The slaughter of innocent tribal women and children at sites such as Sand Creek and Wounded Knee indisputably refutes this notion.

Although *Sitting Bull and His World* appears to be richly annotated, the sources exclude essential accounts. This historical leader and his people are among the most famous and most written about tribal peoples in the country, but Marrin's writing does not reflect this richness. Although the need to consult with the people most directly concerned with this history, those inheriting its legacy, seems apparent, there is no evidence that the author did so with this publication. The sources, too, often slanted or dated, incorporate only a few Native works. Lakota/Dakota authors such as Ella Deloria, Zitkala-Sa (Gertrude Bonnin), Beatrice Medicine, Vine Deloria, Elizabeth Cook-Lynn, Tim Giago, Mario Gonzalez, and Virginia Driving Hawk Sneve are missing altogether. Information about Sitting Bull's people (the "world" part of Marrin's title) is also lacking, including any contemporary facts about the Standing Rock Reservation, where Sitting Bull lived out his life after returning from exile in Canada and where he was killed on December 15, 1890. One fact that Marrin could have readily ascertained is that there is a tribal college named for the leader at Standing Rock, manifesting his philosophy, "Let us put our minds together to see what we can build for our children."[8] Consistent with Marrin's lack of Lakota perspectives or information, he fails to cite the Wounded Knee Survivors Association, an organization of descendants who keep the memories of those who perished at Wounded Knee alive. Marrin could have consulted other sources as well, including *Wiping the Tears of Seven Generations*, a film that documents a Lakota commemoration of the Wounded Knee massacre of 1890.[9] In addition, he could have incorporated information about the federal legislation signed into law in 1991 by President George H. W. Bush authorizing a name change from

Custer to the Little Bighorn National Monument at the famous battle
site as well as a memorial to honor the battle's fallen American Indians.
This information could have contributed to Marrin's book, illustrating
the impact of this history today. While *Sitting Bull and His World* has
been lauded in publications such as *Publishers Weekly, School Library
Journal*, and *Booklist*, readers would do well to consider the assess-
ments of Oyate's Doris Seale and Beverly Slapin. "It is absolutely as-
tonishing," these authors comment, "that anyone could, at the beginning
of the 21st century, write a book that incorporates nearly every stereotype and misrepresentation about Indian peoples ever uttered. Albert
Marrin has."[10] They designate his publication a "book to avoid," deeming it "another apologia for 'westward expansion' and the destruction of
Native cultures and lives" (Oyate, 1).

Russell Freedman covers aspects of the same history in *The Life and
Death of Crazy Horse*, a biography of the revered nineteenth-century
Oglala Lakota leader.[11] In contrast to Marrin's treatment of Quanah
Parker and Sitting Bull, Freedman's account is characterized by careful
research and informed writing. He identifies the sources he consulted to
learn about Crazy Horse's life, among them Eleanor Hinman and Mari
Sandoz, who conducted interviews to gather information about the
leader on the Pine Ridge Reservation in 1930. "They interviewed Crazy
Horse's surviving friends and relatives," Freedman writes, "old-timers
such as He Dog, Red Feather, Short Bull, and Little Killer, men who had
lived with Crazy Horse and fought beside him. Even though these ancient warriors were recalling events from long before, their memories
were sharp and they did not often disagree" (Freedman, 3). Their accounts help enliven the portrait of the legendary leader. He Dog, for instance, said of Crazy Horse: "He never spoke in council and attended
very few. There was no special reason for this, it was just his nature. He
was a very quiet man except when there was fighting" (Freedman, 3).
Freedman explains that before the Hinman and Sandoz interviews,
"published sources on the life of Crazy Horse were almost exclusively
the accounts of the white men who fought against him" (Freedman,
159). As he also notes, many details about the life of Crazy Horse remain unknown.

The Life and Death of Crazy Horse is richly enhanced by some fifty
black and white drawings by renowned Oglala Lakota artist-historian
Amos Bad Heart Bull. Bad Heart Bull, born in 1869 and descended

from a long line of historians in his family and band, served as the historian of the Oglala Lakota at a critical time in history. Before his death in 1913, he documented pivotal historical events and traditional ways that the reservation system was rapidly dismantling. Bad Heart Bull eventually completed over four hundred drawings, among them sixty works centered on the Battle of the Little Bighorn. His ledger sketchbook was photographed page by page by graduate student Helen Blish before it was buried with Bad Heart Bull's sister at her death in 1947. Twenty years later, all of the drawings and the text of Blish's study were published for the first time by the University of Nebraska Press in *A Pictographic History of the Oglala Sioux*.[12] The drawings illustrating Freedman's biography are a study in their own right, rich contributions to historical documentation and interpretation. They provide an introduction to Amos Bad Heart Bull's life and work to young adults and other readers.

Arlene Hirschfelder's *Photo Odyssey: Solomon Carvalho's Remarkable Western Adventure, 1853–1854*, while focusing on a non-Indian figure, brings to life a little-known dimension of western history.[13] In this young adult biography, she writes of Solomon Carvalho, a thirty-eight-year-old Jewish painter/photographer who accompanied explorer and military leader Colonel John Charles Fremont on his fifth, and final westward expedition. Drawing from source materials, including Carvalho's diary and letters, Hirschfelder documents the photographer's life as well as his experiences on the expedition's arduous journey to survey the best railroad route between the Mississippi River and the Pacific coast. Carvalho, an observant Sephardic Jew from Baltimore, Maryland, consented to join the expedition to take pictures. "A half hour previously," he wrote, "if anybody had suggested to me the probability of my undertaking an overland journey to California, even over the emigrant route, I should have replied there were no inducements sufficiently powerful to have tempted me. Yet, in this instance, I impulsively, without even a consultation with my family, passed my word to join an exploring party, under command of Col. Fremont . . . with the full expectation of being exposed to all the inclemencies of an arctic winter" (Hirschfelder, 16). Carvalho had a number of challenges to overcome, including learning how to ride a horse. "This animal was given into my own charge," he admitted, "and I only then began to realize that I had entered into duties which I was unqualified to perform.

I had never saddled a horse myself. My sedentary employment in a city, never having required me to do such offices; and now I was to become my own ostler [hostler], and ride him to water twice a day, besides running after him on the prairie for an hour sometimes before I could catch him" (Hirschfelder, 25). This novice member of Fremont's expedition also had to figure out a way to transport and safeguard heavy photographic equipment and adhere to the strict dietary laws of his religion.

Although the several hundred daguerrotypes taken by the photographer on the five-month journey with Fremont became lost to history, Hirschfelder worked around that drawback with writings by Carvalho, who "kept the only known published record of the entire trip," as well as other images of the period to write the story (Hirschfelder, 5). The book, which is well illustrated, includes a picture of a daguerrotype outfit, a self-portrait of the photographer, a map outlining Fremont's fifth expedition, Carvalho's painting of Ute leader Wakara, and pictures from Carvalho's *Incidents of Travel and Adventure in the Far West with Col. Fremont's Last Expedition.* Hirschfelder's account includes important firsthand observations about the photographer's experiences, among them his interactions with the Native peoples he met on the journey.

My World: Young Native Americans Today, a series by the Smithsonian Institution's National Museum of the American Indian, features Gabrielle Tayac's *Meet Naiche: A Native Boy from the Chesapeake Bay Area* as its first entry.[14] The author tells the story of her young cousin Naiche Woosah Tayac, the son of a San Carlos Apache mother and a Piscataway father, and his life in rural Maryland. "Hi, I'm Naiche, and I'm an American Indian," he begins. "My life is probably a lot like yours. I have a dog, a bike that I love to ride, and my own room, which is sometimes very messy! I live with my mom and dad and go to public school. I have a lot of friends. Some are Native, some are not" (Tayac, 11). The book, more snapshot or brief portrayal, incorporates information about Naiche's family, tribal background, and cultural ceremonies, such as the Piscataway Awakening of Mother Earth celebration. Illustrated with photographs by John Harrington, the publication is also enhanced by images from the National Museum of the American Indian's collections. The book's strengths include its portrayal of a contemporary young adult with parents from two diverse tribal cultures and its emphasis on refuting stereotypes. "A lot of people think that all Native Americans live on reservations," the author writes, "or only in the western or southwestern United States. But that isn't true" (Tayac, 6). As this book is more introductory than comprehensive, readers will need to look to other sources for additional historical and contemporary information about the tribal groups represented. The most recent books in this new series are *Meet Mindy: A Native Girl from the Southwest* by Susan Secakuku and *Meet Lydia: A Native Girl from Alaska* by Miranda Belarde-Lewis.[15]

Although not written specifically for young adults, biographies by Tiana Bighorse and Kenn Harper are among the many possible choices in this genre for this age group. In *Bighorse the Warrior*, Bighorse retells the story of her father Gus Bighorse and his life during a crucial period of Navajo history.[16] Born in about 1846, Bighorse led bands of warriors under Chief Manuelito during the Navajo Long Walk of 1864. At that time, over 8,000 Navajos were marched from their homeland to Bosque Redondo in southern New Mexico, a distance of some three hundred miles. Held there for four years by the U.S. government, they suffered enormously from inhumane conditions and brutal treatment. "The Long Walk," Tiana Bighorse relates, "is a tragic journey over frozen snow and rough rocks. There are a few wagons to haul some food and some things that belong to the white soldiers. The trip is on foot. People are shot down on the spot if they say they are tired or sick or if they stop to help someone. If a woman is in labor with a baby, she is killed. There is absolutely no mercy" (Bighorse, 34). Countless Navajo died during the forced march and during their exile; others suffered heartbreak at the loss of family members along the way. "To the Navajo," author Peter Iverson comments, "the Long Walk happened last week" (Bighorse, n.p.).

"I want to talk about my tragic story," Gus Bighorse said, "because if I don't, it will get into my mind and get into my dream and make me crazy. I know some people died of their tragic story. They think about it and think about how many relatives they lost. Their parents got shot. They get into shock. That is what kills them. That is why we warriors have to talk to each other. We wake ourselves up, get out of the shock. And that is why I tell my kids what happened, so it won't be forgot" (Bighorse, 81–82). His daughter, who listened to her father's stories when she was a young child, retold them in his voice in the book. Noël Bennett, who edited *Bighorse the Warrior*, first met Tiana Bighorse in 1968 when she began taking weaving instruction from her. Their publication is an important contribution, providing firsthand perspectives

from Gus Bighorse on a grim chapter of American history. Readers
would do well to turn to this book rather than Ann Turner's *The Girl
Who Chased Away Sorrow: The Diary of Sarah Nita, A Navajo Girl*,
young adult fiction centered on the Long Walk.[17] Oyate's reviewer,
Beverly Slapin, designates Turner's fictional diary a "book to avoid," in
part for its denial and distortion of history and culture.[18] Melissa Kay
Thompson concurs, writing that Turner "avoids the central themes in
U.S. government/tribal relations: extermination and land theft."[19] In
contrast, authors such as Tiana Bighorse, Luci Tapahonso, Rex Lee Jim,
Irvin Morris, and Lori Arviso Alvord offer readers authentic insider per-
spectives on Navajo life. Joseph Bruchac's nonfiction *Trails of Tears,
Paths of Beauty*, which centers on the Cherokee Trail of Tears and the
Navajo Long Walk, represents another outstanding choice.[20]

  Give Me My Father's Body: The Life of Minik, The New York Eskimo
by Kenn Harper also documents a compelling story via biography.[21]
Minik was one of six Inuit brought to New York City from northwest-
ern Greenland by Arctic explorer Robert Peary and presented to the
American Museum of Natural History as "specimens" in 1897. With lit-
tle resistance to disease and suffering from culture shock, Minik's father
Quisuk and three other members of the group quickly died from strains
of influenza. After another member of the group was returned home to
Greenland, seven-year-old Minik found himself alone in New York
City, an orphan and an exile. He was taken into the family of William
Wallace, the superintendent of buildings for the American Museum of
Natural History, a placement that was envisioned as temporary but
lasted for over a decade. "When he first went to the home of the Wal-
laces," Harper writes, "Minik was broken in spirit and in health. He
cried most of the time and 'lived in mortal fear of having to return to the
Museum'" (Harper, 44). His experiences at that institution included being stared at by visitors, examined by scientists, and treated as a live
specimen.

  During the course of his twelve years in New York, Minik and his
foster family endured a number of downturns. William Wallace lost his
job and suffered financial disgrace as well as the death of his wife. He
continued to care for Minik as well as his biological son without the
help of Peary and museum officials, who refused to provide support to
the young Inuit or return him home to Greenland. Instead, they know-
ingly let him live in poverty in an unstable family situation. Minik's suf-

ferings were intensified by the realization that museum officials had staged a fake burial for his father to cover up the fact that they had kept Qisuk's remains for study and display as a "curiosity." The title of the book is drawn from that dimension of the story, the efforts of Minik to retrieve his father's remains for proper burial. Despite newspaper coverage and repeated requests, Minik's efforts were unsuccessful, met by stonewalling and denial on the part of the officials involved. Although Minik finally returned to Greenland in 1909, he had to relearn his native language and fill other gaps in knowledge created by living in a different culture and environment during his formative years. Minik remained among his people for seven years, but his marginalizing childhood experiences led him back to the United States in 1916. He died two years later of the great influenza epidemic.

Kenn Harper, who originally published Minik's story in 1986, has lived in the Arctic for over thirty years, serving as a teacher, historian, linguist, and businessman. He speaks Inuktitut, the language of the eastern Canadian Arctic, and has family ties, through his wife, to Minik's people. "Following the first publication of this book in 1986," he writes, "the American Museum of Natural History was embarrassed. They had succeeded for many years in covering up the story of Minik and their treatment of the remains of Qisuk and his fellow Eskimos. Now, almost a century after the events in question, the story had come back to haunt them" (Harper, 225). However, it was not until 1993 that the remains of the four who died in New York were finally repatriated to Greenland for burial in their home community of Qaanaaq. Four years later, a memorial plaque was unveiled, beginning with the words "NUNAMINGNUT UTEQIHUT," which translates simply as "They have come home" (Harper, 228). Minik, who died in New Hampshire, is buried in that state. Harper concludes: "He died among friends, the Hall family, perhaps the truest friends he ever had. At their own expense, they placed a tiny marker over his grave and tended his final resting place. Minik died among friends. Let him remain there" (Harper, 229). A good companion book to this story is *Battlefields and Burial Grounds: The Indian Struggle to Protect Ancestral Graves in the United States* by Roger C. Echo-Hawk and Walter R. Echo-Hawk.[22]

Native American autobiographies and memoirs represent another rich area of choice for readers. One of them is *Mankiller: A Chief and Her People: An Autobiography by the Principal Chief of the Cherokee*

Nation.[23] The book, coauthored with Michael Wallis, chronicles the life of Wilma Mankiller, the first woman to lead a major Native American tribal nation. The text intersperses Mankiller's personal journey with the history of the Cherokee Nation. The Mankiller name, unusual to most outsiders, has origins as a military title or rank in the Cherokee Nation and has served as a family surname within the tribal group for several generations. The daughter of a Dutch-Irish mother and a Cherokee father, Wilma Mankiller, one of eleven children, was born in Tahlequah, Oklahoma, in 1945. She and her family lived on her grandfather's land, Mankiller Flats, until she was ten years old. At that time, the Mankillers moved to San Francisco through a federal program aimed at relocating American Indians from their rural and reservation homelands to urban areas. "One day I was living in a rural Cherokee community," she comments, "and a few days later I was living in California and trying to deal with the mysteries of television, neon lights, and elevators. It was total culture shock" (Mankiller, xx). After considerable difficulty, Mankiller adjusted to the new environment. She came of age in San Francisco and, in the 1960s, married her first husband and had two daughters. During that period, her political activism also began to awaken.

Mankiller participated in the American Indian occupation of Alcatraz Island in the San Francisco Bay area in 1969, activism that helped call attention to the injustices suffered by tribal peoples across the country. She also did volunteer work with Native organizations in California before divorcing her husband and returning to Oklahoma during the 1970s. Mankiller initially worked for the Cherokee Nation recruiting young Native Americans to pursue university training. She also continued her studies, completing a college degree in 1979 and enrolling in graduate studies at the University of Arkansas. While commuting to school, Mankiller was involved in a head-on automobile collision and nearly died from her injuries. During her lengthy recovery, she turned to what Cherokees call "being of good mind," meaning "one has to think positively, to take what is handed out and turn it into a better path" (Mankiller, 226). By 1981, Mankiller had become the founding director of the Cherokee Nation Community Development Department, which spearheaded revitalization projects in the rural community of Bell, Oklahoma. Two years later, she became the first female Deputy Chief in Cherokee history. In 1985, the Principal Chief resigned and Mankiller assumed the office. Two years later, she was elected to the post and, in

1991, won reelection with nearly 83 percent of the vote. Under Mankiller's leadership, the tribal membership of the Oklahoma Cherokee grew to 170,000, the annual budget reached some $90 million, and the number of tribal employees increased. Mankiller, a recipient of the Presidential Medal of Freedom, married fellow Cherokee Charlie Soap in 1986. After leaving office, she has pursued a range of other activities, including writing and teaching, while also overcoming debilitating health problems. Mankiller's autobiography is a valuable contribution for a number of reasons, including its focus on the governance of a large tribal nation. It addresses the authority and jurisdiction of tribal government, a neglected area of instruction in schools. A 2000 paperback issue of Mankiller's autobiography provides an update of her life after 1994.

Delphine Red Shirt, a member of the Oglala Sioux Tribe from the Pine Ridge Reservation in South Dakota, is the author of *Bead on an Anthill: A Lakota Childhood.*[24] This memoir, which tells the story of Red Shirt's growing up years, was followed by *Turtle Lung Woman's Granddaughter*, which interweaves the life stories of the author's mother and great-grandmother into the narrative.[25] Red Shirt's first language is Lakota, a critically important dimension of her books. "It is the custom in my tribe to begin any public speech or presentation with an autobiographical statement," Red Shirt writes in her introduction to *Bead on an Anthill*, "giving my status in the tribe and telling why I am qualified to speak" (*Bead*, n.p.). Her qualifications are many and varied.[26] A child of the Northern Plains, she grew up in Nebraska and on the Pine Ridge Reservation in the 1960s and 1970s. Red Shirt attended public and government schools, among them Red Cloud Indian School, a Catholic high school on the reservation. A military veteran, she has served in the United States Marine Corps. Red Shirt has held adjunct professor posts at Yale University and Connecticut College. In addition, she serves as series editor for "Race and Ethnicity in the American West" for the University of Nebraska Press. Her writings have appeared in publications such as *Indian Country Today*, the *Lakota Nation Journal*, and the *Hartford Courant*.

"I grew up in a time before the old ways disappeared completely," Red Shirt writes, "and the new ways emerged in their place" (*Bead*, 91). She addresses the impact of these transitions in numerous ways, including the adverse consequences for her first language. "In a conversation," she relates, "my mother utters the old words effortlessly, words that I have to repeat silently to myself, my tongue and throat adjusting to the guttural, to the tone, and to the feeling that I could never speak it as smoothly as she did" (*Bead*, 93). Red Shirt compares Lakota and English, drawing from her experience as a bilingual speaker of both languages. "In Lakota," she explains, "everything is black or white, unpleasant or pleasant, indirect or direct, disrespectful or respectful. In English the nuances are many, and they can be overwhelming to one whose native language is not English" (*Bead*, 92). In *Turtle Lung Woman's Granddaughter*, she translated her mother's story from the Lakota language. Red Shirt received support from the Endangered Languages Fund, Department of Linguistics, at Yale University for her work in preserving the Lakota language as it was spoken by her mother's generation. *Turtle Lung Woman's Granddaughter*, part of the American Indian Lives series of the University of Nebraska Press, was nominated for an American Book Award in 2002 and a Spur Award in 2003.

Lori Arviso Alvord's *The Scalpel and the Silver Bear: The First Navajo Woman Surgeon combines Western Medicine and Traditional Healing*, is also an autobiographical account of a contemporary Native woman's life.[27] Assisted by Elizabeth Cohen Van Pelt, these authors tell the story of Alvord's arduous journey to becoming a physician. The daughter of a white mother and a Navajo father, Alvord grew up in Crownpoint, New Mexico, attending reservation schools that were approximately 95 percent Navajo. "People in Crownpoint," she writes, "lived a hard life. Many families had no running water or electricity. They lived in hogans, or traditional eight-sided dwellings built to face the east, and they herded sheep. Growing up there, I never dreamed that I would someday become a doctor, much less a surgeon" (Alvord, 9). During her youth, there were no Navajo doctors, lawyers, or other such professionals. Alvord, who believed she would attend a nearby state college, applied to Dartmouth instead. Her decision to apply there was influenced by a chance meeting with a Navajo student who was attending Princeton. Arriving on the Dartmouth campus at the age of sixteen, she comments, "I was in complete culture shock. I thought people talked too much, laughed too loud, asked too many personal questions, and had no respect for privacy. They seemed overly competitive and put a higher value on material wealth than I was used to" (Alvord, 27). In contrast, "Navajos placed much more emphasis on a person's relations to family, clan, tribe, and the other inhabitants of the earth, both human and nonhuman, than on possessions" (Alvord, 27). Despite homesickness and feelings of alienation and invisibility, Alvord persisted, drawing comfort from the students in Dartmouth's Native American program. She graduated in 1979 and later wrote of her experiences in *First Person, First Peoples: Native American College Graduates Tell Their Life Stories*, a book of essays, written by alumni representing richly diverse tribal backgrounds and perspectives.[28]

Following her graduation from Dartmouth, Alvord returned home and found work as a research assistant on brain physiology for Dr. Gary Rosenberg, a medical researcher at the University of New Mexico. Encouraged to go to medical school by Dr. Rosenberg, she eventually attended Stanford University, overcoming a number of obstacles in the process. One of them concerned dissecting a cadaver, which forced her to break an important cultural rule. "Navajos do not touch the dead," she explains. "Ever" (Alvord, 40). During her training at Stanford, Alvord returned to New Mexico for periodic rotations at Canyoncito-Laguna Hospital, where she met Taos Pueblo surgeon Dr. Ron Lujan, who served as her mentor and "greatest challenger" (Alvord, 45). After completing medical school, Alvord returned home and took a position at the Gallup Indian Medical Center in Gallup, New Mexico, fifty miles from Crownpoint. She soon realized that to improve her surgical practice, she needed to learn more about traditional medicine. "For Navajos," she writes, "healer and holy man were merged, and doctor and priest were one and the same. . . . Their medicine was for the whole human creature—body, mind, and spirit, their community, and even the larger world. I had come to think of this philosophy as a gift that could be given by Navajos to the medical world" (Alvord, 112).

Alvord left her work in Gallup to become associate dean of minority and student affairs at Dartmouth Medical School. "One of my long-term goals," she writes, "was to gain the ability to help improve national health care policies for Native Americans" (Alvord, 193). The Dartmouth work, in her estimation, helped provide that opportunity. She continued to draw from Navajo knowledge to enhance her medical teaching and practice. "Beauty to Navajos," she explains, "means living in balance and harmony with yourself and the world. It means caring for yourself—mind, body, and spirit—and having the right relationships with your family, community, the animal world, the environment—earth, air, and water—our planet and universe" (Alvord, 186).

Virginia Driving Hawk Sneve, renowned for her children's books based on Lakota life and culture, is also the author of *Completing the Circle*, a memoir chronicling her family's history.[29] A member of the Rosebud Sioux Tribe from the Rosebud Reservation in South Dakota and the daughter of Episcopal minister James Driving Hawk and his wife Rose Ross, the author traces her ancestry to Santee, Yankton, and Teton bands of her people, intermingled with Ponca, French, Scots, and English lineage. "The story of my grandmothers and other women of the circle," she writes, "is found in a gleaning of both oral and written sources and is the thread that stitched the pieces of knowledge into a beautiful star quilt" (Sneve, xvi). Sneve was influenced by the instruction and example of these relatives. "In just about every Sioux family," she observes, "there is a woman who is honored for her beautifully crafted star quilts" (Sneve, xvi). In Sneve's family, that included her paternal grandmother, Flora Clairmont Driving Hawk, who was also a gifted storyteller. "She was a short woman," Sneve comments, "but I never thought her small because of the size of her spirit. *Strong willed* and *determined* are the adjectives that come to mind" (Sneve, 1).

Sneve incorporates information about her own life in the memoir, including her path to becoming a writer. She started writing short stories and poems in high school, striving to become a published author after college. Sneve was interested in focusing on Native American themes aimed at adult audiences, but "found no market" for her work (Sneve, 6). It was not until her daughter Shirley began reading Laura Ingalls Wilder's books that she began writing for young people. "I read *Little House on the Prairie*," Sneve explained, "and found the only reference to Indians in the whole series: 'The naked wild men stood by the fireplace. . . . Laura smelled a horrible bad smell. . . . Their faces were bold and fierce'" (Sneve, 6). She wondered about the impact of such passages on her daughter and other students. "I began to read children's literature," she notes, "and found that Indians were a popular theme, but always Indians of the past—brave boy warriors and cute princesses, or brutal savages. I found no stories of modern Indian children" (Sneve, 6). Sneve's first novel (and her first published work), "*Jimmy Yellow Hawk*, a story of a modern Sioux boy on a South Dakota reservation," was published in 1972 (Sneve, 7). This book was the start of her twenty-year association with Holiday House publishing company in New York. During that period, Sneve completed numerous other novels for young readers, among them *High Elk's Treasure*, *When Thunders Spoke*, and

The ChiChi HooHoo Bogeyman.[30] *Grandpa Was a Cowboy & an Indian and Other Stories*, published by the University of Nebraska Press in 2000, incorporates both contemporary and historical storylines.[31] This collection has great appeal to a wide range of intergenerational readers. "Grandparents told these stories to *Takoža* (grandchild)," the author writes in a note to the book, "a representative of all Native American children—every tribe's most treasured possession" (*Grandpa*, ix).

Sneve is the recipient of numerous awards, among them the Writer of the Year Award from the Western Heritage Hall of Fame in 1984, the North American Indian Prose Award for *Completing the Circle* in 1992, the South Dakota Living Indian Treasure Award presented by the Northern Plains Tribal Arts and South Dakotans for the Arts in 1997, and the National Humanities Medal in 2000. In presenting the humanities medal to her, President Clinton said in part: "A gifted teacher and story teller, she has devoted the past three decades to educating children and others about Native American culture, to breaking down stereotypes and replacing them with knowledge and understanding."[32]

NOTES

1. Patricia Riley, ed., *Growing Up Native American: An Anthology* (New York: William Morrow, 1993), 21; hereafter referred to in text as Riley.

2. Francis La Flesche, *The Middle Five: Indian Schoolboys of the Omaha Tribe* (1900; Lincoln: University of Nebraska Press, 1963); and Basil H. Johnston, *Indian School Days* (Norman: University of Oklahoma Press, 1989).

3. Ann Rinaldi, *My Heart Is on the Ground: The Diary of Nannie Little Rose, A Sioux Girl* (New York: Scholastic, 1999); and Bebe Faas Rice, *The Place at the Edge of the Earth* (New York: Clarion Books, 2002).

4. See the American Indian Lives series. Available online at www .hanksville.org/storytellers/AmIndLives.html (accessed August 7, 2004).

5. See Gretchen Bataille and Kathleen Mullen Sands, *American Indian Women: Telling Their Lives* (Lincoln: University of Nebraska Press, 1984); Arnold Krupat, *For Those Who Come After: A Study of Native American Autobiography* (Berkeley: University of California Press, 1985); H. David Brumble III, *American Indian Autobiography* (Berkeley: University of California Press, 1988); and Hertha Dawn Wong, *Sending My Heart Back Across the Years: Tradition and Innovation in Native American Autobiography* (New York: Oxford University Press, 1992).

6. Albert Marrin, *Plains Warrior: Chief Quanah Parker and the Comanches* (New York: Atheneum Books for Young Readers, 1996); hereafter referred to in text as *Plains Warrior*. The second Marrin title considered here is *Sitting Bull and His World* (New York: Dutton Children's Books, 2000); hereafter referred to in text as *Sitting Bull*.

7. Lisa Mitten, review of *Plains Warrior: Chief Quanah Parker and the Comanches*, by Albert Marrin, *School Library Journal* 42, no. 6 (June 1996), 161.

8. Sitting Bull College, available online at www.kevinlocke.com/sitbulcol.htm (accessed August 7, 2004).

9. *Wiping the Tears of Seven Generations* (documentary film by Kifaru Productions, 1992), available online at www.der.org/films/wiping-the-tears.html (accessed August 7, 2004).

10. Doris Seale and Beverly Slapin, Review of *Sitting Bull and His World* by Albert Marrin. *Oyate—Avoid Sitting Bull and His World*, 1. Available online at www.oyate.org/books-to-avoid/sittingBull.html; hereafter referred to in text as Oyate. For additional comments about this book, see "Turning a Battle into a Massacre" by Beverly Slapin at the same website. (accessed August 7, 2004).

11. Russell Freedman, *The Life and Death of Crazy Horse* (New York: Holiday House, 1996); hereafter referred to in text as Freedman.

12. Amos Bad Heart Bull et al., *A Pictographic History of the Oglala Sioux* (Lincoln: University of Nebraska Press, 1967).

13. Arlene B. Hirschfelder, *Photo Odyssey: Solomon Carvalho's Remarkable Western Adventure, 1853–54* (New York: Clarion Books, 2000); hereafter referred to in text as Hirschfelder.

14. Gabrielle Tayac, with photographer John Harrington, *Meet Naiche: A Native Boy from the Chesapeake Bay Area* (Washington, DC: National Museum of the American Indian, Smithsonian Institution in association with Beyond Words Publishing in Hillsboro, Oregon, 2002); hereafter referred to in text as Tayac.

15. Susan Secakuku, with photographer John Harrington, *Meet Mindy: A Native Girl from the Southwest* (Washington, DC: National Museum of the American Indian, Smithsonian Institution in association with Beyond Words Publishing in Hillsboro, Oregon, 2003); Miranda Belarde-Lewis, with photographer John Harrington, *Meet Lydia: A Native Girl from Southeast Alaska* (same publisher, 2004).

16. Tiana Bighorse, *Bighorse the Warrior*, ed. Noël Bennett (Tucson: University of Arizona Press, 1990); hereafter referred to in text as Bighorse.

17. Ann Turner, *The Girl Who Chased Away Sorrow: The Diary of Sarah Nita, A Navajo Girl, New Mexico, 1864* (New York: Scholastic, 1999).

18. Beverly Slapin, "A Critical Review of Ann Turner's *The Girl Who Chased Away Sorrow: The Diary of Sarah Nita, A Navajo Girl, New Mexico, 1864*." Oyate—Avoid *The Girl Who Chased Away Sorrow*. Available online at http://oyate.org/books-to-avoid/theChased.html (accessed 2004 August 7).

19. Melissa Kay Thompson, "A Sea of Good Intentions: Native Americans in Books for Children," *The Lion and the Unicorn* 25, no. 3 (September 2001), 363.

20. Joseph Bruchac, *Trails of Tears, Paths of Beauty* (Washington, DC: National Geographic Society, 2000).

21. Kenn Harper, *Give Me My Father's Body: The Life of Minik, The New York Eskimo* (1986; South Royalton, VT: Steerforth Press, 2000); hereafter referred to in text as Harper.

22. Roger C. Echo-Hawk and Walter R. Echo-Hawk, *Battlefields and Burial Grounds: The Indian Struggle to Protect Ancestral Graves in the United States* (Minneapolis: Lerner Publications, 1994).

23. Wilma Mankiller and Michael Wallis, *Mankiller: A Chief and Her People: An Autobiography by the Principal Chief of the Cherokee Nation* (New York: St. Martin's Press, 1993); hereafter referred to in text as Mankiller.

24. Delphine Red Shirt, *Bead on an Anthill, A Lakota Childhood* (Lincoln: University of Nebraska Press, 1998); hereafter referred to in text as *Bead*.

25. Delphine Red Shirt, *Turtle Lung Woman's Granddaughter* (Lincoln: University of Nebraska Press, 2002).

26. For more information on Delphine Red Shirt, see www.hanksville .org/storytellers/redshirt; and *Delphine Red Shirt—Voices from the Gaps*. http://voices.cla.umn.edu/newsite/authors/REDSHIRTdelphine.htm (accessed August 7, 2004).

27. Lori Arviso Alvord and Elizabeth Cohen Van Pelt, *The Scalpel and the Silver Bear: The First Navajo Woman Surgeon Combines Western Medicine and Traditional Healing* (New York: Bantam Books, 1999); hereafter referred to in text as Alvord.

28. Andrew Garrod and Colleen Larimore, eds., *First Person, First Peoples: Native American College Graduates Tell Their Life Stories* (Ithaca, NY: Cornell University Press, 1997).

29. Virginia Driving Hawk Sneve, *Completing the Circle* (Lincoln: University of Nebraska Press, 1995); hereafter referred to in text as Sneve.

30. For more information on *Virginia Driving Hawk Sneve,* see *Voices from the Gaps: Virginia Driving Hawk Sneve*, available online at http://voices.cla.umn .edu/newsite/authors/SNEVEvirginia.htm; and "Sneve to Receive 1997 Living Indian Treasure Award (9/12/97)," available online at www.usd.edu/urelations/ news/archives/1997/September/september10.html (accessed August 12, 2004).

31. Virginia Driving Hawk Sneve, *Grandpa Was a Cowboy & an Indian and Other Stories*. (Lincoln: University of Nebraska Press, 2000); hereafter referred to in text as *Grandpa*.

32. Jennifer Sanderson—The Argus Leader. "South Dakota Author Given Prestigious Award," in *Canku Ota* (Many Paths), December 30, 2000, 1. Available online at www.turtletrack.org/Issues00/Co12302000/CO_12302000_ Sneve.htm (accessed August 12, 2004).

Bibliography

This bibliography consists of eight sections, incorporating fiction, nonfiction, poetry, articles and essays, book reviews, and other references and resources cited in this publication. As the bibliographic entries include both recommended and non-recommended works, readers may need to consult the text for additional information about specific authors and titles for young adults. For sources with evaluative criteria to use in selecting materials, see the teacher resource section, with titles such as *American Indian Stereotypes in the World of Children* by Arlene Hirschfelder and others, and *Through Indian Eyes: The Native Experience in Books for Children* by Beverly Slapin and Doris Seale. A number of Internet sites, among them the American Indian Library Association and Oyate, are excellent resources as well.

SELECTED FICTION FOR YOUNG ADULTS AND ADULTS

Alexie, Sherman. *Ten Little Indians: Stories.* New York: Grove Press, 2003.
———. *The Lone Ranger and Tonto Fistfight in Heaven.* New York: The Atlantic Monthly Press, 1993.
Bennett, James. *Dakota Dream.* New York: Scholastic, 1994.
Brashear, Charles. *Killing Cynthia Ann.* Fort Worth: Texas Christian University, 1999.
✓ Broker, Ignatia. *Night Flying Woman: An Ojibway Narrative.* St. Paul: Minnesota Historical Society Press, 1983.
Brooks, Martha. *Bone Dance.* New York: Bantam Doubleday Dell Books for Young Readers, 1997.

Bruchac, Joseph. *Eagle Song*. New York: Dial Books, 1997.

———. *The Heart of a Chief*. New York: Puffin Books, 2001.

———. *The Journal of Jesse Smoke: A Cherokee Boy, Trail of Tears, 1838*. New York: Scholastic, 2001.

———. *Sacajawea*. New York: Silver Whistle, Harcourt, 2000.

———. *Skeleton Man*. New York: HarperCollins, 2001.

———. *The Winter People*. New York: Dial Books, 2002.

Cannon, A. E. *The Shadow Brothers*. New York: Bantam Doubleday Dell Books for Young Readers, 1992; originally published in 1990.

Carvell, Marlene. *Who Will Tell My Brother?* New York: Hyperion Paperbacks for Children, 2002.

Charbonneau, Eileen. *The Ghosts of Stony Clove*. New York: Scholastic, 1988.

———. *Honor to the Hills*. New York: Tor, 1996.

———. *In the Time of the Wolves*. New York: Tor, 1994.

———. *Rachel LeMoyne*. New York: Forge, 1998.

Chibbaro, Julie. *Redemption*. New York: Atheneum, 2004.

Conley, Robert. *Mountain Windsong: A Novel of the Trail of Tears*. Norman: University of Oklahoma Press, 1992.

Cook-Lynn, Elizabeth. *From the River's Edge*. New York: Arcade Publishing, 1991.

Cooney, Caroline B. *The Ransom of Mercy Carter*. New York: Delacorte, 2001.

Culleton, Beatrice. *In Search of April Raintree*. Winnipeg, Manitoba: Pemmican Publications, 1983.

Deloria, Ella Cara. *Waterlily*. Lincoln: University of Nebraska Press, 1988.

Dorris, Michael. *Cloud Chamber*. New York: Scribner, 1997.

———. *Guests*. New York: Hyperion, 1994.

———. *Morning Girl*. New York: Hyperion Books for Children, 1992.

———. *Sees Behind Trees*. New York: Hyperion, 1996.

———. *The Window*. New York: Hyperion, 1997.

———. *A Yellow Raft in Blue Water*. New York: Henry Holt and Company, 1987.

Durrant, Lynda. *The Beaded Moccasins: The Story of Mary Campbell*. New York: Clarion Books, 1998.

———. *Echohawk*. New York: Clarion Books, 1996.

———. *Turtle Clan Journey*. New York: Clarion Books, 1999.

Easley, MaryAnn. *I Am the Ice Worm*. New York: Bantam Doubleday Dell Books for Young Readers, 1996.

Erdrich, Louise. *The Birchbark House*. New York: Hyperion Books for Children, 1999.

Fleischman, Paul. *Saturnalia*. New York: Harper & Row, 1990.

Gregory, Kristiana. *The Legend of Jimmy Spoon*. New York: Harcourt Brace Jovanovich, 1990.

Hale, Janet Campbell. *The Owl's Song*. New York: Doubleday, 1974.

Hardy, Aurora. *Terror at Black Rapids*. Baltimore: PublishAmerica, 2004.

Harrell, Beatrice Orcutt. *Longwalker's Journey: A Novel of the Choctaw Trail of Tears*. New York: Dial Books for Young Readers, 1999.

Harris, Christie. *Raven's Cry*. 1966. Reprint, Seattle: University of Washington, 1992.

Hesse, Karen. *Aleutian Sparrow*. New York: Margaret K. McElderry Books, 2003.

Hobbs, Will. *Beardance*. New York: Bradbury Press, 1993; New York: Avon Camelot, 1995.

———. *Bearstone*. New York: Atheneum, 1989; New York: Avon Camelot, 1991.

———. *Far North*. New York: William Morrow, 1996.

———. *Ghost Canoe*. New York: William Morrow, 1997.

———. *Kokopelli's Flute*. New York: Atheneum, 1995.

Hoklotubbe, Sara Sue. *Deception on All Accounts*. Tucson: University of Arizona Press, 2003.

Hotze, Sollace. *A Circle Unbroken*. New York: Clarion Books, 1988.

Hudson, Jan. *Dawn Rider*. New York: Philomel Books, 1990; New York: Puffin Books, 2000.

———. *Sweetgrass*. Canada: Tree Frog Press, 1984; New York: Penguin Putnam Books for Young Readers, 1999.

Keehn, Sally M. *I am Regina*. New York: Philomel Books, 1991.

———. *Moon of Two Dark Horses*. New York: Philomel Books, 1995.

Kersey, Colin. *Soul Catcher*. New York: St. Martin's Press, 1995.

King, Thomas. *Medicine River*. Toronto: Penguin Books Canada Limited, 1989.

———. *Truth & Bright Water*. Toronto: HarperCollins, 1999.

Kirkpatrick, Katherine. *Trouble's Daughter: The Story of Susanna Hutchinson, Indian Captive*. New York: Delacorte Press, 1998.

Lenski, Lois. *Indian Captive: The Story of Mary Jemison*. 1941. Reprint, New York: First Harper Trophy edition, 1995.

Lipsyte, Robert. *The Brave*. New York: Harper Trophy, 1991.

———. *The Chief*. New York: Harper Trophy, 1993.

———. *The Contender*. New York: Harper Trophy, 1967.

———. *Warrior Angel*. New York: HarperCollins, 2003.

Markoosie. *Harpoon of the Hunter*. Montreal: McGill-Queen's University Press, 1970.

Matcheck, Diane. *The Sacrifice*. New York: Puffin Books, 1999.

Meyer, Carolyn. *Where the Broken Heart Still Beats: The Story of Cynthia Ann Parker*. New York: Harcourt Brace, 1992.

Mikaelsen, Ben. *Touching Spirit Bear*. New York: Scholastic, 2002.

Moore, Robin. *Maggie among the Seneca*. New York: J. B. Lippincott, 1987.

Mosioner, Beatrice Culleton. *In Search of April Raintree*, Critical Edition, ed. Cheryl Suzack. Winnipeg, MB: Portage & Main Press, 1999.

Northrup, Jim. *Walking the Rez Road.* Stillwater, MN: Voyageur Press, 1993.

Osborne, Mary Pope. *Standing in the Light: The Captive Diary of Catherine Carey Logan.* New York: Scholastic, 2000.

Power, Susan. *The Grass Dancer.* New York: G. P. Putnam's Sons, 1994.

———. *Roofwalker.* Minneapolis, MN: Milkweed Editions, 2002.

Rice, Bebe Faas. *The Place at the Edge of the Earth.* New York: Clarion Books, 2002.

Rinaldi, Ann. *The Blue Door.* New York: Scholastic Press, 1996.

———. *My Heart Is on the Ground: The Diary of Nannie Little Rose, A Sioux Girl.* New York: Scholastic, 1999.

———. *The Second Bend in the River.* New York: Scholastic, 1997.

Robinson, Margaret A. *A Woman of Her Tribe.* New York: Charles Scribner's Sons, 1990.

Rockwood, Joyce. *To Spoil the Sun.* New York: Holt, Rinehart and Winston, 1976.

———. *Apalachee.* Athens: University of Georgia Press, 2000.

———. *Groundhog's Horse.* New York: Holt, Rinehart and Winston, 1978.

———. *Long Man's Song.* New York: Henry Holt and Company, 1975.

Sawyer, Don. *Where the Rivers Meet.* Winnipeg, MB: Pemmican Publications, 1988.

Smith, Cynthia Leitich. *Indian Shoes.* New York: HarperCollins, 2002.

———. *Jingle Dancer.* New York: Morrow, 2002 [children's book].

———. *Rain Is Not My Indian Name.* New York: HarperCollins, 2001.

Smith, Patricia Clark. *Weetamoo: Heart of the Pocassets.* New York: Scholastic, 2003.

Sneve, Virginia Driving Hawk. *Grandpa Was a Cowboy & an Indian & Other Stories.* Lincoln: University of Nebraska Press, 2000.

Speare, Elizabeth George. *Calico Captive.* 1957. New York: Bantam Doubleday Dell Books for Young Readers, 1989.

———. *The Sign of the Beaver.* New York: Bantam Doubleday Dell Books for Young Readers, 1984.

Sterling, Shirley. *My Name Is Seepeetza.* Toronto, ON: Douglas & McIntyre, 1992.

Strete, Craig. *The Bleeding Man and Other Science Fiction Stories.* New York: Greenwillow Books, 1974.

Turner, Ann. *The Girl Who Chased Away Sorrow: The Diary of Sarah Nita, A Navajo Girl, New Mexico, 1864.* New York: Scholastic, 1999.

Van Camp, Richard. *The Lesser Blessed.* Vancouver, BC: Douglas & McIntyre, 1996.

Wilder, Laura Ingalls. *Little House in the Big Woods.* 1932. Reprint, New York: Harper Trophy Edition, 1971.

Willis, Patricia. *Danger Along the Ohio.* New York: Clarion Books, 1997.

Young Bear, Ray A. *Remnants of the First Earth.* New York: Grove Press, 1996.

POETRY AND OTHER WRITINGS
BY AMERICAN INDIAN YOUTH*

*See the text and other sections of the bibliography for additional publications incorporating writings and other creative expression by American Indian youth.

Francis, Lee et al., eds. *When the Rain Sings: Poems by Young Native Americans.* New York: Simon & Schuster Books for Young Readers, 1999.

Hirschfelder, Arlene B., and Beverly R. Singer, selectors. *Rising Voices: Writings of Young Native Americans.* New York: Charles Scribner's Sons, 1992 [poems and essays by younger writers].

Ochoa, Annette Piña, Betsy Franco, and Traci L. Gourdine, eds. *Night Is Gone, Day Is Still Coming: Stories and Poems by American Indian Teens and Young Adults.* Cambridge, MA: Candlewick Press, 2003.

Philip, Neil, selector. *Earth Always Endures: Native American Poems.* New York: Viking, 1996.

SELECTED NONFICTION FOR
YOUNG ADULTS AND ADULTS

Allen, Paula Gunn and Patricia Clark Smith. *As Long as the Rivers Flow: The Stories of Nine Native Americans.* New York: Scholastic, 1996.

Alvord, Lori Arviso, and Elizabeth Cohen Van Pelt. *The Scalpel and the Silver Bear: The First Navajo Woman Surgeon Combines Western Medicine and Traditional Healing.* New York: Bantam Books, 1999.

Bad Heart Bull, Amos et al. *A Pictographic History of the Oglala Sioux.* Lincoln: University of Nebraska Press, 1967.

Bataille, Gretchen, and Kathleen Mullen Sands. *American Indian Women: Telling Their Lives.* Lincoln: University of Nebraska Press, 1984.

Belarde-Lewis, Miranda, with photographer John Harrington. *Meet Lydia: A Native Girl from Southeast Alaska.* Washington, DC: National Museum of the American Indian, Smithsonian Institution, in association with Beyond Words Publishing in Hillsboro, Oregon, 2004.

Bergstrom, Amy, Linda Miller Cleary, and Thomas D. Peacock. *The Seventh Generation: Native Students Speak about Finding the Good Path.* Charleston, WV: ERIC Clearinghouse on Rural Education and Small Schools, 2003.

Bighorse, Tiana. *Bighorse the Warrior*, ed. Noël Bennett. Tucson: University of Arizona Press, 1990.

Brashear, Charles. *Killing Cynthia Ann*. Fort Worth: Texas Christian University, 1999.

Brown, Tricia and Roy Corral (Photographer). *Children of the Midnight Sun: Young Native Voices of Alaska*. Portland, OR: Alaska Northwest Books, 1998.

Bruchac, Joseph. *Bowman's Store: A Journey to Myself*. New York: Dial Books, 1997.

————. *Trails of Tears, Paths of Beauty: The Story of the Navajos and the Cherokees*. Washington, DC: National Geographic Society, 2000.

Brumble, H. David, III. *American Indian Autobiography*. Berkeley: University of California Press, 1988.

Cox, Loretta Outwater. *The Winter Walk: A Century-Old Survival Story from the Arctic*. Anchorage: Alaska Northwest Books, 2003.

Eastman, Charles Alexander. *Indian Boyhood*. 1902. Reprint, Norman: University of Nebraska Press, 1991.

Echo-Hawk, Roger C., and Walter R. Echo-Hawk. *Battlefields and Burial Grounds: The Indian Struggle to Protect Ancestral Graves in the United States*. Minneapolis, MN: Lerner Publications Company, 1994.

Erdrich, Louise. *Books and Islands in Ojibwe Country*. Washington, DC: National Geographic Society, 2003.

Freedman, Russell. *The Life and Death of Crazy Horse*. New York: Holiday House, 1996.

Garrod, Andrew, and Colleen Larimore, eds. *First Person, First Peoples: Native American College Graduates Tell Their Life Stories*. Ithaca, NY: Cornell University Press, 1997.

Greenberg, Henry, and Georgia Greenberg. *Power of a Navajo: Carl Gorman: The Man and His Life*. Santa Fe, NM: Clear Light Publishers, 1996.

Hager, Barbara. *Honour Song: A Tribute*. Vancouver, BC: Raincoast Books, 1996.

Hale, Frederick. *Janet Campbell Hale*. Boise, ID: Boise State University, 1996.

Harper, Kenn. *Give Me My Father's Body: The Life of Minik, the New York Eskimo*. 1986. South Royalton, VT: Steerforth Press, 2000.

Harris, LaDonna, and H. Henrietta Stockel, ed. *LaDonna Harris: A Comanche Life*. Lincoln: University of Nebraska Press, 2000.

Hirschfelder, Arlene B. *Photo Odyssey: Solomon Carvalho's Remarkable Western Adventure, 1853–54*. New York: Clarion Books, 2000.

Hogan, Linda. *The Woman Who Watches Over the World: A Native Memoir*. New York: W. W. Norton, 2001.

Hoig, Stanley. *Night of the Cruel Moon: Cherokee Removal and the Trail of Tears*. New York: Facts On File, 1996.

Hubbard, Jim, ed. *Shooting Back: A Photographic View of Life by Homeless Children*. San Francisco: Chronicle Books, 1991.

———. *Shooting Back from the Reservation: A Photographic View of Life by Native American Youth*. New York: The New Press, 1994.

Hucko, Bruce. *Where There Is No Name for Art: The Art of Tewa Pueblo Children*. Santa Fe, NM: School of American Research, 1996.

———. *A Rainbow at Night: The World in Words and Pictures by Navajo Children*. San Francisco: Chronicle Books, 1997.

Johnston, Basil H. *Crazy Dave*. Toronto: Key Porter Books, 1999; St. Paul: Minnesota Historical Society Press, 2002.

Katz, William Loren and Paula A. Franklin. *Proudly Red and Black: Stories of African and Native Americans*. New York: Atheneum, 1993.

———. *Indian School Days*. Norman: University of Oklahoma Press, 1989.

Kawano, Kenji. *Warriors: Navajo Code Talkers*. Flagstaff, AZ: Northland Publishing Company, 1990.

Krupat, Arnold. *For Those Who Come After: A Study of Native American Autobiography*. Berkeley: University of California Press, 1985.

LaDuke, Winona. *All Our Relations: Native Struggles for Land and Life*. Cambridge, MA: South End Press, 1999.

La Flesche, Francis. *The Middle Five: Indian Schoolboys of the Omaha Tribe*. Lincoln: University of Nebraska Press, 1978 (reprint, originally published in 1900).

Lee, George P. *Silent Courage, An Indian Story: The Autobiography of George P. Lee, A Navajo*. Salt Lake City, UT: Deseret Book Company, 1987.

Lipsyte, Robert. *Jim Thorpe: 20th-Century Jock*. New York: HarperCollins, 1993.

MacDonald, Peter. *The Last Warrior: Peter MacDonald and the Navajo Nation*. New York: Crown Publishers, 1993.

Mankiller, Wilma, and Michael Wallis. *Mankiller: A Chief and Her People: An Autobiography by the Principal Chief of the Cherokee Nation*. New York: St. Martin's Press, 1993.

Marrin, Albert. *Plains Warrior: Chief Quanah Parker and the Comanches*. New York: Atheneum Books for Young Readers, 1996.

———. *Sitting Bull and His World*. New York: Dutton Children's Books, 2000.

Meadows, William C. *The Comanche Code Talkers of World War II*. Austin: University of Texas Press, 2003.

Nabokov, Peter. *Indian Running*. Santa Barbara, CA: Capra Press, 1981.

Nasdijj. *The Blood Runs Like a River Through My Dreams*. New York: Houghton Mifflin, 2000.

Northrup, Jim. *The Rez Road Follies*. New York: Kodansha America, 1997.

Red Shirt, Delphine. *Bead on an Anthill: A Lakota Childhood*. Lincoln: University of Nebraska Press, 1998.

———. *Turtle Lung Woman's Granddaughter*. Lincoln: University of Nebraska Press, 2002.

Riley, Patricia, ed. *Growing Up Native American: An Anthology.* New York: William Morrow, 1993.

Sarris, Greg. *Mabel McKay: Weaving the Dream.* Berkeley: University of California Press, 1994.

Secakuku, Susan, with photographer John Harrington. *Meet Mindy: A Native Girl from the Southwest.* Washington, DC: National Museum of the American Indian, Smithsonian Institution in association with Beyond Words Publishing in Hillsboro, Oregon, 2003.

Silverstone, Michael. *Winona LaDuke: Restoring Land and Culture in Native America.* New York: The Feminist Press at the City University of New York, 2001.

Smith, Donald B. *Chief Buffalo Child Long Lance: The Glorious Impostor.* Red Deer, Alberta: Red Deer Press, 1999.

Sneve, Virginia Driving Hawk. *Completing the Circle.* Lincoln: University of Nebraska Press, 1995.

Standing Bear, Luther. *My People the Sioux.* Lincoln: University of Nebraska Press, 1975.

Tayac, Gabrielle, with photographer John Harrington. *Meet Naiche: A Native Boy from the Chesapeake Bay Area.* Washington, DC: National Museum of the American Indian, Smithsonian Institution, in association with Beyond Words Publishing in Hillsboro, Oregon, 2002.

Viola, Herman J. *It Is a Good Day to Die: Indian Eyewitnesses Tell the Story of the Battle of the Little Bighorn.* New York: Crown Publishers, 1998.

Wallis, Velma. *Raising Ourselves: A Gwichi'in Coming of Age Story from the Yukon River.* Kenmore, WA: Epicenter Press, 2002.

Welch, James, with Paul Stekler. *Killing Custer: The Battle of the Little Bighorn and the Fate of the Plains Indians.* New York: W. W. Norton & Company, 1994.

Wong, Hertha Dawn. *Sending My Heart Back Across the Years: Tradition and Innovation in Native American Autobiography.* New York: Oxford University Press, 1992.

Young Bear, Ray A. *Black Eagle Child: The Facepaint Narratives.* Iowa City: University of Iowa Press, 1992.

ARTICLES AND ESSAYS*

*Other articles and essays are cited in the Internet section.

Bader, Barbara. "Multiculturalism in the Mainstream." *The Horn Book Magazine* (May/June 2003): 265–91.

Bevis, William. "Native American Novels: Homing In." In *Recovering the Word: Essays on Native American Literature,* ed. Brian Swann and Arnold Krupat. Berkeley: University of California Press, 1987.

Bigelow, Bill. "Good Intentions Are Not Enough: Recent Children's Books on the Columbus-Taino Encounter." In *Rethinking Columbus: The Next 500 Years*, 2nd ed., ed. Bill Bigelow and Bob Peterson. Milwaukee, WI: Rethinking Schools, 1998.

Bovey, Seth. "Markoosie's Harpoon of the Hunter: A Story of Cultural Survival." *American Indian Quarterly* XV, no. 2 (Spring 1991): 217–23.

Bruchac, Joseph. "All Our Relations." *The Horn Book Magazine* (March-April 1995): 158–62.

———. "Indian Scenes from a Renaissance." *National Geographic* 206, no. 3 (September 2004): 76–95.

Bush, Elizabeth. "A Conversation with Ann Rinaldi, Author." *The New Advocate* 14, no. 4 (2001): 311–19.

Byler, Mary Gloyne. "The Image of American Indians Projected by Non-Indian Writers." *Library Journal* (February 1974): 546–49.

Charles, Jim. "Contemporary American Indian Life in *The Owl's Song* and *Smoke Signals*." *English Journal* 90, no. 3 (January 2001): 54–59.

———. "Out of the Cupboard and into the Classroom: Children and the American Indian Literary Experience." *Children's Literature in Education* 27, no. 3 (1996): 167–79.

Churchill, Ward. "Literature as a Weapon in the Colonization of the American Indian." In *Fantasies of the Master Race: Literature, Cinema and the Colonization of American Indians*, ed. M. Annette Jaimes. Monroe, ME: Common Courage Press, 1992.

Cohen, Sandra. "The Sign of the Beaver: The Problem and the Solution." In *American Indian Stereotypes in the World of Children*, 2nd edition, ed. Arlene Hirschfelder, Paulette Fairbanks Molin, and Yvonne Wakim. Lanham, MD: Scarecrow Press, 1999.

Damm, Kateri. "Dispelling and Telling: Speaking Native Realities in Maria Campbell's *Halfbreed* and Beatrice Culleton's *In Search of April Raintree*." In *Looking at the Words of Our People: First Nations Analysis of Literature*, ed. Jeannette Armstrong. Penticton, British Columbia: Theytus Books, 1993.

Deloria, Vine, Jr. "Secularism, Civil Religion, and the Religious Freedom of American Indians." *American Indian Culture and Research Journal* 16, no. 2 (1992): 9–20.

Dorris, Michael. "'I' Is Not for Indian." In *Through Indian Eyes: The Native Experience in Books for Children*, ed. Beverly Slapin and Doris Seale. 1987. Reprint, Philadephia: New Society Publishers, 1992.

———. "Indians on the Shelf." In *The American Indian and the Problem of History*, ed. Calvin Martin. New York: Oxford University Press, 1987.

———. "Trusting the Words." *Booklist* 89, no. 19–20 (1 June 1993): 1820–1822.

——. "Waiting to Listen." *The Horn Book Magazine* (November-December 1995): 698-703.

——. "Why I'm Not Thankful for Thanksgiving." In *Through Indian Eyes: The Native Experience in Books for Children*, ed. Beverly Slapin and Doris Seale. 1987. Reprint, Philadelphia: New Society Publishers, 1992.

Erdrich, Louise. "Where I Ought to Be: A Writer's Sense of Place." *New York Times Book Review*, 28 July 1985, 1, 23–24.

Fee, Margery. "Deploying Identity in the Face of Racism." In *In Search of April Raintree*, Critical Edition, Beatrice Culleton Mosioner and ed. Cheryl Suzack. Winnipeg, Manitoba: Portage & Main Press, 1999.

Gardner, Susan. "The Education of Joseph Bruchac, Conversations: 1995–1997." *Paintbrush* XXIV (Autumn 1997): 16–44.

——. "My First Rhetoric of Domination: The Columbian Encounter in Children's Biographies." *Children's Literature in Education*, 22, no. 4 (1991): 275–90.

Giago, Tim. "Indians Don't Rely on Gambling, Charity." *Daily Press*, 22 January 2004, A11.

Grant, Agnes. "Abuse and Violence: April Raintree's Human Rights (If She Had Any)." In *In Search of April Raintree*, Critical Edition, Beatrice Culleton Mosioner and ed. Cheryl Suzack. Winnipeg: Portage & Main Press, 1999.

Green, Rayna. "The Tribe Called Wannabee: Playing Indian in America and Europe." In *Aniyunwiya/Real Human Beings: An Anthology of Contemporary Cherokee Prose*, ed. Joseph Bruchac. Greenfield Center, NY: Greenfield Review Press, 1995.

Hale, Frederick. "Dreams and Vision Quests in Janet Campbell Hale's *The Owl's Song*." *Studies in American Indian Literatures* 12, no. 1 (Spring 2000): 69–82.

Herbst, Laura. "That's One Good Indian: Unacceptable Images in Children's Novels." *Top of the News* (January 1975): 192–98.

Hirschfelder, Arlene B. "Native American Literature for Children and Young Adults." *Library Trends* 41, no. 3 (Winter 1993): 414–36.

Horning, Kathleen T., and Ginny Moore Kruse. "Looking into the Mirror: Considerations behind the Reflections." In *The Multicolored Mirror: Cultural Substance in Literature for Children and Young Adults*, ed. Merri V. Lindgren. Fort Atkinson, WI: Highsmith, 1991.

Hoy, Helen. "'Nothing But the Truth': Discursive Transparency in Beatrice Culleton." In *In Search of April Raintree*, Critical Edition. Beatrice Culleton Mosionier and ed. Cheryl Suzack. Winnipeg: Portage & Main Press, 1999.

Hunter, Sally M. "American Indian Literature." *The Five Owls* VII, no. 3 (January/February 1993): 49–51.

LaBonty, Jan. "A Demand for Excellence in Books for Children." *Journal of American Indian Education* (Winter 1995): 1–9.

LaRocque, Emma. "Here Are Our Voices—Who Will Hear?" Preface to *Writing the Circle: Native Women of Western Canada*, compiled and edited by Jeanne Perreault and Sylvia Vance. Norman: University of Oklahoma Press, 1993.

Lehman, Carolyn. "Gold Rush and Genocide: What Are We Telling Children about Our Bloody Past." *School Library Journal* 44, no. 9 (September 1998): 118–19.

Lewis, Magda. "'Are Indians Nicer Now?': What Children Learn from Books about Native North Americans." In *How Much Truth Do We Tell the Children? The Politics of Children's Literature*, ed. Betty Bacon. Minneapolis, MN: MEP Publications, 1988.

MacCann, Donnarae. "Native Americans in Books for the Young." In *Teaching Multicultural Literature in Grades K–8*, ed. Violet J. Harris. Norwood, MA: Christopher-Gordon Publishers, 1993.

Mihesuah, Devon A., ed. Special Issue, "Writing about (Writing about) American Indians," *American Indian Quarterly* 20, no. 1 (Winter 1996).

Mitten, Lisa, ed. Special Issue, "Children's Literature," *Studies in American Indian Literatures* 12, no. 1 (Spring 2000).

Mosionier, Beatrice Culleton. "The Special Time." In *In Search of April Raintree*, Ciritical Edition, Beatrice Culleton Mosionier and ed. Cheryl Suzack. Winnipeg: Portage & Main Press, 1999.

Murphy, Nora. "Starting Children on the Path to the Past: American Indians in Children's Historical Fiction." *Minnesota History* 57, no. 6 (Summer 2001): 184–95.

Neubauer, Paul. "Indian Captivity in American Children's Literature: A Pre-Civil War Set of Stereotypes." *The Lion and the Unicorn* 25 (2001): 70–80.

Pearce, Roy Harvey. "The Significance of the Captivity Narrative." *American Literature* 19 (March 1949): 1–20.

Reese, Debbie. "Authenticity and Sensitivity: Goals for Writing and Reviewing Books with Native American Themes." *School Library Journal* 45, no. 11 (Novermber 1999): 36–37.

———. "Mom, Look! It's George, and He's a TV Indian!" *The Horn Book* (September–October 1998): 636–43.

Reese, Debbie A., and Naomi Caldwell-Wood. "Native Americans in Children's Literature." In *Using Multiethnic Literature in the K–8 Classroom*, ed. Violet J. Harris. Norwood, MA: Christopher-Gordon Publishers, 1997.

Roberts, David. "The Long Walk to Bosque Redondo." *Smithsonian* 28, no. 9 (December 1997): 46–57.

Seale, Doris. "Bibliographies about Native Americans—A Mixed Blessing." *Interracial Books for Children* 12, no. 3 (1981): 11–15.

Shanley, Kathryn. "The Indians America Loves to Love and Read: American Indian Identity and Cultural Appropriation." *American Indian Quarterly* 21, no. 4 (Fall 1997): 675–702.

———. "The Lived Experience: American Indian Literature After Alcatraz." *Native Expressive Culture*, XI, nos. 3 and 4 (Fall/Winter 1994): 119–27.

Strong, Pauline Turner. "Captive Images." *Natural History* (December 1985): 50–57.

Taxel, Joel. "The Politics of Children's Literature: Reflections on Multiculturalism and Christopher Columbus." In *Teaching Multicultural Literature in Grades K–8*, ed. Violet J. Harris. Norwood, MA: Christopher-Gordon Publishers, 1993.

Thom, Jo-Ann. "The Effects of Readers' Responses on the Development of Aboriginal Literature in Canada: A Study of Maria Campbell's *Halfbreed*, Beatrice Culleton's *In Search of April Raintree*, and Richard Wagamese's *Keeper'n Me*." In *In Search of April Raintree*, Critical Edition, Beatrice Culleton Mosioner and ed. Cheryl Suzack. Winnipeg: Portage & Main Press, 1999.

Thompson, Melissa Kay. "A Sea of Good Intentions: Native Americans in Books for Children." *The Lion and the Unicorn* 25, no. 3 (September 2001): 353–74.

Trafzer, Clifford E. "'The Word Is Sacred to a Child': American Indians and Children's Literature." *American Indian Quarterly* 16, no. 3 (Summer 1992): 381–95.

Weaver, Jace. "Native American Authors and Their Communities." *Wicazo Sa Review* 12, no. 1 (Spring 1997): 47–87.

BOOK REVIEWS CITED*

*Other book reviews are cited in the Internet section.

Alexie, Sherman. "Some of My Best Friends." Review of *On the Rez*, by Ian Frazier. *Los Angeles Times*, 23 January 2000, 3.

Atleo, Marlene et al. "Fiction Posing as Truth: A Critical Review of Ann Rinaldi's *My Heart Is on the Ground: The Diary of Nannie Little Rose, A Sioux Girl*." *Rethinking Schools* (Summer 1999): 14–16.

———. "*My Heart Is on the Ground* and the Boarding School Experience." *Multicultural Review* 8 (September 1999): 41–46.

Bliss, Liza. Review of *Danger Along the Ohio*, by Patricia Willis. *School Library Journal* 43, no. 5 (May 1997): 140.

Brautigam, Faith. Review of *My Heart Is on the Ground: The Diary of Nannie Little Rose, A Sioux Girl*, by Ann Rinaldi. *School Library Journal* 45, no. 4 (April 1999): 141.

Bush, Elizabeth. Review of *My Heart Is on the Ground: The Diary of Nannie Little Rose, A Sioux Girl*, by Ann Rinaldi. *The Bulletin of the Center for Children's Books* 52, no. 6 (February 1999): 215.

Edwards, Carol A. Review of *The Place at the Edge of the Earth*, by Bebe Faas Rice. *School Library Journal* 48, no. 12 (December 2002): 146.

Frey, Yvonne A. Review of *Sweetgrass*, by Jan Hudson. *School Library Journal* 35, no. 8 (April 1989): 102.

Gleason, George. Review of *The Shadow Brothers*, by A. E. Cannon. *School Library Journal* 36, no. 6 (June 1990): 137.

Jaffee, Cyrisse. Review of *I Am the Ice Worm*, by MaryAnn Easley. *School Library Journal* 42, no. 11 (November 1996): 104.

Kirkus Reviews 61 (May 15, 1993): 664. Review of *The Chief*, by Robert Lipsyte.

Kirkus Reviews 67 (February 1, 1999): 228. Review of *My Heart Is on the Ground: The Diary of Nannie Little Rose, A Sioux Girl*, by Ann Rinaldi.

Korbeck, Sharon. Review of *Earth Always Endures: Native American Poems*, by Neil Philip. *School Library Journal* 42, no. 11 (November 1996): 130.

McDougall, M. Colleen. Review of *Battlefields and Burial Grounds: The Indian Struggle to Protect Ancestral Graves in the United States*, by Roger C. Echo-Hawk and Walter R. Echo-Hawk. *School Library Journal* 40, no. 7 (July 1994): 122.

Meyer, Randy. Review of *Children of the Midnight Sun: Young Native Voices of Alaska*, by Tricia Brown. *Booklist* 94, no. 21 (July 1998): 1874.

Mitten, Lisa. Review of *Plains Warrior: Chief Quanah Parker and the Comanches*, by Albert Marrin. *School Library Journal* 42, no. 6 (June 1996): 161.

Molin, Paulette F. "Dear Diary, Dear America: Commentary on Ann Rinaldi's *My Heart Is on the Ground*." *HONOR Digest* 10, no. 3 (May/June 1999): 4.

——. "Dear Diary, Dear America: Commentary on Ann Rinaldi's *My Heart Is on the Ground*. In *They Taught You Wrong: Raising Cultural Consciousness of Stereotypes and Misconceptions about American Indians*, Kathy Kerner. 1995. Lynchburg, VA: O.L. and Carole Durham Publishers, 2000 edition.

Moore, MariJo. "'Artistic License' Should Be Revoked If It Involves the Rewriting of History." Review of *My Heart Is on the Ground: The Diary of Nannie Little Rose, A Sioux Girl*, by Ann Rinaldi. *Studies in American Indian Literature* 12, no. 1 (Spring 2000): 83–85.

Morning, Todd. Review of *Beardance*, by Will Hobbs. *School Library Journal* 39, no. 12 (December 1993): 134.

Publishers Weekly 242, no. 38 (18 September 1995): 110. Review of *Soul Catcher*, by Colin Kersey.

—— 244, no. 2 (13 January 1997): 76–77. Review of *The Second Bend in the River*, by Ann Rinaldi.

Roback, Diane. Review of *Saturnalia*, by Paul Fleischman. *Publishers Weekly* 237, no. 11 (16 March 1990): 72.

Rochman, Hazel. Review of *The Birchbark House*, by Louise Erdrich. *Booklist* 95, no. 15 (1 April 1999): 1427.

Schadle, Carrie. Review of *The Second Bend in the River*, by Ann Rinaldi. *School Library Journal* 43, no. 6 (June 1997): 126.

Soltan, Rita. Review of *The Winter People*, by Joseph Bruchac. *School Library Journal* 48, no. 11 (November 2002): 154–55.

Weisman, Kay. Review of *The Second Bend in the River*, by Ann Rinaldi. *Booklist* 93, no. 12 (February 15, 1997): 1016.

Zvirin, Stephanie. Review of *My Heart Is on the Ground: The Diary of Nannie Little Rose, A Sioux Girl*, by Ann Rinaldi. *Booklist* 95, no. 15 (1 April 1999):1428.

SELECTED RESOURCES FOR TEACHERS

Bigelow, Bill, and Bob Peterson, eds. *Rethinking Columbus: The Next 500 Years: Resources for Teaching about the Impact of the Arrival of Columbus in the Americas*. 2nd ed. Milwaukee: Rethinking Schools, 1998.

Cleary, Linda Miller, and Thomas D. Peacock. *Collected Wisdom: American Indian Education*. Boston: Allyn and Bacon, 1998.

Davis, Mary B., ed. *Native America in the Twentieth Century: An Encyclopedia*. New York: Garland Publishing, 1994.

Francis, Lee, and James Bruchac, eds. *Reclaiming the Vision: Native Voices for the Eighth Generation*. New York: Greenfield Review Press, 1996.

Hirschfelder, Arlene, and Yvonne Beamer. *Native Americans Today: Resources and Activities for Educators, Grades 4–8*. Englewood, CO: Teacher Ideas Press, 2000.

Hirschfelder, Arlene, Paulette Fairbanks Molin, and Yvonne Wakim. *American Indian Stereotypes in the World of Children*. 2nd ed. Lanham, MD: Scarecrow Press, 1999.

Hoxie, Frederick E., ed. *Encyclopedia of North American Indians: Native American History, Culture, and Life from Paleo-Indians to the Present*. New York: Houghton Mifflin, 1996.

Kuipers, Barbara J. *American Indian Reference and Resource Books for Children and Young Adults*. 2nd edition. Englewood, CO: Libraries Unlimited, 1995.

Mihesuah, Devon. *American Indians: Stereotypes & Realities*. Atlanta: Clarity Press, 1996.

Seale, Doris, Beverly Slapin, and Carolyn Silverman, eds. *Thanksgiving: A Native Perspective*. Berkeley: Oyate, 1995.

Slapin, Beverly, and Doris Seale, eds. *Through Indian Eyes: The Native Experience in Books for Children*. Philadelphia, PA: New Society Publishers, 1992.

Smith, Linda Tuhiwai. *Decolonizing Methodologies: Research and Indigenous Peoples*. London and New York: Zed Books, 1999.

Susag, Dorothea M. *Roots and Branches: A Resource of Native American Literature—Themes, Lessons, and Bibliographies*. Urbana, IL: National Council of Teachers of English, 1998.

OTHER WORKS OF FICTION AND NONFICTION

Alfred, Taiaiake. *Peace, Power, Righteousness: An Indigenous Manifesto.* Toronto: Oxford University Press, 1999.

Archuleta, Margaret L., Brenda J. Child, and K. Tsianina Lomawaima, eds. *Away from Home: American Indian Boarding School Experiences, 1879–2000.* Phoenix, AZ: The Heard Museum, 2000.

Armstrong, Jeannette, ed. *Looking at the Words of Our People: First Nations Analysis of Literature.* Penticton, British Columbia: Theytus Books, 1993.

Axtell, James. *The Invasion Within: The Contest of Cultures in Colonial North America.* New York: Oxford University Press, 1985.

Bell, Genevieve. "Telling Stories Out of School: Remembering the Carlisle Indian Industrial School, 1879–1918." Ph.D. diss., Stanford University, 1998.

Benson, Robert, ed. *Children of the Dragonfly: Native American Voices on Child Custody and Education.* Tucson: University of Arizona Press, 2001.

Blaeser, Kimberly, ed. *Stories Migrating Home: A Collection of Anishinaabe Prose.* Bemidji, MN: Loonfeather Press, 1999.

Bruchac, Joseph, ed. *Raven Tells Stories: An Anthology of Alaskan Native Writing.* Greenfield Center, NY: The Greenfield Review Press, 1991.

———, ed. *Returning the Gift: Poetry and Prose from the First North American Native Writers' Festival.* Tucson: University of Arizona Press, 1994.

Byler, Mary Gloyne. *American Indian Authors for Young Readers: A Selected Bibliography.* New York: Asociation on American Indian Affairs, 1973.

Cajete, Gregory. *Look to the Mountain: An Ecology of Indigenous Education.* Durango, CO: Kivakí Press, 1994.

Child, Brenda. *Boarding School Seasons: American Indian Families, 1900–1940.* Lincoln: University of Nebraska Press, 1998.

Commire, Anne, ed. *Something about the Author: Facts and Pictures about Authors and Illustrators of Books for Young People*, Vol. 39. Detroit, MI: Gale Research Company, 1985.

Cook-Lynn, Elizabeth. *Why I Can't Read Wallace Stegner and Other Essays: A Tribal Voice.* Madison: University of Wisconsin Press, 1996.

Costo, Rupert, ed., and Jeannette Henry, writer. *Textbooks and the American Indian.* San Francisco: Indian Historian Press, 1970.

Council on Interracial Books for Children. *Unlearning "Indian" Stereotypes: A Teaching Unit for Elementary Teachers and Children's Librarians.* New York: Racisim and Sexism Resource Center for Educators, 1977.

Cutler, Charles L. *O Brave New Words! Native American Loanwords in Current English.* Norman: University of Oklahoma Press, 1994.

Deloria, Philip J. *Playing Indian.* New Haven, CT: Yale University Press, 1998.

———. *Indians in Unexpected Places.* Lawrence: University Press of Kansas, 2004.

Edmunds, R. David. *Tecumseh and the Quest for Indian Leadership*. New York: Addison Wesley Longman, 1984.

Erdrich, Heid E., and Laura Tohe, eds. *Sister Nations: Native American Women Writers on Community*. St. Paul: Minnesota Historical Society Press, 2002.

Fedullo, Mick. *Light of the Feather: Pathways Through Contemporary Indian America*. New York: William Morrow, 1992.

Fleming, Walter C. *The Complete Idiot's Guide to Native American History*. New York: Alpha Books, 2003.

Francis, Lee. *Native Time: A Historical Time Line of Native America*. New York: St. Martin's Press, 1996.

Gonzalez, Mario and Elizabeth Cook-Lynn. *The Politics of Hallowed Ground: Wounded Knee and the Struggle for Indian Sovereignty*. Urbana: University of Illinois Press, 1999.

Grant, Agnes, ed. *Our Bit of Truth: An Anthology of Canadian Native Literature*. Winnipeg, MB: Pemmican Publications, 1990.

Green, Rayna. *Native American Women: A Contextual Bibliography*. Bloomington: Indiana University Press, 1983.

Harjo, Joy, and Gloria Bird, eds. *Reinventing the Enemy's Language: Contemporary Native Women's Writings of North America*. New York: W. W. Norton, 1997.

Harris, Violet J., ed. *Teaching Multicultural Literature in Grades K–8*. Norwood, MA: Christopher-Gordon Publishers, 1993.

———, ed. *Using Multiethnic Literature in the K–8 Classroom*. Norwood, MA: Christopher-Gordon Publishers, 1997.

Henry, Gordon, Jr. *The Light People*. Norman: University of Oklahoma Press, 1994.

Hill, Barbara-Helen. *Shaking the Rattle: Healing the Trauma of Colonization*. Penticton, BC: Theytus Books, 1995.

Hodgkinson, Harold L. et al. *The Demographics of American Indians: One Percent of the People; Fifty Percent of the Diversity*. Washington, DC: Institute for Education Leadership/Center for Demographic Policy, 1990.

Hoy, Helen. *How Should I Read These? Native Women Writers in Canada*. Toronto: University of Toronto Press, 2001.

Joe, Rita, with Lynn Henry. *Song of Rita Joe: Autobiography of a Mi'kmaq Poet*. Charlottetown, PEI: Ragweed Press, 1996 and Lincoln: University of Nebraska Press, 1996.

Johansen, Bruce E., and Donald A. Grinde, Jr. *The Encyclopedia of Native American Biography: Six Hundred Life Stories of Important People, from Powhatan to Wilma Mankiller*. New York: Henry Holt and Company, 1997.

Keoke, Emory Dean, and Kay Marie Porterfield. *Encyclopedia of American Indian Contributions to the World: 15,000 Years of Inventions and Innovations*. New York: Facts On File, 2001.

Kerner, Kathy. *They Taught You Wrong: Raising Cultural Consciouness of Stereotypes and Misconceptions about American Indians*. 1995. Lynchburg, VA: O.L. and Carole Durham Publishers, 2000.

King, Thomas, ed. *All My Relations: An Anthology of Contemporary Canadian Native Fiction*. Toronto: McClelland & Stewart, 1990; Norman: University of Oklahoma Press, 1992.

Krupat, Arnold. *The Voice in the Margin: Native American Literature and the Canon*. Berkeley: University of California Press, 1989.

LaDuke, Winona. *The Winona LaDuke Reader: A Collection of Essential Writings*. Stillwater, MN: Voyageur Press, 2002.

Lepore, Jill. *The Name of War: King Philip's War and the Origins of American Identity*. New York: Vintage Books, 1999.

Lincoln, Charles H., ed. *Narratives of the Indian Wars, 1675–1699*. 1913; reprint, New York: Barnes & Noble, 1959.

Lincoln, Kenneth. *Native American Renaissance*. Berkeley: University of California Press, 1983.

Lomawaima, K. Tsianina. *They Called It Prairie Light: The Story of the Chilocco Indian School*. Lincoln: University of Nebraska Press, 1994.

Marshall, Joseph, III. *The Dance House: Stories from Rosebud*. Santa Fe, NM: Red Crane Books, 1998.

McGlinn, Jeanne M. *Ann Rinaldi: Historian & Storyteller*. Lanham, MD: Scarecrow Press, 2000.

McMaster, Gerald, and Clifford E. Trafzer, eds. *Native Universe: Voices of Indian America*. Washington, DC: National Museum of the American Indian, Smithsonian Institution in association with National Geographic, 2004.

McTaggart, Fred. *Wolf That I Am: In Search of the Red Earth People*. Boston: Houghton Mifflin, 1976.

Namias, June. *White Captives: Gender and Ethnicity on the American Frontier*. Chapel Hill: University of North Carolina, 1993.

Niatum, Duane, ed. *Harper's Anthology of 20th Century Native American Poetry*. New York: HarperCollins, 1988.

Norman, Howard. *The Northern Lights*. New York: Picador USA, 2001 (reprint edition).

Pejsa, Jane. *The Life of Emily Peake: One Dedicated Ojibwe*. Minneapolis, MN: Nodin Press, 2003.

Peltier, Leonard. *Prison Writings: My Life Is My Sundance*, ed. Harvey Arden. New York: St. Martin's Press, 1999.

Perreault, Jeanne, and Sylvia Vance, comps. and eds. *Writing the Circle: Native Women of Western Canada*. Norman: University of Oklahoma Press, 1993.

Pratt, Richard Henry. *Battlefield and Classroom: Four Decades with the American Indian, 1867–1904*, ed. Robert M. Utley. Lincoln: University of Nebraska Press, 1964.

Revard, Carter. *Winning the Dust Bowl*. Tucson: The University of Arizona Press, 2001.

Rowlandson, Mary. *The Soveraignty & Goodness of God, Together, With the Faithfulness of His Promises Displayed; Being a Narrative of the Captivity and Restauration of Mrs. Mary Rowlandson*. In *So Dreadfull a Judgment: Puritan Responses to King Philip's War, 1676–1677*. eds. Richard Slotkin and James Folsom. Middletown, CT: Wesleyan University Press, 1978.

Ruoff, A. Lavonne Brown. *Literatures of the American Indian*. New York: Chelsea House, 1991.

Sarris, Greg. *Keeping Slug Woman Alive: A Holistic Approach to American Indian Texts*. Berkeley: University of California Press, 1993.

Singer, Beverly R. *Wiping the War Paint Off the Lens: Native American Film and Video*. Minneapolis: University of Minnesota Press, 2001.

Stedman, Raymond William. *Shadows of the Indian: Stereotypes in American Culture*. Norman: University of Oklahoma, 1982.

Steinbeck, John. *America and Americans and Selected Nonfiction*, ed. Susan Shillinglaw and Jackson J. Benson. 1966. New York: Viking Penguin, 2002.

Stensland, Anna Lee. *Literature by and about the American Indian, An Annotated Bibliography*, 2nd edition. Urbana, IL: National Council of Teachers of English, 1979.

Stott, Jon C. *Native Americans in Children's Literature*. Phoenix, AZ: Oryx Press, 1995.

Vizenor, Gerald. *Interior Landscapes: Autobiographical Myths and Metaphors*. Minneapolis: University of Minnesota Press, 1990.

Witmer, Linda F. *The Indian Industrial School, Carlisle, Pennsylvania, 1879–1918*. Carlisle, PA: Cumberland County Historical Society, 1993.

Womack, Craig S. *Red on Red: Native American Literary Separatism*. Minneapolis: University of Minnesota Press, 1999.

INTERNET SOURCES AND RESOURCES

Alexie, Sherman. Official website of author Sherman Alexie. shermanalexie .com (accessed August 7, 2004).

American Indian College Fund. www.collegefund.org (accessed August 7, 2004).

American Indian Library Association Home Page. www.nativeculture.com/ lisamitten/aila.html (accessed August 7, 2004).

American Indian Lives Series. www.hanksville.org/storytellers/AmIndLives .html (accessed August 7, 2004).

American Indian Science & Engineering Society—AISES. www.aises.org (accessed 16 August 2004).

American Native Press Archives, Sequoyah Research Center. http://anpa.uair.edu/bibliography/bibliography.htm#Tribal_Writers_Archives (accessed August 16, 2004).

Atleo, Marlene et al. "A Critical Review of Ann Rinaldi's *My Heart Is on the Ground: The Diary of Nannie Little Rose, A Sioux Girl*." Oyate—Avoid *My Heart Is on the Ground*. www.oyate.org/books-to-avoid/myHeart.html (accessed August 7, 2004).

Bell, Genevieve. "The Politics of Representation: A Response to the Publication of Ann Rinaldi's *My Heart Is on the Ground*." May 1999. http://home.epix.net/~landis/review.html (accessed August 24, 2004).

Bias by Omission. www.panamgames.net/mainpage/s1Intro/s1intro.html (accessed August 7, 2004).

Brooks, Martha. www.stemnet.nf.ca/easternhorizons/presenters/martha_brooks.html (accessed August 7, 2004).

Caldwell-Wood, Naomi, and Lisa A. Mitten, comps. "Selective Bibliography and Guide for '*I' Is Not for Indian: The Portrayal of Native Americans in Books for Young People*." Program of the ALA/OLOS Subcommittee for Library Services to American Indian People. American Indian Library Association. June 29, 1991, 1–11. www.nativeculture.com/lisamitten/ailabib.htm (accessed August 24, 2004).

Canku Ota (Many Paths), An Online Newsletter Celebrating Native America. www.turtletrack.org (accessed August 7, 2004).

Carlisle Indian Industrial School Research Pages. http://home.epix.net/~landis/index.html (accessed August 7, 2004). Follow the links to information that includes primary and secondary sources as well as biographies.

Cradleboard Teaching Project. www.cradleboard.org (accessed August 7, 2004).

Dorris, Michael. "Mixed Blood," *Hungry Mind Review*. www.bookwire.com/hmr/Review/dorris.html (accessed August 7, 2004).

Greenfield Review Press: Multicultural Books and Recordings. http://greenfieldreview.org (accessed August 7, 2004).

Grossman, Mary Ann. "Ojibwe Tale Is 2004 Book Selection," twincities.com, Pioneer Press. February 10, 2004. www.twincities.com/mld/twincities/news/local/7915097.htm (accessed August 7, 2004).

Indian Country Today. Leading Native American news source (weekly). www.indiancountry.com (accessed August 7, 2004).

Kaupp, P. Ann, compiler. "A Critical Bibliography on North American Indians, For K–12." Anthropology Outreach Office, Smithsonian Institution. http://nmnhwww.si.edu/anthro/outreach/Indbibl/bibliogr.html (accessed August 7, 2004).

"'Kill the Indian, and Save the Man': Capt. Richard [H.] Pratt on the Education of Native Americans." http://historymatters.gmu.edu/d/4929 (accessed August 7, 2004).

Bibliography

Kirkus Reviews. Review of *Bone Dance,* by Martha Brooks. 15 September 1997. www.kirkusreviews.com (accessed August 7, 2004). Subscription required.

Kunuk, Zacharias. "The Art of Inuit Storytelling." www.isuma.ca/ about_us/isuma/our_style/kunuk.html (accessed August 7, 2004).

Leopold, Wendy. "Seeing Beyond Tonto: How the News Media Perpetuate Indian Stereotypes." *Northwestern News.* May 20, 1996. www.northwestern .edu/univ-relations/media/news-releases/*archives/*media-comm (accessed August 7, 2004).

Lindsay, Nina. "'I' Still Isn't for Indian: A Look at Recent Publishing about Native Americans." *School Library Journal* (1 November 2003). www .schoollibraryjournal.com/article/CA332697?display=searchResults&stt=00 1&te . . . (accessed August 7, 2004).

Lipsyte, Robert—HarperCollins. www.harpercollins.com/catalog/author_xml .asp?authorid=12397 (accessed August 9, 2004).

Lomawaima, K. Tsianina. Letter sent to Scholastic Press (editor Tracy Mack), June 14, 1999. http://home.epix.net/~landis/lomawaima.html (accessed August 7, 2004).

McAlister, Melani. "Saving Private Lynch." *New York Times,* 6 April 2003, Section 4, Col. 2, p. 13. www.nytimes.com/2003/04/06/opinion/06MCAL.html (accessed August 7, 2004). Purchase required.

Mendoza, Jean, and Debbie Reese. "Examining Multicultural Picture Books for the Early Childhood Classroom: Possibilities and Pitfalls." *Early Childhood Research & Practice* 3, no. 2 (Fall 2001). http://ecrp.uiuc.edu/v3n2/mendoza .html (accessed August 7, 2004).

National Museum of the American Indian. www.nmai.si.edu (accessed August 7, 2004).

"Native American Author [Cynthia Leitich Smith] Shows Off Indian Shoes." www.bookflash.com/releases/100594.html (accessed August 7, 2004).

Native American Authors Project, The Internet Public Library. www.ipl .org/div/natam (accessed August 7, 2004).

Native American Books: Lists and Bibliographies. www.kstrom.net/ isk/books/lists.html (accessed August 7, 2004).

News from Indian Country. Independent, Indian-owned newspaper (twice-monthly). www.indiancountrynews.com (accessed August 7, 2004).

Noley, Grayson B. "Historical Research and American Indian Education." *Journal of American Indian Education* 20, no. 1 (January 1981). http://jaie.asu.edu/v20/V20S2his.html (accessed August 7, 2004).

Oyate. A Berkeley-based Native organization providing reviews of books by and about American Indians, a catalog of print and non-print materials, and other resources. www.oyate.org (accessed August 7, 2004).

Power, Susan. "Voices from the Gaps," English Department, University of Minnesota http://voices.cla.umn.edu/newsite/authors/POWERsusan.htm (accessed August 7, 2004).

"President Bush Honors Navajo Code Talkers." 26 July 2001. www.whitehouse .gov/news/releases/2001/07/print/20010726-5.html (accessed August 7, 2004).

Red Shirt, Delphine. www.hanksville.org/storytellers/redshirt (accessed August 7, 2004). Information on this author.

———. "Voices from the Gaps," English Department, University of Minnesota. http://voices.cla.umn.edu/newsite/authors/REDSHIRTdelphine.htm (accessed August 7, 2004).

Reese, Debbie. "Authenticity and Sensitivity: Goals for Writing and Reviewing Books with Native American Themes." *School Library Journal* (December 1, 1999). www.schoollibraryjournal.com/article/CA153126.html (accessed August 7, 2004).

"Resources for Selecting Fair and Accurate American Indian Books for Libraries, Schools and Home," by Kay Marie Porterfield and Emory Dean Keoke, authors of *The Encyclopedia of American Indian Contributions to the World: 15,000 Years of Inventions and Innovations.* www.kporterfield.com/ aicttw/excerpts/antibiasbooks.html (accessed August 7, 2004).

Sanderson, Jennifer. "South Dakota Author Given Prestigious Award" [Virginia Driving Hawk Sneve]. www.turtletrack.org/Issues00/Co12302000/ CO_12302000_Sneve.htm (accessed August 12, 2004).

Seale, Doris. Oyate—Avoid *The Sign of the Beaver.* Review of *The Sign of the Beaver*, by Elizabeth George Speare. http://oyate.org/books-to- avoid/sign-Beaver.html (accessed August 7, 2004).

Seale, Doris, and Beverly Slapin. Oyate—*Avoid Sitting Bull and His World.* Review of *Sitting Bull and His World*, by Albert Marrin. www.oyate .org/books-to-avoid/sittingBull.html (accessed August 7, 2004).

Sitting Bull College. www.kevinlocke.com/sitbulcol.htm (accessed August 7, 2004).

Slapin, Beverly. "'Literary License' or 'Mutated Plagiarism'? Additional Comments about Ann Rinaldi's *My Heart Is on the Ground.*" http://oyate. org/books-to-avoid/myHeartMore.html (accessed August 7, 2004).

———. Oyate—Avoid *The Girl Who Chased Away Sorrow.* Review of *The Girl Who Chased Away Sorrow: The Diary of Sarah Nita, A Navajo Girl, New Mexico, 1864*, by Ann Turner. http://oyate.org/books-to-avoid/theChased .html (accessed August 7, 2004).

———. "Turning a Battle into a Massacre: Additional Comments about Albert Marrin's *Sitting Bull and His World.*" www.oyate.org/books-to-avoid/sitting-BullMore.html (accessed August 7, 2004).

Slapin, Beverly, and Doris Seale. Oyate—Avoid *The Place at the Edge of the Earth.* Review of *The Place at the Edge of the Earth*, by Bebe Faas Rice. http://oyate.org/books-to-avoid/edgeEarth.html (accessed August 7, 2004).

Smith, Cynthia Leitich. Children's and Young Adult Book Author Cynthia Leitich Smith Official Web Site. www.cynthialeitichsmith.com/index.html (accessed August 7, 2004).

————. "Native Now: Contemporary Indian Stories." American Library Association Book Links 10, no. 3 (December/January 2000–2001): 1–7. www.ala.org/BookLinks/native.html (accessed August 7, 2004).

"Sneve to Receive 1997 Living Indian Treasure Award (9/12/97)." www.usd.edu/urelations/news/archives/1997/September/september10.html (accessed August 7, 2004).

Sneve, Virginia Driving Hawk. "Voices from the Gaps," English Department, University of Minnesota. http://voices.cla.umn.edu/newsite/authors/SNEVEvirginia.htm (accessed August 12, 2004).

Starrwatcher Online. www.arigonstarr.com/lyrics_all/wind-up/myheart.html (accessed March 10, 2005).

Storytellers: Native American Authors Online. www.hanksville.org/storytellers (accessed August 7, 2004).

Techniques for Evaluating American Indian Web Sites. www.u.arizona.edu/~ecubbins/webcrit.html (accessed August 7, 2004).

West, Alexandra. "Christie Harris: Biocritical Essay." University of Calgary Library, 2000, revised 2002. www.ucalgary.ca/library/SpecColl/harrisbio.htm (accessed August 7, 2004).

Wiping the Tears of Seven Generations (documentary film by Kifaru Productions, 1992). www.der.org/films/wiping-the-tears.html (accessed August 7, 2004).

Wordcraft Circle of Native Writers & Storytellers. www.wordcraftcircle.org (accessed August 7, 2004).

Younge, Gary. "What about Private Lori?" *The Guardian*, April 10, 2003. www.guardian.co.uk/print/0,3858,4644802-103550,00.html (accessed August 7, 2004).

Index

I Am Regina (Keehn), 67; cruelty to children in, 70–72
I Am the Ice Worm (Easley), discussed, 20–21
identity, Native peoples: adoption and, 50, 68, 69, 71; appropriation of, 13–17, 84–85; boarding school fiction and, 61, 88, 89; issues explored about, 12, 31, 36, 37, 38, 84; mistaken as a role or occupation, 15; tribal citizenship/enrollment and, 16. *See also* American Indian tribes; Eskimos; First Nations; images or stereotypes of Native peoples, "playing Indian"; Inuit; Métis
images or stereotypes of Native peoples: anachronistic (also static, frozen-in-time), 15, 40, 59, 76, 77, 82, 121, 126, 140; animal-like (also wild), 6, 7, 20, 52, 55, 57, 140; childlike or simplistic, 6, 49, 50, 53, 74; dirty, 12, 55, 74, 140; drunken (or alcoholic), 6, 18, 21, 24, 48, 72; exotic, 9, 77; generic, 8, 13, 15, 20, 87, 126–30, 132–33; good/bad duality, 47, 58, 73; language, pidgin or distorted speech, 18, 53, 86–87, 88; language, stereotypical words and names, 4, 5, 33, 15, 16, 17, 50, 51, 57, 58, 59, 60, 61, 62, 71, 72, 73, 82, 126, 127, 128; noble savage, 51, 52; objectified, 50, 53, 77, 100, 134; "playing Indian," 13, 14, 15, 16, 50; primitive, 8, 12, 20, 21, 24, 74; rapists, 71, 72, 73, 74, 127; romanticized, 6, 40, 51, 52, 53, 140; symbol of defeat, 11, 87; torn between cultures, 5, 24; vanished or vanishing, 6, 17, 18,

24, 35, 37, 39, 59, 76, 95, 96, 99; violent, 19, 20, 47, 48, 50, 51, 52, 53, 58, 60, 61, 65, 66, 68, 69, 70, 71, 72, 77, 127, 128, 129, 140. *See also* stereotyping of Native peoples
In Search of April Raintree (Culleton), discussed, 30–32
Indian Boyhood (Eastman), 96
Indian Captive: The Story of Mary Jemison (Lenski), 67
Indian Child Welfare Act of 1978, 11
Indian Country Today, 137
Indian Running (Nabokov), 6
Indian School Days (Johnston), 125
Indian Student Placement Services program, 10–11
Inuit, 17, 29, 112, 134. *See also* Alaska Natives; Eskimos; First Nations
It Is a Good Day to Die (Viola), discussed, 114–15
Iverson, Peter, comment on Navajo Long Walk by, 133

Jack-Maldonado, Cokata Aupi/Quinton, "Ration Day," 122
Jacob, Murv (illustrator), 102
Jaffee, Cyrisse (reviewer), 21
Jenkins, Melissa, and *My Heart Is on the Ground* (Rinaldi), 83
Jim, Rex Lee (author), 134
Jimmy Yellow Hawk (Sneve), 140
Johnson, E. Pauline (author), 29
Johnson, Elias (author), 29
Johnston, Basil H., 28; *Indian School Days*, 125; Ojibway code delineated by, 112
The Journal of Jesse Smoke (Bruchac), discussed, xii, 101–2, 103

About the Author

Paulette F. Molin, a member of the Minnesota Chippewa Tribe from the White Earth Reservation, has worked in the field of education for many years. She has directed a curriculum development project and an American Indian scholarship program and served as a school social worker, teacher, and assistant dean. Molin has also completed curatorial work, especially in connection with boarding school history. She is the coeditor of *American Indian Stereotypes in the World of Children*, 2nd edition, with Arlene Hirschfelder and Yvonne Wakim. This book received the Writer of the Year Award from Wordcraft Circle of Native Writers & Storytellers in 1999. Molin has contributed writings to *Away from Home: American Indian Boarding School Experiences, 1879–2000*, edited by Margaret L. Archuleta, Brenda J. Child, and K. Tsianina Lomawaima; and *Stories Migrating Home: A Collection of Anishinaabe Prose*, edited by Kimberly Blaeser. She has also authored numerous journal articles, encyclopedia entries, and curriculum materials. A two-part series, "To Be Examples to . . . Their People: Standing Rock Sioux Students at Hampton Institute, 1878–1923," coauthored with Mary Lou Hultgren, was named best article in *North Dakota History* journal for 2001. Molin lives in Hampton, Virginia.